// Y0-AWK-342

TRENDS IN FEDERAL SUPPORT OF RESEARCH AND GRADUATE EDUCATION

Stephen A. Merrill, Editor

Committee on Trends in Federal Spending on Scientific and Engineering Research
Board on Science, Technology, and Economic Policy
Policy and Global Affairs
National Research Council

NATIONAL ACADEMY PRESS
Washington, D.C.

NATIONAL ACADEMY PRESS   2101 Constitution Avenue, N.W.   Washington, D.C. 20418

NOTICE: The project that is the subject of this report was approved by the Governing Board of the National Research Council, whose members are drawn from the councils of the National Academy of Sciences, the National Academy of Engineering, and the Institute of Medicine. The members of the committee responsible for the report were chosen for their special competencies and with regard for appropriate balance.

This study was supported by Contract No. NASW-99037, Task Order 103, between the National Academy of Sciences and the National Aeronautics and Space Administration and by a grant from the New York Community Trust. Any opinions, findings, conclusions, or recommendations expressed in this publication are those of the author(s) and do not necessarily reflect the views of the organizations or agencies that provided support for the project.

International Standard Book Number 0-309-07589-0

A separately published Executive Summary is available as a pdf file at www.nap.edu and in hard copy from:

Board on Science, Technology, and Economic Policy
National Research Council
1055 Thomas Jefferson Street, N.W.
Washington, D.C. 20007
Phone: 202-334-2200
Fax: 202-334-1505

Copies of this report are available from National Academy Press, 2101 Constitution Avenue, N.W., Lockbox 285, Washington, D.C. 20055; (800) 624-6242 or (202) 334-3313 (in the Washington metropolitan area); Internet, http://www.nap.edu

Printed in the United States of America
Copyright 2001 by the National Academy of Sciences. All rights reserved.

The cover design incorporates medallions from the mosaic ceiling of the Great Hall of the National Academy of Sciences. They represent the disciplines of mathematics, botany, chemistry, and physics.

THE NATIONAL ACADEMIES

National Academy of Sciences
National Academy of Engineering
Institute of Medicine
National Research Council

The **National Academy of Sciences** is a private, nonprofit, self-perpetuating society of distinguished scholars engaged in scientific and engineering research, dedicated to the furtherance of science and technology and to their use for the general welfare. Upon the authority of the charter granted to it by the Congress in 1863, the Academy has a mandate that requires it to advise the federal government on scientific and technical matters. Dr. Bruce M. Alberts is president of the National Academy of Sciences.

The **National Academy of Engineering** was established in 1964, under the charter of the National Academy of Sciences, as a parallel organization of outstanding engineers. It is autonomous in its administration and in the selection of its members, sharing with the National Academy of Sciences the responsibility for advising the federal government. The National Academy of Engineering also sponsors engineering programs aimed at meeting national needs, encourages education and research, and recognizes the superior achievements of engineers. Dr. Wm. A. Wulf is president of the National Academy of Engineering.

The **Institute of Medicine** was established in 1970 by the National Academy of Sciences to secure the services of eminent members of appropriate professions in the examination of policy matters pertaining to the health of the public. The Institute acts under the responsibility given to the National Academy of Sciences by its congressional charter to be an adviser to the federal government and, upon its own initiative, to identify issues of medical care, research, and education. Dr. Kenneth I. Shine is president of the Institute of Medicine.

The **National Research Council** was organized by the National Academy of Sciences in 1916 to associate the broad community of science and technology with the Academy's purposes of furthering knowledge and advising the federal government. Functioning in accordance with general policies determined by the Academy, the Council has become the principal operating agency of both the National Academy of Sciences and the National Academy of Engineering in providing services to the government, the public, and the scientific and engineering communities. The Council is administered jointly by both Academies and the Institute of Medicine. Dr. Bruce M. Alberts and Dr. Wm. A. Wulf are chairman and vice chairman, respectively, of the National Research Council.

COMMITTEE ON TRENDS IN FEDERAL SPENDING ON SCIENTIFIC AND ENGINEERING RESEARCH
BOARD ON SCIENCE, TECHNOLOGY, AND ECONOMIC POLICY
NATIONAL RESEARCH COUNCIL

Chairman

Dale Jorgenson
Frederic Eaton Abbe Professor of Economics
Harvard University

Vice Chairman

Bill Spencer
The Washington Advisory Group

Committee

John Armstrong
Vice President, Science and Technology (retired)
IBM

M. Kathy Behrens
Managing Partner
Robertson Stephens Investment Management

Vinton G. Cerf
Senior Vice President, Internet Architecture and
    Technology
WorldCom

David Challoner
Director
Institute for Science and Health Policy
and
Vice President for Health Affairs Emeritus
University of Florida

Bronwyn Hall
Professor of Economics
University of California, Berkeley

James Heckman
Henry Schultz Distinguished Service Professor of
    Economics
University of Chicago

Ralph Landau
Senior Fellow
Stanford Institute for Economic Policy Research
Stanford University

Richard Levin
President
Yale University

David Morgenthaler
Founding Partner
Morgenthaler Ventures

Mark Myers
Senior Vice President (retired)
Corporate Research and Technology
Xerox Corporation

Roger Noll
Morris M. Doyle Centennial Professor of Economics
Director, Public Policy Program
Stanford University

Edward E. Penhoet
Dean, School of Public Health
University of California at Berkeley

William Raduchel
Chief Technology Officer
AOL TimeWarner

Warren M. Washington
Senior Scientist and head of the Climate Change Research
    Section
National Center for Atmospheric Research

Alan Wm. Wolff
Managing Partner
Dewey Ballantine, DC

Staff

Stephen A. Merrill
Project Director

Michael McGeary
Consultant

Peter Henderson
Senior Staff Officer

Camille Collett
Program Associate

Craig Schultz
Research Associate

Julie Schneider
NRC Intern

NATIONAL RESEARCH COUNCIL
BOARD ON SCIENCE, TECHNOLOGY, AND ECONOMIC POLICY

Chairman

Dale Jorgenson
Frederic Eaton Abbe Professor of Economics
Harvard University

Vice Chairman

Bill Spencer
The Washington Advisory Group

Committee

M. Kathy Behrens
Managing Partner
Robertson Stephens Investment Management

Vinton G. Cerf
Senior Vice President, Internet Architecture and
    Technology
WorldCom

Bronwyn Hall
Professor of Economics
University of California, Berkeley

James Heckman
Henry Schultz Distinguished Service Professor of
    Economics
University of Chicago

Ralph Landau
Senior Fellow
Stanford Institute for Economic Policy Research
Stanford University

Richard Levin
President
Yale University

David Morgenthaler
Founding Partner
Morgenthaler Ventures

Mark Myers
Senior Vice President (retired)
Corporate Research and Technology
Xerox Corporation

Roger Noll
Morris M. Doyle Centennial Professor of Economics and
Director, Public Policy Program
Stanford University

Edward E. Penhoet
Dean, School of Public Health
University of California at Berkeley

William Raduchel
Chief Technology Officer
AOL Time Warner

Alan Wm. Wolff
Managing Partner
Dewey Ballantine, DC

Ex-Officio Members

Bruce Alberts
President
National Academy of Sciences

Wm. A. Wulf
President
National Academy of Engineering

Kenneth I. Shine
President
Institute of Medicine

Staff

Stephen A. Merrill
Executive Director

Charles Wessner
Deputy Director

Philip Aspden
Program Officer

Craig Schultz
Research Associate

McAlister T. Clabaugh
Program Associate

Camille Collett
Program Associate

David E. Dierksheide
Program Associate

Preface and Acknowledgments

The improved competitive performance of much of U.S. industry in the 1990s derived from a combination of corporate strategies and supportive public policies, including steady and conservative fiscal policy, economic deregulation, trade liberalization, relatively lenient antitrust enforcement, and previous decades' research investments. These were conclusions of an in-depth study of 11 manufacturing and service industries by the National Academies' Board on Science, Technology, and Economic Policy (STEP), published in 1999.[1] Although cautiously optimistic about the future performance of the economy, the STEP Board articulated four concerns that continue to guide much of its work: the adequacy of measures and statistical data to inform policy making; the availability of skilled human capital to sustain resurgence; the implications for research and innovation of some aspects of the extension of intellectual property rights; and the adequacy of public and private investment in long-range research, especially in the physical sciences and engineering. The Board included in its report a commissioned analysis providing the first detailed picture of changes in the federal research portfolio in the 1990s.[2]

The present study was undertaken to update and extend the Board's 1999 effort. In approving this project the National Research Council decided to assemble a study committee that included members of the STEP Board and representatives of a range of scientific disciplines, including the biological, atmospheric, and physical sciences. David Challoner, Warren Washington, and John Armstrong were appointed to the study committee, and we are grateful for their contributions to the report.

This report has been reviewed in draft form by individuals chosen for their diverse perspectives and technical expertise, in accordance with procedures approved by the NRC's Report Review Committee. The purpose of this independent review is to provide candid and critical comments that will assist the institution in making its published report as sound as possible and to ensure that the report meets institutional standards for objectivity, evidence, and responsiveness to the study charge. The review comments and draft manuscript remain confidential to protect the integrity of the deliberative process. We wish to thank the following individuals for their review of this report:

Daniel C. Drucker, University of Florida
Susan M. Fitzpatrick, James S. McDonnell Foundation
Pierre C. Hohenberg, Yale University
Anita Jones, University of Virginia
Kei Koizumi, American Association for the Advancement of Science
M. Granger Morgan, Carnegie Mellon Univeristy
Georgine M. Pion, Vanderbilt University
Paul M. Romer, Hoover Institute, Stanford University
Richard N. Zare, Stanford University

Although the reviewers listed above have provided many constructive comments and suggestions, they were not asked to endorse the conclusions or recommendations nor did they see the final draft of the report before its release. The review of this report was overseen by R. Stephen Berry, University of Chicago, and Ronald Ehrenberg, Cornell University. Appointed by the National Research Council, they were responsible for making certain that an independent examination of this report was

---

[1] Board on Science, Technology, and Economic Policy. 1999. *Securing America's Industrial Strength*, Washington, D.C.: National Academy Press; and Board on Science, Technology, and Economic Policy. 1999. *U.S. Industry in 2000: Studies in Competitive Performance*, Washington, D.C.: National Academy Press.

[2] Michael McGeary and Stephen A. Merrill. 1999. "Recent Trends in Federal Spending on Scientific and Engineering Research: Impacts on Research Fields and Graduate Training," in Board on Science, Technology, and Economic Policy, *Securing America's Industrial Strength*, pp. 53-97. Washington, D.C.: National Academy Press. A version of the analysis was published under the authors' names as "Who's Balancing the Federal Research Portfolio and How?" *Science* 285:1679–1680, 1999.

carried out in accordance with institutional procedures and that all review comments were carefully considered. Responsibility for the final content of this report rests entirely with the authoring committee and the institution.

The Board owes a special debt to Stephen Merrill, STEP Executive Director, and Michael McGeary, consultant, for repeating and extending the analysis that they performed in 1999. They were assisted by Peter Henderson, Director of the Board on Higher Education and the Scientific Workforce, who analyzed data from the Survey of Graduate Students and Postdoctorates in Science Engineering (GSPSE) and drafted the section of the report addressing graduate student support. Craig Schultz, STEP Research Associate, and Julie Schneider, a National Research Council summer 2000 intern and now a research scientist with Genaissance Corporation in New Haven, Connecticut, provided indispensable help compiling and deciding how to present the data. Finally, Camille Collett applied her considerable editorial skills to preparing the manuscript for publication. Rona Briere helped with the editing and design of the publication.

Dale Jorgenson,
Chairman

William Spencer,
Vice Chairman

Contents

EXECUTIVE SUMMARY 1

INTRODUCTION 9

1 AGGREGATE TRENDS IN FEDERAL RESEARCH 13
General Trends, 13
Agencies' Research Budgets, 14
Research Performers, 15
Recent Appropriations, 17
Annex   Data Tables, 18

2 FIELD TRENDS IN FEDERAL RESEARCH SUPPORT 21
Historical Trends in Research Funding, 23
Recent Trends in Research Funding, 23
Engineering, 23
Physical Sciences, 27
Mathematics and Computer Science, 30
Life Sciences, 32
Environmental Sciences, 35
Social Sciences, 37
Psychology, 38
Changing Funding Base of Some Fields, 39
Annex   Data Tables, 43

3 FIELD TRENDS IN GRADUATE EDUCATION SUPPORT 49
Physical, Environmental, and Mathematical Sciences, 51
Engineering, 53
Computer Science, 55
Life Sciences, 56
Social and Behavioral Sciences, 57
Recent Trends in Doctoral Awards, 57
Trends Across Fields, 59
Annex   Data Tables, 61

4 AGENCY TRENDS IN RESEARCH AND GRADUATE EDUCATION SUPPORT 65
Portfolio Changes in Agencies with Reduced Research Funding, 65
Portfolio Changes in Agencies with Increased Research Funding, 67
Annex   Data Tables, 71

5 TRENDS IN NONFEDERAL SUPPORT OF RESEARCH 79
    Nonfederal Support of University Research and Development, 79
    States' Support of Research, 80
    Philanthropy, 81
    Industry Research Investment, 81
    Annex   Data Tables, 82

6 FINDINGS, CONCLUSIONS, AND RECOMMENDATIONS 85

APPENDIX   NOTE ON SOURCES OF DATA 93

List of Figures, Tables, and Boxes

FIGURES

ES-1 Federal funding of research, by agency, FY 1993 and FY 1999 (constant dollars), 2
ES-2 Changes in federal research obligations for all performers and university/college performers, FY 1993–FY 1999 (constant dollars), 3
ES-3 Percent change in full-time graduate enrollment, by field and primary source of support, 1993–1999, 4

1-1 Federal obligations for research, FY 1990-FY 1999 (in constant dollars), 14

2-1 Federal obligations for research, total and by broad field FY 1970–FY 2000 (in constant dollars), 24
2-2 Federal funding of engineering research, FY 1990–FY 1999 (in constant dollars), 25
2-3 Federal funding of aeronautical engineering research, FY 1990–FY 1999 (in constant dollars), 25
2-4 Federal funding of civil engineering research FY 1990–FY 1999 (in constant dollars), 26
2-5 Federal funding of astronautical engineering research, FY 1990–FY 1999 (in constant dollars), 26
2-6 Federal funding of chemical engineering research, FY 1990–FY 1999 (in constant dollars), 27
2-7 Federal funding of mechanical engineering research, FY 1990–FY 1999 (in constant dollars), 27
2-8 Federal funding of electrical engineering research, FY 1990–FY 1999 (in constant dollars), 28
2-9 Federal funding of metallurgy/materials engineering research, FY 1990–FY 1999 (in constant dollars), 28
2-10 Federal funding of other engineering research FY 1990–FY 1999 (in constant dollars), 29
2-11 Federal funding of physical sciences research, FY 1990–FY 1999 (in constant dollars), 29
2-12 Federal funding of chemistry research, FY 1990–FY 1999 (in constant dollars), 30
2-13 Federal funding of astronomy research, FY 1990–FY 1999 (in constant dollars), 30
2-14 Federal funding of physics research, FY 1990–FY 1999 (in constant dollars), 31
2-15 Federal funding of mathematics research, FY 1990–FY 1999 (in constant dollars), 31
2-16 Federal funding of computer science research, FY 1990–FY 1999 (in constant dollars), 32
2-17 Federal funding of life sciences research, FY 1990–FY 1999 (in constant dollars), 33
2-18 Federal funding of medical sciences research, FY 1990–FY 1999 (in constant dollars), 33
2-19 Federal funding of biological sciences research, FY 1990–FY 1999 (in constant dollars), 34

2-20 Federal funding of environmental biology research, FY 1990–FY 1999 (in constant dollars), 34
2-21 Federal funding of agricultural sciences research, FY 1990–FY 1999 (in constant dollars), 35
2-22 Federal funding of environmental sciences research, FY 1990–FY 1999 (in constant dollars), 35
2-23 Federal funding of atmospheric sciences research, FY 1990–FY 1999 (in constant dollars), 36
2-24 Federal funding of oceanography research, FY 1990–FY 1999 (in constant dollars), 36
2-25 Federal funding of geology research, FY 1990–FY 1999 (in constant dollars), 37
2-26 Federal funding of social sciences research, FY 1990–FY 1999 (in constant dollars), 37
2-27 Federal funding of psychology research, FY 1990–FY 1999 (in constant dollars), 38
2-28 Agency funding of physics research, FY 1993 and FY 1999 (in constant dollars), 39
2-29 Agency funding of electrical engineering research, FY 1993 and FY 1999 (in constant dollars), 39
2-30 Agency funding of computer science research, FY 1993 and FY 1999 (in constant dollars), 40
2-31 Agency funding of materials/metallurgy research, FY 1993 and FY 1999 (in constant dollars), 40
2-32 Agency funding of medical sciences research, FY 1993 and FY 1999 (in constant dollars), 41
2-33 Agency funding of oceanography research, FY 1993 and FY 1999 (in constant dollars), 41
2-34 Agency funding of mathematical sciences research, FY 1993 and FY 1999 (in constant dollars), 42
2-35 Agency funding of chemical engineering research, FY 1993 and FY 1999 (in constant dollars), 42

3-1 Full-time graduate enrollment in physics, 1993–1999, 51
3-2 Full-time graduate enrollment in chemistry, 1993–1999, 51
3-3 Full-time graduate enrollment in astronomy, 1993–1999, 52
3-4 Full-time graduate enrollment in mathematical sciences, 1993–1999, 52
3-5 Full-time graduate enrollment in geosciences, 1993–1999, 52
3-6 Full-time graduate enrollment in atmospheric sciences, 1993–1999, 52
3-7 Full-time graduate enrollment in ocean sciences, 1993–1999, 53
3-8 Full-time graduate enrollment in aerospace engineering, 1993–1999, 53
3-9 Full-time graduate enrollment in chemical engineering, 1993–1999, 54
3-10 Full-time graduate enrollment in civil engineering, 1993–1999, 54
3-11 Full-time graduate enrollment in electrical engineering, 1993–1999, 55
3-12 Full-time graduate enrollment in mechanical engineering, 1993–1999, 55
3-13 Full-time graduate enrollment in metallurgical and materials engineering, 1993–1999, 56
3-14 Full-time graduate enrollment in computer science, 1993–1999, 56
3-15 Full-time graduate enrollment in agricultural sciences, 1993–1999, 57
3-16 Full-time graduate enrollment in biological sciences, 1993–1999, 57
3-17 Full-time graduate enrollment in health fields, 1993–1999, 58
3-18 Full-time graduate enrollment in social sciences, 1993–1999, 58
3-19 Full-time graduate enrollment in psychology, 1993–1999, 59

4-1 Research funding by field, Department of Defense, FY 1993 vs. FY 1999, 66
4-2 Research funding by field, Department of Energy, FY 1993 vs. FY 1999, 67
4-3 Research funding by field, National Institutes of Health, FY 1993 vs. FY 1999, 68
4-4 Research funding by field, National Science Foundation, FY 1993 vs. FY 1999, 69

TABLES

1-1 Trends by Agency and Character of Research, 1990–1999 (millions of 1999 dollars), 18

2-1 Percent Change in Federal Funding for Research, by Field, FY 1993–1999 (in constant dollars), 43
2-2 Trends by Field and Character of Research, 1990–1999 (millions of 1999 dollars), 44

3-1 Percent Change in Federal Funding for University Research, Full-time Graduate Enrollment, and Doctorate Degrees Awarded, by Field, 1993–1999, 61
3-2 Full-time Graduate Enrollment in Science and Engineering, by Field and by Selected Source and Mechanism of Support, 1993–1999, 62

4-1 Trends in DOD Support of Research, by Field, 1993 to 1997, 1999 (constant dollars), 71
4-2 Full-time Graduate Students Whose Primary Source of Support is the Department of Defense, by Field, 1993–1999, 72
4-3 Trends in DOE Support of Research, by Field, 1993 to 1997, 1999 (constant dollars), 73
4-4 Trends in NIH Support of Research, by Field, 1993 to 1997, 1999 (constant dollars), 74
4-5 Full-time Graduate Students Whose Primary Source of Support is the National Institutes of Health, by Field, 1993–1999, 75
4-6 Trends in NSF Support of Research, by Field, 1993 to 1997, 1999 (constant dollars), 76
4-7 Full-time Graduate Students Whose Primary Source of Support is the National Science Foundation, by Field, 1993–1999, 77

5-1 Nonfederally Funded Academic R&D in 1999 Dollars, 82
5-2 1995 Recipients of State R&D Support, by Field (Percent), 83
5-3 Foundation Grants for Research in Millions of Current Dollars, 83
5-4 Corporate Funded Industrial Research (Basic and Applied) in Millions of Current Dollars, 83

BOXES

1 Classification of Research, 13
2 Classification of Research Fields, 22

Executive Summary

This report updates and extends a 1999 study of trends in federal research funding commissioned by the National Academies' Board on Science, Technology, and Economic Policy (STEP).[1] Analysis of more recent data supports that study's principal conclusion that a substantial shift has been occurring in the composition of the federal research portfolio. This shift in funding is affecting both the allocation of resources by research field and the supply of human resources. In particular, there has been a significant reduction in federal funding for research in certain of the physical science and engineering fields. These include fields whose earlier advances contributed to the surge in productivity and economic growth of the late 1990s[2] and fields that underlie progress in energy production and conservation, pollution abatement, medical diagnosis and treatment, and other national priorities.

BACKGROUND

In the early 1990s shifting national priorities stemming from the end of the Cold War and a political consensus to eliminate the federal budget deficit began to reduce federal funding of research and development in real terms.[3] Defense R&D, funded mostly by the Department of Defense (DOD) but also by the Department of Energy (DOE), was most affected by the cuts. The purpose of the STEP Board's 1999 study was to see if, in fact, longer range research in disciplines that received most of their federal funding from DOD and other agencies with reduced R&D budgets was being cut accordingly. The study analyzed data on actual federal obligations for basic and applied research from FY 1990 through FY 1997 (the last year for which data were available), especially trends after 1993 (the last year of real growth in federal research budgets until 1998).[4]

The study showed that in 1997, although the level of federal research spending was nearly the same as it had been in 1993, a number of agencies were spending less on research than they had in 1993, including DOD (–27.5 percent), Department of the Interior (–13.3 percent), Department of Agriculture (–6.2 percent), and DOE (–5.6 percent).[5] Meanwhile, the research budget of the National Institutes of Health (NIH) had increased by 11 percent. The cuts disproportionately affected most fields in the physical sciences (physics, chemistry, and geology), engineering (chemical, civil, electrical, and mechanical) and mathematics, because those fields received most of their support from agencies with reduced research funding and only a few were able to obtain increased support from other agencies. Nevertheless, the funding of particular fields did not necessarily mirror the budgets of their

---

[1] Michael McGeary and Stephen A. Merrill. 1999. "Recent Trends in Federal Spending on Scientific and Engineering Research: Impacts on Research Fields and Graduate Training," Appendix A in National Research Council, *Securing America's Industrial Strength*. Washington, D.C.: National Academy Press.

[2] Dale Jorgenson, "Information Technology and the U.S. Economy," *American Economic Review* 91(1):1-32, 2001 and Kevin J. Stiroh, "Information Technology and the U.S. Productivity Revival: What Do the Industry Data Say?" Staff Report, Federal Reserve Bank of New York, no. 95, 2001. Available online at: http://www.ny.frb.org/rmaghome/staff_rp/2001/2001.html

[3] Unless otherwise specified, all funding numbers in this report have been converted to constant (1999) dollars using GDP deflators in Office of Management and Budget. 2001. *Historical Tables, Budget of the United States Government, Fiscal Year 2002*, Table 10.1, Washington, D.C.: U.S. Government Printing Office.

[4] Obligations are commitments to spend money, regardless of when the funds were appropriated and of whether actual payment is made later, for example, under multiyear contracts. The data on federal obligations are based on the federal fiscal year that begins October 1 each year. Data on expenditures by other sponsors of research are for calendar years.

[5] Michael McGeary and Stephen A. Merrill. 1999. "Recent Trends in Federal Spending on Scientific and Engineering Research: Impacts on Research Fields and Graduate Training," Appendix A, Table A-1 in National Research Council, *Securing America's Industrial Strength*. Washington, D.C.: National Academy Press.

principal supporting agencies. Some of these fields were subject to reductions in support by agencies with growing budgets. Based on these findings, the Board expressed its concern about the long-term implications of reduced federal investment in fields important to such industries as electronics, software, networking, and materials processing and to advances in the life sciences.

KEY FINDINGS

The following findings form support the conclusions and recommendations of this study, based on trends through 1999:

- Federal research funding in the aggregate turned a corner in FY 1998 after 5 years of stagnation. Total expenditures were up 4.5 percent in FY 1998 over their level in 1993. A year later, in FY 1999, they were up 11.7 percent over 1993. FY 2000 and FY 2001 saw continued growth in budget authority for research. These increases are accounted for primarily by NIH. Indeed, increases in NIH appropriations kept federal research funding from falling even lower in the mid-1990s and have dominated more recent growth in overall research funding (see Figure ES-1). Moreover, NIH is slated by the current administration for substantial increases in the next several years while most other agencies would receive flat or reduced funding for research.
- Although federal research funding began to increase after 1997, the new composition of federal support remained relatively unchanged. In 1999, the life sciences had 46 percent of federal funding for research, compared with 40 percent in 1993. During the same period, physical science and engineering funding went from 37 to 31 percent of the research portfolio.
  - Whereas 12 of the 22 fields examined had suffered a real loss of support in the mid-1990s (four by 20 percent or more), by FY 1999 the number of fields with reduced support was seven. However, five of these—physics, geological sciences, and chemical, electrical, and mechanical engineering—were down 20 percent or more from 1993.[6]
  - The fields of chemical and mechanical engineering and geological sciences had less funding in 1999 than in 1997. Funding of some fields—including electrical engineering and physics—improved somewhat from 1997 to 1999 but not enough to raise them back up to their 1993 levels.
  - Other fields that failed to increase or had less funding after 1997 included astronomy, chemistry, and atmospheric sciences.
  - One field that had increased funding in the mid-1990s, materials engineering, experienced declining support at the end of the decade. Its funding was 14.0 percent larger in 1997 than in 1993, but that margin fell to 3.0 percent in 1998 and 1.5 percent in 1999.
  - The fields whose support was up in 1997 and has continued to increase include aeronautical, astronautical, civil, and other engineering;[7] biological and medical sciences; computer sciences; and oceanography.
  - Fields that, like overall research expenditures, turned a corner were environmental biology, agricultural sciences, mathematics, social sciences, and psychology. Their funding, which was less in 1997 than in 1993, exceeded the 1993 level by 1999 (see Figure ES-2).
- More recent actions on federal budgets for research, including the first installments in doubling of the NIH budget over the 5 years ending in FY 2003, will increase

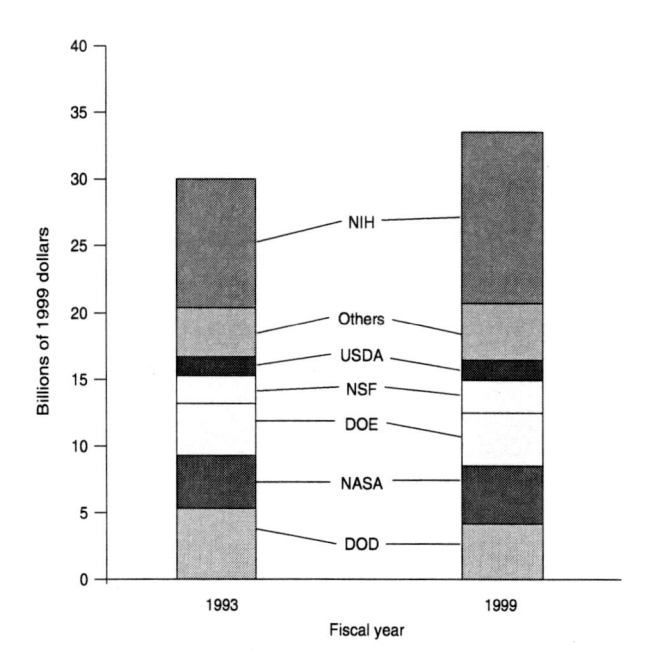

FIGURE ES-1 Federal funding of research, by agency, FY 1993 and FY 1999 (constant dollars).

---

[6]From time to time, agencies responding to the NSF survey of federal funds for research and development change their procedures for classifying funding by field of research. In 1996, for example, NSF changed its classification of engineering and the environmental sciences research activities so that its support of mechanical engineering appeared to be much less and its funding of oceanography much greater. In this case, if NSF did not actually change what it was funding, the drop in overall federal funding of mechanical engineering was somewhat less than reported, and the apparent increase in oceanography may not be real. Most fine fields were not affected by such changes during the 1993-1999 period, and the broad trends documented in this report—expansion of life sciences funding relative to funding of the physical sciences and engineering—are not affected.

[7]"Other engineering" includes agricultural, bioengineering, biomedical, industrial and management, nuclear, ocean, and systems engineering.

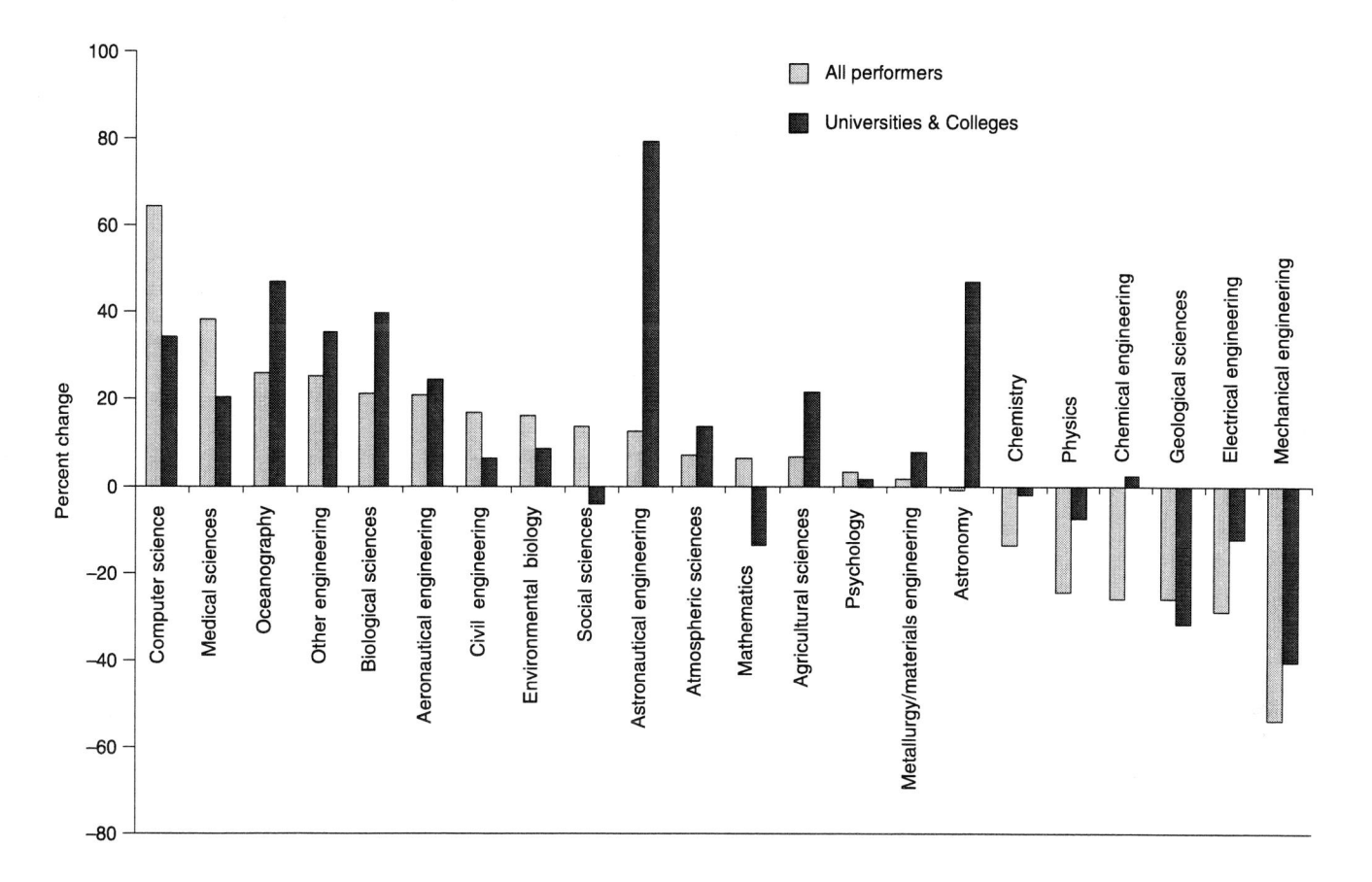

FIGURE ES-2 Changes in federal research obligations for all performers and university/college performers, FY 1993–FY 1999 (constant dollars).

the current divergence between the life sciences and other fields unless other fields receive substantially larger increases than proposed.

• The decline in the support of many of the physical science and engineering fields is partly attributable to the fact that the budgets of their principal sponsoring agencies [e.g., DOD, DOE, and the National Aeronautics and Space Administration (NASA)] did not fare as well as the NIH budget and partly to the fact that the agencies with growing budgets, especially NIH and NSF, did not increase their support of those fields and in some cases reduced it. At the same time, some fields—e.g., computer sciences, oceanography, and aeronautical engineering—experienced substantial growth even though their largest 1993 funders were agencies with shrinking budgets—e.g., DOD and NASA. These fields did so by maintaining their level of funding from agencies with declining budgets and by picking up additional support from other agencies.

• The patterns in federal funding of basic research and research performed at universities are similar to that for overall funding of research but somewhat more favorable, suggesting that by the late 1990s agencies were tending to protect basic and university research relative to applied research and other performers.

• Although federal funding of research assistant positions through research grants and contracts is but one factor among many in determining the number of graduate students in training and the number of Ph.D.'s produced in a field, graduate enrollments and Ph.D. production were generally down in fields that had less federal funding in 1999 than in 1993. Over the next few years, these declines will contribute to an ongoing reduction in the supply of new talent for positions in governmental/nonprofit organizations, industry, academia, and other employment sectors (see Figure ES-3).

• Although the data are much more limited, it appears that states and philanthropies have shared the research priorities of the federal government in the last decade. For both states and foundations, biomedical research consumes a majority of research funding and has grown at a faster rate than support of other scientific and engineering fields.

• Data on the composition of industry-funded research are classified by sector rather than by field and thus are not directly comparable to those on federal expenditures. The

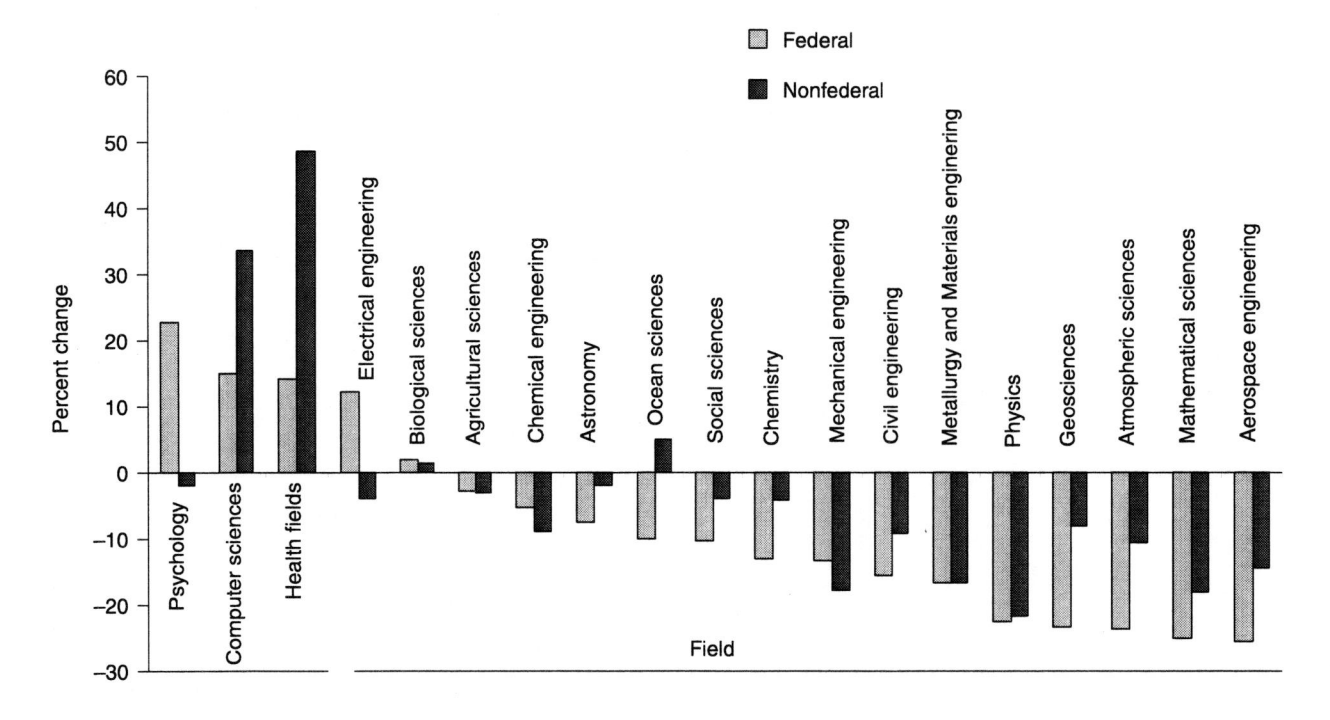

FIGURE ES-3 Percent change in full-time graduate enrollment, by field and primary source of support, 1993–1999.

data show that corporations' spending on research has been increasing but is concentrated in a few sectors such as the pharmaceutical industry and the information technology sector. Electronic components was one industry in which research investment increased as federal support of the most closely related research field, electrical engineering, declined over the decade. Nevertheless, except for a few industries such as pharmaceuticals, only a small fraction (less than 4 percent in computers and semiconductors, for example) of all corporate research and development is basic research. Moreover, private research investment is quite volatile, sometimes subject to wide fluctuation from year to year with or independent of the business cycle.

• The shifts in federal funding of fields were partly the result of congressional (e.g., biomedical research) and presidential priorities (e.g., high-performance computing research and development); but the funding reductions were substantially the product of decentralized decision making by officials in various departments, agencies, and congressional committees, adjusting resources to agency mission needs in a constrained budget environment. Impacts on the overall composition of the federal research portfolio were not considered until FY 2000, when the administration and Congress began to discuss the balance of funding among fields, and the FY 2001 budget cycle, when for the first time balance became an explicit criterion used by the administration in developing its budget request.

CONCLUSIONS

The recent shift in composition of the federal research portfolio is significant. Although nonfederal entities increased their share of national funding for R&D from 60 to 74 percent between 1990 and 2000, federal funding still supports a substantial component, 27 percent, of the nation's total research expenditures, 49 percent of basic research spending. Reductions in federal funding of a field of 20 percent or more have a substantial impact unless there are compensating increases in funding from nonfederal sources, which does not appear to be the case in the last few years. Generally speaking, moreover, federal funding for research has a longer time horizon and can be more stable than investments from other sources.

The funding trends leading to shifts in the federal research portfolio will continue under the administration's budget plan. The administration's request for NIH for FY 2002 would increase its budget authority for research by 12.9 percent over the 2001 level in constant dollars. All other non-defense research would be reduced by 1.5 percent. There is also provision for an increase in DOD's budget authority for research but its allocation awaits the results of the administration's strategic review.

There is little indication, based on their portfolios from 1993 to 1999, that NIH would allocate substantial funds to fields outside of the biological and medical sciences or that DOD would rebuild funding for fields the department previously cut or increased less. NSF, with the broadest research portfolio, has tended to increase its support of fields whose funding from other sources is growing and reduce support of some fields whose support is declining elsewhere. In any case, its research budget is small compared with those of DOD and NIH.

There are compelling reasons for the federal government to invest across the range of scientific and engineering disciplines.[8] Increasingly, the most important problems in both the life and physical sciences and engineering require collaboration across disciplines. Examples include genomics and bioinformatics, which rely on mathematics and computer science as much as biology for progress; nanotechnology, which depends on chemistry and chemical engineering, physics, materials science and technology, and electrical engineering; and understanding of climate change, which relies on collaboration among oceanographers, atmospheric chemists, geologists and geophysicists, paleontologists, and computer scientists.

Furthermore, research, by its nature, is highly uncertain. It is not possible to know when and where breakthroughs will occur, what practical applications they may have, and when those applications may pay off. Important advances in one field sometimes come from apparently unrelated work in another field. For example, who knew in 1945 that the discovery of nuclear magnetic resonance in condensed matter by basic research physicists would lead to the development of MRI technology 30 years later?[9] Increasing interdisciplinarity and uncertainty about where advances will take place and if or when they will be commercially successful argue for the prudence of investing in a broad portfolio of research activities.

There is cause for concern about the allocation of funding among fields in the federal research portfolio, in particular with respect to most of the physical sciences and engineering whose funding, in contrast with the biomedical sciences, has with few exceptions stagnated or declined. The current level of funding in some fields may not be optimal from a national perspective or from the viewpoint of those who support expanded funding of biomedical or computer science research. Advances in both of the latter fields will be dependent on progress in a broad range of fields of fundamental research, including physics, chemistry, electrical engineering, and chemical engineering, all fields with less funding at the end of the 1990s than they received earlier in the decade.

Although it may be wise policy to reduce the linkage between research funding and training support,[10] *research allocation decisions should take into account the need for trained people in a field.* Curtailing research in a field may constrict the supply of trained people with advanced technical degrees (not only Ph.D.'s) who are capable of applying and exploiting research advances in a variety of settings including but not limited to the laboratory. Increasingly, there is a premium on scientific and engineering training in a range of service as well as manufacturing industries. The effect of cutting research is both direct, in reducing the number of research assistant positions, and indirect, in signaling to prospective graduate students that some fields offer poor career opportunities.

The current system for allocating research funding does not necessarily ensure that national priorities are taken into account. In the highly decentralized U.S. system of support for science and engineering, most research funding is tied to the missions of federal agencies rather than national needs more broadly conceived, such as technological innovation and economic growth. If a mission changes—for example, defense strategy in the post-Cold War world—support of certain fields of research may decline for reasons that are entirely defensible in terms of the affected agency's priorities but not necessarily defensible in terms of the research opportunities in and productivity of those fields and their potential contributions to national goals.

The evidence of changing agency priorities and portfolios is actually encouraging. In a rapidly changing world, it would be disturbing if spending patterns were static. But there is no process for reviewing systematically the effects of these decentralized decisions on the health of research fields and the supply of human resources with reference to a set of national goals. It may be that funding reductions are entirely warranted by diminished research opportunities or productivity or less need for people in those specialties. On the other hand, funding increments may be justified. Simply increasing the research funding of certain agencies (for example, DOD, DOE, or NSF) will not necessarily achieve the desired allocation by itself. A single agency's research budget may be comparatively small and widely dispersed or the agency may continue to

---

[8] The rationale for a diverse portfolio is articulated in National Academy of Sciences, National Academy of Engineering, and Institute of Medicine. 1993. *Science, Technology, and the Federal Government: National Goals for a New Era.* Washington, D.C.: National Academy Press; and National Research Council. 1995. *Allocating Federal Funds for Science and Technology*, Washington, D.C.: National Academy Press.

[9] National Academy of Sciences. March 2001. *A Life-Saving Window on the Mind and Body: The Development of Magnetic Resonance Imaging*, Washington, D.C.: National Academy of Sciences. At: www/beyonddiscovery.org/beyond/BeyondDiscovery.nsf/files/PDF MRI.pdf/$file/MRI PDF.pdf.

[10] A position taken by the Committee on Science, Engineering, and Public Policy in its report, *Reshaping the Graduate Education of Scientists and Engineers*, Washington, D.C.: National Academy Press, 1995.

allocate any increases to its current priorities. The task requires some centralized oversight, similar to the mechanisms for advancing presidential priorities that cut across agency programs and budgets.[11]

Improvements in data and analysis would support a better informed process of allocating federal funding for research. Current surveys are valuable and underutilized tools for assessing the nation's allocation of resources to the conduct of science and development of technology, but their utility could be improved by modest changes in the surveys and in the presentation of their results. Moreover, there are significant gaps in information, especially on non-unversity performers of federal research and on nonfederal research sponsors — states, philanthropic institutions, and businesses at a fine level of detail. There needs to be a good deal more qualitative evaluation of the output of research fields and the effects on outputs of changes in funding levels as well as more rigorous analysis of the influences on the supply of and demand for scientists and engineers with advanced training.

RECOMMENDATIONS

Based on these conclusions, the committee recommends action in three areas. For the most part our recommendations reaffirm previous Academy statements on the budget allocation process for research,[12] priorities for the National Science Foundation's statistical arm, the Division of Science Resources Studies,[13] international benchmarking of scientific performance,[14] and federal support of graduate training in science and engineering.[15]

Evaluation and Adjustment of the Research Portfolio

The U.S. system for funding and performing research has many strengths and accounts in large part for the productivity of American science and technology. In making the following recommendations, we are not calling for centralization of decision making about research priorities and spending. What is needed is a mechanism or mechanisms to monitor the aggregate results of a very decentralized system of selecting and carrying out research projects to see if adjustments are needed to close gaps or reduce shortfalls that occur when policy makers make decisions in a narrow framework.

Recommendation 1. The White House Office of Science and Technology Policy (OSTP) and the Office of Management and Budget (OMB), with assistance from federal agencies and appropriate advisory bodies, should evaluate the federal research portfolio, with an initial focus on fields related to industrial performance and other national priorities and a recent history of declining funding. Examples are physics, electrical engineering, chemistry, chemical engineering, mechanical engineering, and geological sciences. Fields with flat funding or only small real increases through the 1990s also merit attention. These include materials engineering, atmospheric sciences, mathematics, psychology, and astronomy. The conclusions of the evaluation should be reflected in budget allocations.

Recommendation 2. Congress should conduct its own evaluation of the federal research portfolio through the budget, appropriations, or authorization committees.

Recommendation 3. For the longer term, the executive branch and Congress should sponsor the following types of studies: (1) in-depth qualitative case studies of selected fields, taking into account not only funding trends across federal agencies and nonfederal supporters and international comparisons but also subtler differences in the foci, time horizons, and other research characteristics that are obscured by quantitative data; (2) studies of agency research portfolios and decision making to understand the reasons for shifts in funding by field and the extent to which the health of individual fields and interrelationships among fields are taken into account; and (3) studies of methodologies for allocating federal research funding according to national rather than merely departmental criteria and priorities.

Recommendation 4. The executive branch and Congress should institutionalize processes for conducting and, if necessary, acting on an integrated analysis of the federal budget for research, by field as well as by agency, national purpose, and other perspectives.

Data Improvements

National data systems need to be expanded and improved to support better policy making.

Recommendation 5. NSF should annually report and interpret data from its survey of federal R&D obliga-

---

[11]National Science Board, "The Scientific Allocation of Scientific Resources" [Discussion Draft for Comment], March 28, 2001, p. 3.

[12]National Research Council, *Allocating Federal Funds for Science and Technology*, 1995. *Op. Cit.*

[13]National Research Council, *Measuring the Science and Engineering Enterprise*, Washington, D.C.: National Academy Press, 2000; and *Industrial Research and Innovation Indicators*, Washington, D.C.: National Academy Press, 1997.

[14]National Academy of Sciences, National Academy of Engineering, and Institute of Medicine, *Experiments in International Benchmarking of U.S. Research Fields*, Washington, D.C.: National Academy Press, 2000.

[15]National Academy of Sciences, National Academy of Engineering, and Institute of Medicine, *Reshaping the Graduate Education of Scientists and Engineers*, 1995. *Op. Cit.*

tions in a form (e.g., adjusted for inflation) and on a schedule useful to policy makers. Improvements in the data that should be given careful consideration include reporting of data on university research support by all agencies that support a major share of research in certain fields [e.g., Department of Interior (DOI) in geological sciences and Department of Commerce (DOC) in oceanography], obtaining data by field on performers other than universities (e.g., in industry and government laboratories), evaluating and revising the field classification, and making the field classification and research typology uniform across surveys (e.g., the surveys of academic R&D expenditures and earned doctorates as well as the survey of federal R&D obligations). Agencies should make sure that the data they provide NSF are accurate and timely.

Recommendation 6. Although it may be impractical to obtain data on industrial R&D spending by research field, NSF should administer the Industrial R&D survey at the business unit level to make data on the composition of private R&D more meaningful.

Recommendation 7. NSF should consider ways of obtaining data on the allocation of state expenditures on a regular basis.

Recommendation 8. The philanthropic community should cooperate in collecting and publishing data on a basis comparable to federal research statistics.

Analytical Improvements

The analysis presented here, a gathering of existing data from various sources, is a first step that raises more questions than it answers.

Recommendation 9. NSF and other federal agencies funding research should support benchmarking studies that compare inputs and outputs across countries and sponsor other efforts to develop techniques for assessing the productivity of various fields of research.

Recommendation 10. NSF should continue and expand its efforts to develop innovation indicators other than R&D expenditure inputs, collect data on them, and fund researchers to analyze them. Other agencies (e.g., NASA, DOD, DOE, and the National Institute of Standards and Technology) interested in the role of federal research in technological innovation, could fund or jointly fund such analyses.

Recommendation 11. Researchers, professional societies, industry associations, and federal research agencies should explore the relationships between federal research funding and other factors (e.g., population flows through the educational system, domestic and foreign student demand, labor market conditions, etc.) in the development and use of scientific and engineering talent. Only then can we evaluate the trends in student enrollment and in graduate study programs' output and determine how to influence those trends if that is the conclusion of the analysis.

Introduction

In the early 1990s, shifting national priorities stemming from the end of the Cold War and strong pressures to eliminate the federal budget deficit began to reduce federal funding of research and development in real terms.[1] The level of federal R&D funding decreased by 9.2 percent from FY 1992, its historical high, to FY 1996 and did not surpass its 1992 level until 2001.[2] Defense R&D, funded mostly by DOD but also DOE, was most affected by the cuts. It decreased by 14.4 percent between 1992 and 1996. That trend raised concern about how cuts would be imposed by discipline and agency, given the decentralization of decisionmaking concerning federal R&D programs. In 1995, a National Research Council committee chaired by former National Academy of Sciences President Frank Press observed that historically DOD had provided the majority of federal funding for academic research and training in electrical engineering, metallurgy and materials, and computer science, and DOE was the largest federal contributor to materials science through its national laboratories. The committee said that all science and engineering depend critically on those fields, and cuts in Department of Defense and Department of Energy programs made for other purposes might well have significant and inadvertent impacts on diverse research and development programs conducted in many other agencies and having clear importance to the country.[3]

In 1999, the National Academies' Board on Science, Technology, and Economic Policy sponsored a study of trends in federal funding of fields to see if, in fact, research in disciplines that received most of their federal funding from DOD and other agencies with reduced R&D budgets were being cut accordingly.[4] At that time, data were available on actual funding of research obligations from FY 1990 through FY 1997, especially trends after 1993, when pressures to reduce the federal budget deficit and reductions in the defense budget had stopped real growth in federal research budgets for a 5-year period.[5]

The principal findings of the 1999 report were as follows:

• In the period 1993-1997 the research fields with declining constant dollar support outnumbered the fields with growing support by 12 to 10. The support for four fields dropped by 20 percent or more. The reductions were concentrated in engineering (especially mechanical and electrical) and the physical sciences (especially physics and geology). Exceptions were computer science and materials engineering, whose support increased 39.4 and 12.6 percent, respectively. Other fields given substantial funding increases in the mid-1990s were medical sciences and oceanography.

• Computer science and materials research, heavily supported by the Department of Defense (DOD), illustrated that fields may receive increased funding even though the overall research budgets of their principal

---

[1] Unless otherwise specified, all funding numbers in this report have been converted to constant (1999) dollars using GDP deflators in the OMB. 2001. *Historical Tables, Budget of the United States Government, Fiscal Year 2002*, Table 10.1. Washington, D.C.: U.S. Government Printing Office. The data are based on the federal fiscal year, which begins October 1 each year.

[2] American Association for the Advancement of Science, "Historical Data on Federal R&D, FY 1976–2002." At www.aaas.org/spp/dspp/rd/hist02p2.pdf.

[3] National Research Council. 1995. *Allocating Federal Funds for Science and Technology*, pp. 8–9. Washington, D.C.: National Academy Press.

[4] Michael McGeary and Stephen A. Merrill. 1999. "Recent Trends in Federal Spending on Scientific and Engineering Research: Impacts on Research Fields and Graduate Training," Appendix A in National Research Council, *Securing America's Industrial Strength*. Washington, D.C.: National Academy Press.

[5] Before 1993 there had been a long period of real growth in research funding overall if not in all research fields or by all federal agencies supporting research.

agency sponsors decline. By the same token, fields primarily funded by agencies with rising budgets do not necessarily fare accordingly. In the FY 1993-1997 period, medical sciences (up 14.4 percent) received far more from growth in the National Institutes of Health budget than did the biological sciences (up only 1.1 percent).

- In the constrained budget environment of the mid-1990s there was no consistent pattern of protecting support of university research relative to in-house research and research performed in the corporate sector.
- No single agency was serving as a "balance wheel" to ensure some stability of funding in fields whose support is declining elsewhere. In the 1990s, NSF, with the broadest research portfolio, appeared to be amplifying changes in other agencies, in most cases boosting funding for fields prospering elsewhere and reducing funding for fields being cut elsewhere.
- In the cases where direct comparisons can be made because of identical field nomenclature in different NSF surveys, changes in university research funding of a field corresponded to changes in the number of graduate students supported by federal fellowships, traineeships, and research assistantships in that field. Where research funding was down (e.g., chemical and mechanical engineering), the number of graduate students also declined. Conversely, the number of federally supported graduate students in computer science increased, as did federal research support.

Based on those findings, the Board expressed its concern about the reduction in federal investment in fields important to such industries as electronics, software, and materials processing and concluded that the trends in federal funding, if they continued, merited "a careful assessment of their long-term implications and what steps, if any, should be taken to change them."[6] At about the same time, concern began to increase about the possible "imbalance" in the federal research portfolio based on the divergence between the declining support of the physical sciences and engineering and the growth of funding of biomedical research through the National Institutes of Health.

In the fall of 2000 the STEP Board decided to revisit its analysis and conclusions for several reasons.

The Board's first motivation was the availability of additional data that were otherwise unlikely to be presented and interpreted in a form useful to policy makers. As a result of efforts by the NSF's Science Resource Studies (SRS) Division to accelerate the availability of results of the Federal Funds and other surveys, data on agencies' research obligations are now available within approximately 15 months of the end of the fiscal year. This enables examination of federal agencies' spending on nearly two dozen research fields in FY 1998 and FY 1999 and their reasonably reliable estimates for FY 2000 by major field of research. Surprisingly, however, none of these data have been reported in the NSF's publications of science and technology statistics—*Science and Engineering Indicators*, *National Patterns of R&D Resources*, or, with few exceptions, SRS' periodic *Data Briefs*.[7] Nor does the American Association for the Advancement of Science examine the subject of field allocation in its annual analyses of the current fiscal year federal R&D budget.

A second motivation was curiosity about the effects on allocations among research fields of the marked turnaround in federal research funding in FY 1998. After 5 years of stagnation, FY 1998 research expenditures were up 4.5 percent in real terms from 1993 and even more (11.7 percent) in FY 1999. Even DOD's research budget showed modest increases over FY 1997 (although it was still much smaller than in 1993), and increases in FY 2000-2001 federal R&D budgets ensure continuing incremental growth through most of 2001. In this improved funding environment, the question arises whether the disparities in how research fields fared in the mid-1990s have been eliminated or moderated.

Third, recent articulations of the importance of "balance" in the publicly supported research portfolio by a number of executive branch and congressional policy makers makes the question of the relative growth in funding among research fields when R&D budgets are increasing even more compelling. What has been the impact of officials' greater attention to how federal research money is being spent and their declared intention to correct any "imbalances"?

Finally, the Board decided to extend the analysis of federal research spending in certain respects. First, although this report deals primarily with changes in (basic and applied) research spending through 1999, it also examines trends in basic research support and research conducted at universities by field.[8] Second, the report looks in greater detail at the relationship between research funding and graduate student support by research field. Third, the report identifies which fields changed their structure of support (principal agency sponsors and their shares) in the 1990s and which did not and with what results. Finally, it considers trends in the composition of research support from nonfederal sources, principally states, philanthropies, and industry, to cast some light on the question of whether other sponsors of research are

---

[6]National Research Council. 1999. *Securing America's Industrial Strength*, pp. 4. Washington, D.C.: National Academy Press.

[7]An exception was Alan I. Rapoport. Feb. 17, 1999. "How Has the Mix of Federal Research Funding Changed Over the Past Three Decades?" Arlington, VA: National Science Foundation.

[8]Occasionally the report refers to trends in research and development expenditures, especially with regard to budgets after 1999 for which separate figures for research are not available.

following federal government priorities or supporting areas whose federal support is declining. The data sources used in this analysis and their principal features are described in the Appendix.

Chapter 1 reviews aggregate support, while Chapter 2 addresses trends in federal support by field. Field trends in graduate education support are examined in Chapter 3, and agency trends in research and graduate education support in Chapter 4. Chapter 5 looks at trends in nonfederal research support. The key findings, conclusions, and recommendations of the study are presented in the final chapter. The Appendix provides a brief discussion of data sources while the Annexes contain data tables for Chapters 2 through 6, respectively.

1

Aggregate Trends in Federal Research

GENERAL TRENDS

Federal investment in research turned a corner in 1998, after 5 years of stagnation (Figure 1-1). Overall federal expenditures on research exhibited a solid increase in FY 1998 (up 4.5 percent in real terms from 1993) and a much more substantial increase in 1999 (up 11.7 percent from 1993). Further increases in budget authority for research and development in the FY 2000 and FY 2001 appropriations have ensured continuing incremental growth into the current year. Substantial increases in appropriations to NIH represent a very large part of this growth, but even excluding NIH, federal obligations for research in 1999 were up by 1.4 percent over 1993, whereas in 1998 non-NIH research expenditures had been 2.3 percent below their 1993 levels.

Federal funding of basic research declined slightly after 1993 but since 1996 has been treated more favorably than research overall. In 1993, federal agencies obligated $15.0 billion for basic research in 1999 dollars. Real spending on basic research surpassed that level in 1996 and has increased steadily every year since. In 1997, funding of basic research was $15.4 billion, 2.8 percent more than in 1993. In 1999, it was $17.4 billion (16.6 percent more) and it was projected to be $18.6 billion (24.5 percent more) in 2000. The comparable increases for total research were 0.6 percent (1993-1997), 11.7 percent (1993-1999), and 18.7 percent (1993-2000). As a result of its high growth rate, basic research constituted 52.0 percent of total research in 1999, compared with 49.8 percent in 1993.

This trend toward basic research relative to applied research did not occur in all agencies or fields. Between 1993 and 1999, funding for basic research increased more than for applied research or was cut less than applied research in 12 of 22 fields we examine. Of the nine major agencies we look at, basic research support increased more than total research support, or decreased less, in four cases. These differences are discussed in Chapters 3 and 4.

BOX 1
Classification of Research[1]

In **basic research** the objective of the sponsoring agency is to gain more complete knowledge or understanding of the fundamental aspects of phenomena and of observable facts, without specific applications toward processes or products in mind.

In **applied research** the objective of the sponsoring agency is to gain knowledge or understanding necessary for determining the means by which a recognized need may be met.

Development is systematic use of the knowledge or understanding gained from research, directed toward the production of useful materials, devices, systems, or methods, including design and development of prototypes and processes. It excludes quality control, routine product testing, and production.

---

[1]The National Academies have for several years recommended use of the concept "federal science and technology (FS&T)" to refer to and highlight in the federal budget investments in investigations aimed at discovering new knowledge of fundamental phenomena and their applications, as distinct from development spending involving initial production, maintenance, and upgrading of weapons, space, and other systems. The FS&T concept is broader than basic and applied research together. See National Research Council. 1995. *Allocating Federal Funds for Science and Technology*, pp. 8-9, Washington, D.C.: National Academy Press. Since 1998 the Academies' Committee on Science, Engineering, and Public Policy has been tracking what it considers to be FS&T expenditures at the agency and program level but not at the level of research fields. National Academy of Sciences, National Academy of Engineering, Institute of Medicine. 1998. *Observations on the President's Fiscal Year 1999 Federal Science and Technology Budget*, Washington, D.C.: National Academy Press. Also same title for FY 2000, FY 2001, and FY 2002. In its FY 2002 budget submission the Office of Management and Budget has included its own FS&T analysis for the coming fiscal year. Office of Management and Budget. 2001. *Analytical Perspectives, Budget of the United States Government, Fiscal Year 2002*, Table 7-3, p. 136, Washington, D.C.: U.S. Government Printing Office. It is possible that more common use of the concept and agreement on its application will lead to systematic collection of data that can be used to assess FS&T allocations over time. For the time being, that is only possible with the NSF Federal Funds Survey relying on the traditional classification of science and engineering activity—basic research, applied research, and development.

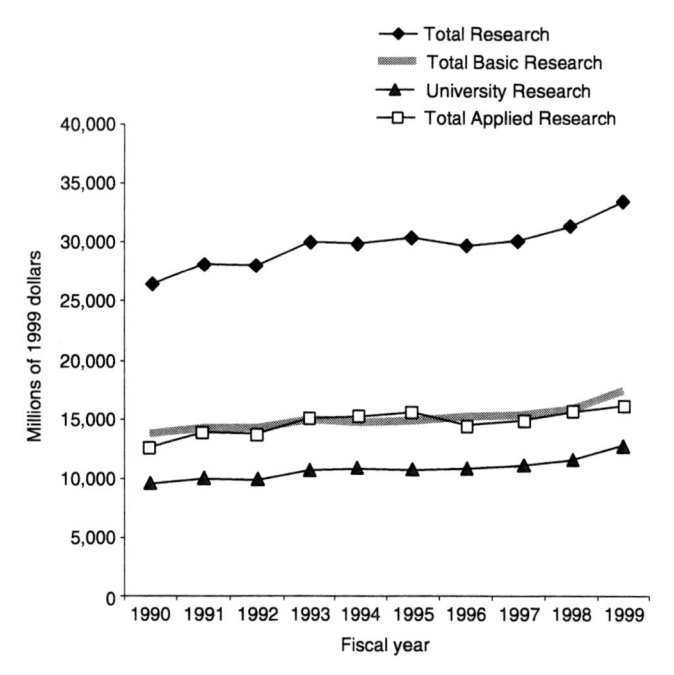

FIGURE 1-1 Federal obligations for research, FY 1990–FY 1999 (in constant dollars).

Like basic research, federal funding of research at universities also fared better than overall federal research funding. The federal agencies with the six largest R&D budgets obligated $13.2 billion for research performed at universities in 1999, compared with $11.0 billion in 1993, a real increase of $2.2 billion. This increase of 19.6 percent was larger than the increase in overall federal support of research of 11.7 percent and was only exceeded by an increase in support for research at nonprofit institutions of 23.2 percent over the same time period. The other major types of performers experienced much smaller increases: intramural laboratories (4.4 percent), industrial laboratories (4.6 percent), and federally funded research and development centers (6.9 percent).

Universities received substantial increases in both basic research support (up 19.4 percent from 1993 to 1999) and applied research support (up 20.0 percent). As a result, universities accounted for 39.4 percent of federally funded research and 52.2 percent of federally funded basic research in 1999, compared with 36.8 percent and 51.0 percent in 1993, respectively. And they were expected to receive even higher percentages of federal research funding in 2000 (40.5 percent and 52.9 percent, respectively).

AGENCIES' RESEARCH BUDGETS

Between 1993 and 1997, only NIH, NSF, NASA, Environmental Protection Agency (EPA), and DOC experienced real growth in research budgets among the nine largest agencies, but in 1998 and 1999 nearly all agencies benefited from the improved budget picture. NIH had the most success. Its budget for research was 33.5 percent larger in 1999 than it was in 1993 in real terms. But the cases of double-digit growth also included the DOC (up 30.5 percent), NSF (up 19.3 percent), EPA (up 13.3 percent) and NASA (up 10.0 percent). The Department of Agriculture (USDA) turned a 5-year decline in research funding (–5.0 percent from 1993 to 1997) into 6.5 percent real growth by 1999. Even the DOD research budget showed modest increases in 1998 and 1999, although the drop from 1993 was not greatly affected (down by 26.6 percent in 1997, compared with 22.4 percent in 1999). Of the major federal agency sponsors of research, other than DOD, only the Department of Interior continued to experience reductions in research funding (off 5.8 percent in 1999 from its 1993 level). (See Annex, Table 1-1.)

Although by 1998 or 1999 most agencies' research budgets were higher than they were in 1993, the divergence in budget success observed in 1997 persists. NIH accounted for much of the growth in federal research funding; all other agencies received 4.9 percent less research funding in 1997 than in 1993, primarily due to the substantial cut at DOD. By 1999, the non-NIH agencies were up by 1.4 percent over 1993. NIH's steady increases pushed up its share of federal research funding from 32.1 percent in 1993 to 38.4 percent in 1999, and it was expected to increase to 40.4 percent in 2000.[1]

The upward trend in agency funding of research is certain to continue through FY 2000 and FY 2001 because of enacted appropriations, but it is by no means certain to persist in future years. In its first budget, the new administration is attempting to reduce to 4 percent the "recent explosive growth" in discretionary spending, which had been growing at a rate of 6 percent in recent years.[2] Proposed overall budget increases of $14.2 billion for DOD, $4.6 billion for the Department of Education, $2.9 billion for NIH, and $5.6 billion for a National Emergency Reserve leave little for growth in other programs and agencies in FY 2002. The FY 2002 budget submission also proposes to limit future growth in discretionary spending to the projected rate of inflation, approximately 2.1 percent a year. The budget requests an increase in nondefense research and development of 4.3 percent in FY 2002 (from $45.1 to $47.1 billion), but excluding NIH, nondefense R&D would decrease by 3.0 percent. Nondefense R&D would increase substantially in 2003, because of the final

---

[1] American Association for the Advancement of Science. December 19, 2000. "A Preview Report for *Congressional Action on Research and Development in the FY 2001 Budget*," Table 2, Washington, D.C.: American Association for the Advancement of Science.

[2] Changes in this paragraph are expressed in current, not constant dollars.

installment of the amount needed to double the NIH budget in 5 years, but according to an analysis by the American Association for the Advancement of Science (AAAS), the annual increases would drop to about 2.2 percent after 2003. AAAS estimates that nondefense R&D funding would be 10.9 percent larger in 2006 than in 2001. If NIH is excluded from the calculation, nondefense R&D funding would be 2.8 percent less in 2006 than in 2001.[3]

Not every agency funded more basic research in 1999 than in 1993. DOD's support of basic research was 26.5 percent less in 1999 than in 1993 in real terms, and several smaller agencies (EPA and Department of the Interior) sustained even larger cuts in basic research, although the absolute amounts were substantially smaller than DOD's.

Much of the increase in funding of basic research has been driven by NIH. In 1993, NIH obligated $6.4 billion for basic research (42.5 percent of all basic research). In 1999, NIH obligated $8.6 billion (49.5 percent of all basic research). NIH support of basic research was 35.8 percent larger in 1999 than in 1993, an annual rate of increase of 5.2 percent. In all, NIH accounted for 91.4 percent of the net increase in federal funding of basic research during the 6 years from 1993 to 1999. NIH estimated that its funding of basic research would increase by more than a billion dollars (11.8 percent) from 1999 to 2000. That would make NIH's support of basic research 51.7 percent more in 2000 than in 1993. As a result, NIH would account for 51.8 percent of all federal support of basic research.

If NIH is taken out of the calculation, federal support of basic research increased only 2.5 percent from 1993 to 1999 (0.4 percent a year) rather than 16.6 percent (2.6 percent a year). Decreases at DOD, EPA, and DOI totaling $615.7 million in 1999 compared with 1993 were offset by increases totaling $829.1 million at the other non-NIH agencies. The largest absolute increases were at NSF ($413.1 million) and DOE ($173.1 million). NASA's spending on basic research increased just 1.6 percent ($31.6 million). All other agencies raised basic research support by a total of $211.3 million.

RESEARCH PERFORMERS

Universities

The majority of federal R&D agencies treated universities more favorably than other performers in the 1990s. Funding of university research increased at about the same or higher rate than funding of total research at five of the nine largest agencies (NASA, NIH, NSF, EPA, and DOC).

At a sixth (DOD), university research was reduced less than total research (-18.7 percent vs. -22.4 percent). At DOE and Interior, however, universities did not fare as well as other performers. For example, DOE support for research was 2.1 percent larger in 1999 than in 1993, but support for university research was 8.0 percent less.

There was a similar pattern in federal support of university basic research. Five of the nine major agencies provided about the same or larger percentage increases in basic support to universities than to other performers (NASA, DOE, NIH, NSF, and DOC) and EPA reduced funding of university basic research by a smaller percentage than total basic research. At the other three agencies, support of basic research increased less, or fell more, than for other performers. DOD, for example, reduced funding of total basic research by 26.5 percent but university basic research by 34.3 percent. At the same time, DOD reduced funding of total applied research by 20.9 percent but increased it at universities by 17.7 percent.

NIH was responsible for most of the increase in federal funding of university research. In 1999, NIH provided $1.9 billion more for research at universities than in 1993, which accounted for 86.5 percent of the net increase in all federal funding for research at universities. Similarly, NIH provided $1.3 billion more for basic research at universities than in 1993, which was 88.4 percent of the net federal increase in funding of university basic research. Without NIH, the increase in federal funding of university research would have been smaller (5.6 percent without NIH vs. 19.6 percent with NIH) and the increase in basic research at universities would have been even less (4.7 percent vs. 19.4 percent).

The other increases in university research were provided by NSF ($332.9 million), NASA ($143.1 million), DOC ($38.8 million), EPA ($18.0 million), and USDA ($2.6 million). Increases were offset by decreases in support from DOD (-$227.8 million), DOE (-$49.1 million), and Interior (-$20.3 million).

The pattern was similar for university basic research except that DOE increased its funding by $59.2 million in 1999 compared with 1993 even as it cut overall funding of research at universities by $49.1 million by making steep cuts in applied research. The EPA cut funding of university basic research by $2.2 million even though it had increased funding of total research at universities by $18.0 million.

In sum, barely half of the nine major agencies supporting research favored universities over other performers for total research or basic research, but one of those agencies was the one with the largest research budget, NIH. Thus, federal support of university research was substantially greater in 1999 than in 1993. As a result, NIH accounted for a greater percentage of federal support of university research in 1999 than in 1993 (58.6 percent vs. 53.1

---

[3]AAAS. 2001. *AAAS Report XXVI: Research and Development FY 2002*, Table I-15, Washington, D.C.: American Association for the Advancement of Science. Outyear projections for defense R&D were not included in the AAAS table, because they will not be available until the Defense Strategic Review is completed in June 2001.

percent). The same was true for university basic research (58.2 percent vs. 52.3 percent).

Other Performers

In 1993, universities received the most federal research funds ($11.0 billion), followed by federal intramural laboratories ($8.3 billion), industry ($4.4 billion), federally funded R&D centers (FFRDCs) ($3.7 billion), nonprofits ($2.3 billion), state and local governments ($0.2 billion), and foreign performers ($0.1 billion). Although the various categories of performers had different rates of increases from 1993 to 1999, the rank order of performers in federal funding did not change.

In 1999, federal agencies obligated $13.2 billion for research performed at universities, 19.6 percent more than in 1993 in real terms. Only nonprofit institutions received a larger percentage increase—23.2 percent—to $2.8 billion. In 1999, other performers (except state and local governments) also had more funds than in 1993, but the increases were much smaller—in the 5 to 7 percent range. As a result, universities increased their share of federal research funding from 36.8 percent in 1993 to 39.4 percent in 1999. Nonprofits also increased their share (from 7.6 to 8.4 percent). The other performers—intramural laboratories, industry, FFRDCs, state and local governments, and foreign organizations—received smaller percentages of federal research funding than they did in 1993. Despite the differential rates of growth, however, the overall allocation of federal research funding among types of performers had not resulted in major shifts.

In the immediate aftermath of the flattening of federal research funding after 1993, federal funding of FFRDCs contracted substantially for several years and did not surpass the 1993 level of funding until 1997. Intramural laboratories also were cut, especially in the period from 1996 to 1998, and only exceeded the 1993 level of funding in 1999. Industry experienced a substantial funding increase in 1995 (19.7 percent more than in 1993) but was cut back in 1996 to a level only slightly larger than it was in 1993. The other sectors had small increases during the several years after 1993 until larger increases came along in 1998 and 1999.

In 1993, universities were the largest performer of federally funded basic research. That year, federal agencies obligated $7.6 billion (in 1999 dollars) for basic research at universities, 51.0 percent of the total. Federal intramural laboratories were the next largest performer category with $3.0 billion (19.9 percent), followed by FFRDCs with $1.9 billion (12.8 percent), nonprofit institutions with $1.3 billion (8.7 percent), and industry with $1.0 billion (6.7 percent). State and local and foreign governments accounted for $0.1 billion (less than 1 percent). In this rank order, industry is further down than it is in total research, reflecting the fact the industry is much more likely to perform applied research.

In 1999, the distribution of funding among basic research performers was largely unchanged. Universities were still the dominant venue for basic research, with 52.2 percent of the funding. This small increase in academia's share of 1.2 percentage points came at the expense of intramural laboratories and industry, which lost 1.2 percentage points and 0.5 percentage points, respectively. Nonprofit research institutions also increased their share, by 0.8 percentage points.

These differences in share came from varying growth rates among types of performers. Funding of basic research at universities was 19.4 percent larger in 1999 than in 1993, 26.9 percent larger at nonprofits, and 16.5 percent larger at FFRDCs. The percentage growth in federal funding of basic research at FFRDCs was much larger than it was for total research at FFRDCs (16.5 percent vs. 6.9 percent). Basic research funding at intramural laboratories and industrial laboratories was also larger, but by less (9.6 percent and 8.2 percent, respectively). Funding of basic research performed by state and local governments and foreign institutions was smaller in 1999 than in 1993, but the amounts were small (the decline was less than $20 million).

It should be noted that there were significant shifts in agency support of intramural laboratories. DOD, DOE, NASA, and Interior together provided 40.4 percent of the funding for basic research in intramural laboratories in 1993 but only 28.9 percent in 1999. Meanwhile, NIH intramural laboratories increased their percentage of funding from 36.6 to 44.1 percent, and other agencies also gained share, including USDA (by 0.9 percentage points) and "other agencies" (mostly VA and DOT, by 3.4 percentage points). Together, the share of intramural research funding accounted for by the two largest biomedical research agencies, NIH and VA, increased from 37.1 percent in 1993 to 48.6 percent in 1999.

Similar shifts were happening in the support of universities. NIH support of basic research at universities increased by one-third from 1993 to 1999 (from $4.0 billion to $5.3 billion in 1999 dollars). As a result, NIH's share of all federal funds for basic research at universities increased from 52.3 percent to 58.2 percent. Meanwhile, federal support other than NIH's for basic research at universities was just 4.7 percent more in 1999 than in 1993. And this is an average of agencies with decreased funding for basic research in universities and those with increased funding. For example, funding at DOD decreased by nearly one-third (from $0.9 billion to $0.6 billion), USDA (by 9.0 percent), Interior (by 86.0 percent), EPA (by 35.9 percent), and "other agencies" (by 12.4 percent). These losses were offset by increases from NSF (21.8 percent), NASA (18.6 percent), DOC (27.6 percent), and DOE (14.3 percent).

RECENT APPROPRIATIONS

The rapid growth of the NIH budget continues to dominate the allocation of funding among agencies and fields. Under a congressional initiative to double the budget of NIH in 5 years, NIH received 15 percent increases in budget authority in 1999 and 2000, which translated into increases in obligations for research of 13 percent and 12 percent in those years. In December 2000, NIH received an increase for FY 2001 of 13 percent ($2.5 billion). As a result, NIH obligations for research were 49.4 percent more in 2000 than in 1993, while obligations for research supported by other federal agencies in 2000 were just 4.2 percent more than in 1993. NIH accounted for 84.7 percent of the net increase in federal funding of research between 1993 and 2000 ($4.8 billion of $5.6 billion) and for 40.4 percent of federal spending on research in 2000, compared with 29.3 percent in 1990. Research in the life sciences accounted for 48.0 percent of the federal research budget in 2000, compared with 40.8 percent in 1990.

This success led to an explicit effort in the FY 2001 budget process to achieve a better balance among agencies and among scientific and engineering disciplines. In President Clinton's last budget proposal, balance took the form of double-digit increases in budget authority requested for NSF (17.3 percent) and DOE science programs (13.0 percent) and a requested increase (instead of a decrease) in DOD basic research was 4.3 percent, whereas the increase requested for NIH—5.6 percent—was substantially less than it had received in recent years.[4] Congress responded favorably, increasing the budget of NSF by 13.6 percent, DOE Office of Science by 10.7 percent, and basic research at DOD by 12.8 percent.[5] The FY 2000 to FY 2001 increase in appropriations for research (basic and applied) at agencies other than NIH was 11.7 percent; the increase in basic research not counting NIH was 9.0 percent.[6] Notwithstanding congressional approval of a 14.2 percent increase in NIH's budget,[7] NIH accounted for only 45.3 percent of the net increase in funding for research from 2000 to 2001, compared with 54.5 percent from 1997 to 1998, 65.7 percent from 1998 to 1999, and 72.6 percent from 1999 to 2000. In 2001, NIH's share of federal funding of research increased by 0.6 percentage points to 40.8 percent, compared with increases of approximately 2.0 percentage points in 1999 and 2000.[8] Thus the divergence between NIH and other agencies' research budgets did not widen as much in 2001 as it had in the several preceding years. The Bush Administration's proposed FY 2002 budget and its projections for future years would return to the previous pattern of large NIH increases and flat or declining research budgets in most other federal agencies.

---

[4]Office of Management and Budget. 2000. *Budget of the United States Government: Fiscal Year 2001*, Table 5-1, Washington, D.C.: U.S. Government Printing Office.

[5]Janice Long, "2001: A Good Year for Federal R&D Funding," *Chemical & Engineering News* (January 8, 2001): 23.

[6]Calculated from Table 2 in AAAS. 2000. *Congressional Action on R&D in the FY 2001 Budget*. Washington, D.C.: American Association for the Advancement of Science.

[7]Janice Long, "2001: A Good Year for Federal R&D Funding," *Chemical & Engineering News* (January 8, 2001):23.

[8]The calculation of change from 2000 to 2001 was based on appropriated budget authority; for the change from 1999 to 2000 it was based on obligations.

ANNEX

TABLE 1-1 Trends by Agency and Character of Research, 1990–1999 (millions of 1999 dollars)

	1990	1991	1992	1993	1994	1995	1996	1997	1998	1999	1993–1997	1993–1999
All Agencies												
Total Research	26,346.3	28,112.1	27,989.3	30,015.1	29,951.0	30,407.9	29,631.8	30,202.2	31,355.0	33,527.5	0.6%	11.7%
Total Basic Research	13,751.2	14,274.9	14,274.2	14,956.0	14,776.6	14,840.1	15,166.2	15,367.6	15,831.5	17,443.7	2.8%	16.6%
Total Applied Research	12,595.1	13,837.2	13,715.1	15,059.0	15,174.5	15,567.7	14,465.5	14,834.5	15,523.5	16,083.9	-1.5%	6.8%
University Research	9,914.1	10,400.6	10,355.1	11,041.7	11,245.3	11,072.4	11,226.3	11,491.6	11,905.3	13,203.8	4.1%	19.6%
DOD												
Total Research	4,300.2	4,360.7	4,655.3	5,339.3	4,633.5	4,489.8	4,189.5	3,918.3	4,025.4	4,142.3	-26.6%	-22.4%
Total Basic Research	1,154.6	1,166.1	1,255.9	1,415.6	1,312.0	1,334.9	1,193.1	1,052.0	1,045.2	1,040.2	-25.7%	-26.5%
Total Applied Research	3,145.6	3,194.7	3,399.4	3,923.7	3,321.7	3,154.8	2,996.3	2,866.3	2,980.2	3,102.1	-26.9%	-20.9%
University Research	968.8	931.1	1,042.6	1,216.8	1,178.6	1,119.6	1,122.8	972.4	978.2	989.0	-20.1%	-18.7%
NASA												
Total Research	3,729.4	3,954.0	3,690.6	3,961.0	4,196.5	4,326.9	4,066.3	4,304.1	4,475.5	4,357.9	8.7%	10.0%
Total Basic Research	1,994.5	2,000.5	1,986.5	2,009.3	2,145.9	2,115.5	2,077.1	2,154.5	2,052.1	2,040.9	7.2%	1.6%
Total Applied Research	1,734.9	1,953.6	1,704.1	1,951.8	2,050.6	2,211.4	1,989.2	2,149.6	2,423.3	2,317.0	10.1%	18.7%
University Research	514.0	556.4	584.9	601.6	606.8	628.4	587.4	613.1	656.6	744.7	1.9%	23.8%
DOE												
Total Research	3,132.1	3,839.5	3,900.0	3,839.9	3,586.6	3,700.0	3,525.4	3,669.3	3,840.5	3,919.8	-4.4%	2.1%
Total Basic Research	1,833.6	1,978.1	1,984.5	1,958.7	1,751.7	1,747.8	2,023.4	2,027.0	2,057.9	2,131.8	3.5%	8.8%
Total Applied Research	1,298.5	1,861.6	1,915.5	1,881.2	1,834.8	1,952.3	1,502.0	1,642.3	1,783.3	1,788.0	-12.7%	-5.0%
University Research	583.6	698.5	691.7	611.0	577.7	596.8	593.9	567.9	571.4	561.9	-7.0%	-8.0%
DHHS*												
Total Research	9,098.5	9,573.7	9,080.6	10,260.7	10,638.5	10,775.3	11,057.9	11,548.0	12,186.6	13,714.6	12.5%	33.7%
Total Basic Research	5,664.7	5,923.2	5,781.4	6,358.6	6,429.2	6,481.8	6,820.4	7,047.0	7,458.3	8,632.5	10.8%	35.8%
Total Applied Research	3,433.8	3,650.5	3,299.2	3,902.1	4,209.5	4,293.6	4,237.5	4,501.0	4,728.4	5,082.1	15.3%	30.2%
University Research	5,391.3	5,688.5	5,302.7	6,001.5	6,161.9	5,988.4	6,325.5	6,613.7	6,949.9	7,922.6	10.2%	32.0%
NIH												
Total Research	7,720.0	7,955.7	8,455.7	9,642.3	9,921.0	9,981.4	10,356.4	10,819.4	11,447.2	12,875.5	12.2%	33.5%
Total Basic Research	5,192.8	5,382.9	5,779.9	6,357.4	6,427.4	6,480.6	6,819.3	7,045.9	7,457.2	8,631.3	10.8%	35.8%
Total Applied Research	2,527.2	2,572.7	2,675.8	3,284.9	3,493.7	3,500.8	3,537.1	3,773.5	3,990.0	4,244.2	14.9%	29.2%
University Research	4,720.9	4,895.0	5,162.4	5,862.9	6,028.6	5,861.3	6,212.0	6,488.3	6,809.8	7,733.2	10.7%	31.9%

continues

TABLE 1-1 Continued

	1990	1991	1992	1993	1994	1995	1996	1997	1998	1999	1993–1997	1993–1999
NSF												
Total Research	2,058.6	2,093.8	2,135.3	2,100.6	2,229.5	2,298.5	2,294.5	2,312.6	2,321.4	2,506.0	10.1%	19.3%
Total Basic Research	1,932.9	1,966.0	1,990.3	1,946.4	2,044.0	2,110.3	2,104.9	2,115.3	2,148.3	2,359.5	8.7%	21.2%
Total Applied Research	125.9	127.8	145.0	154.1	185.4	188.2	189.8	197.3	173.1	146.5	28.0%	-4.9%
University Research	1,609.5	1,683.7	1,760.5	1,743.4	1,835.9	1,853.8	1,824.3	1,870.9	1,901.1	2,076.4	7.3%	19.1%
USDA												
Total Research	1,293.2	1,378.7	1,441.1	1,397.1	1,445.0	1,388.9	1,279.2	1,326.9	1,352.6	1,488.1	-5.0%	6.5%
Total Basic Research	632.6	654.0	680.2	687.5	662.5	636.3	576.7	606.7	612.2	743.3	-11.7%	8.1%
Total Applied Research	660.5	724.7	760.9	709.7	782.6	752.6	702.5	719.9	740.3	744.8	1.4%	4.9%
University Research	421.1	450.3	498.4	479.0	475.9	461.1	391.6	449.1	413.8	481.5	-6.2%	0.5%
DOI												
Total Research	579.0	649.1	652.1	647.5	710.4	569.4	568.4	568.4	509.9	610.0	-12.2%	-5.8%
Total Basic Research	250.3	268.9	263.9	257.1	90.9	59.0	58.7	58.0	49.4	59.1	-77.4%	-77.0%
Total Applied Research	328.7	380.1	388.2	390.4	619.4	510.4	509.6	510.3	460.5	550.9	30.7%	41.1%
University Research	60.2	66.5	64.5	66.1	56.8	52.7	48.0	41.9	47.0	45.7	-36.6%	-30.8%
EPA												
Total Research	384.1	414.1	462.1	403.5	439.6	429.5	399.3	420.8	483.9	457.0	4.3%	13.3%
Total Basic Research	89.7	107.0	126.2	99.5	110.8	75.2	54.2	52.6	58.2	57.0	-47.2%	-42.7%
Total Applied Research	294.4	307.2	335.9	304.1	328.9	354.3	345.1	368.2	425.7	400.0	21.1%	31.6%
University Research	94.4	65.7	155.5	75.1	78.0	97.9	65.1	94.9	107.6	93.0	26.5%	23.9%
DOC												
Total Research	459.4	527.4	681.0	649.7	784.9	954.2	891.9	831.1	818.3	848.0	27.9%	30.5%
Total Basic Research	38.3	40.2	39.4	41.5	43.8	42.0	39.3	40.3	40.2	49.1	-2.9%	18.3%
Total Applied Research	421.1	487.2	641.6	608.2	741.0	912.3	852.6	790.7	778.1	798.9	30.0%	31.3%
University Research	57.7	66.1	86.7	58.0	85.8	88.2	85.0	82.0	100.4	96.8	41.4%	66.9%
All Others												
Total Research	1,312.1	1,321.0	1,291.1	1,415.7	1,286.9	1,475.2	1,359.3	1,303.0	1,341.1	1,483.8	-8.0%	4.8%
Total Basic Research	160.0	171.2	165.9	181.9	185.9	237.4	218.4	213.8	310.3	330.1	17.5%	81.5%
Total Applied Research	1,151.9	1,150.0	1,124.9	1,233.6	1,100.9	1,237.8	1,140.8	1,088.6	1,030.8	1,153.6	-11.8%	-6.5%
University Research	213.5	193.8	167.6	189.4	187.9	185.5	182.7	185.6	179.3	192.1	-2.0%	1.5%

*DHHS includes NIH.

2

Field Trends in Federal Research Support

In recent years, concern has grown about the shifting allocation, or "balance," of federal research funding among fields, with continuing reductions in most fields of engineering and the physical sciences on the one hand, and accelerating growth in funding for biomedical research. FY 1999 marked the first year of a campaign to double NIH's budget in 5 years with annual increases of 15 percent through FY 2003, which promises to increase the gap between fields unless there are substantial funding increases for the other fields.[1]

To characterize the nation's research portfolio in a reasonably comprehensive and quantitative way, we have only two taxonomies: classification by field or discipline for research performed or supported by government and nonprofit institutions, and classification by industrial sector for research supported by and performed in private industry (see Chapter 5).

Disciplinary classifications generally reflect long-standing academic organization of faculty and graduate training. In other words, they correspond relatively closely to university departments and degree programs. A relatively static disciplinary taxonomy is subject to legitimate criticism for obscuring, among other phenomena

- the diversity of some research fields such as physics, encompassing nuclear, particle, and solid state among many sub-disciplines;
- the growing importance of inter- and multidisciplinary research;
- the extent to which some fields have shifted focus and approach—for example, the predominance of biologically-based chemistry relative to physical chemistry;
- the integration of related fields—for example, electrical engineering and computer science and molecular biology and biochemistry; and
- the emergence of new fields and subfields—for example, materials science, computational biology, and biophysics—and the decline of others.

The field taxonomy used by the NSF to obtain data on federal and university research expenditures (see Box 2) has other limitations. It may be difficult for non-academic institutions to use,[2] it is not uniform across surveys,[3] and it is not very detailed. All of these are valid concerns recognized by the NSF. Since its introduction in 1970, the survey of federal R&D obligations has been modified by the addition of the fields of computer science in 1976 and environmental biology and agricultural sciences in 1978. The Foundation nevertheless approaches changes cautiously to minimize discontinuities in the time series. In view of the increased concern about the overall and individual agency research portfolios, the field taxonomy in the Federal Funds Survey deserves even more attention. In the meantime, we are dependent on the classification currently in use to characterize what changes have occurred in the federal research portfolio. To assess the implications of those changes for the health of the research enterprise requires recognition that certain parts of some fields such as physics, astronomy, and oceanography are

---

[1] The funding balance issue has been raised by Donald Kennedy, editor of *Science*, and D. Allan Bromley, science advisor to former-President George Bush, and the House Committee on Science among others. See Donald Kennedy, "A Budget Out of Balance," *Science*, 291(23 March 2001):2337; D. Allan Bromley, "Science and Surpluses," *New York Times*, March 9, 2001; House Committee on Science, "Views and Estimates of the Committee on Science for Fiscal Year 2002," March 16, 2001.

[2] Michael E. Davey and Richard E. Rowberg. January 31, 2000. *Challenges in Collecting and Reporting Federal Research and Development Data*. Report RL30413. Washington, D.C.: Congressional Research Service.

[3] See National Research Council, *Measuring the Science and Engineering Enterprise*, pp. 48-49, esp. Table 3-1, showing the differences among scientific and engineering personnel surveys.

BOX 2
Classification of Research Fields

Engineering

Aeronautical: aerodynamics

Astronautical: aerospace; space technology

Chemical: petroleum; petroleum refining; process

Civil: architectural; hydraulic; hydrologic; marine; sanitary and environmental; structural; transportation

Electrical: communication; electronic; power

Mechanical: engineering mechanics

Metallurgy and materials: ceramic; mining; textile; welding

Engineering, other: agricultural; bioengineering; biomedical; industrial and management; nuclear; ocean; systems

Physical Sciences

Astronomy: laboratory astrophysics; optical astronomy; radio astronomy; theoretical astrophysics; X-ray, gamma-ray, and neutrino astronomy

Chemistry: inorganic; organic; organometallic; physical

Physics: acoustics; atomic and molecular; condensed matter; elementary particle; nuclear structure; optics; plasma

Mathematics and computer science

Mathematics: algebra; analysis; applied mathematics; foundations and logic; geometry; numerical analysis; statistics; topology

Computer science: computer and information sciences (general); design, development, and application of computer capabilities to data storage and manipulation; information sciences and systems; programming languages; systems analysis

Life Sciences

Biological: anatomy; biochemistry; biology; biometry and biostatistics; biophysics; botany; cell biology; entomology and parasitology; genetics; microbiology; neuroscience (biological); nutrition; physiology; zoology

Environmental biology: ecosystem sciences; evolutionary biology; limnology; physiological ecology; population and biotic community ecology; population biology; systematics

Agricultural: agronomy; animal sciences; food science and technology; fish and wildlife; forestry; horticulture; phytopathology; phytoproduction; plant sciences; soils and soil science; general agriculture

Medical: dentistry; internal medicine; neurology; obstetrics and gynecology; ophthalmology; otolaryngology; pathology; pediatrics; pharmacology; pharmacy; preventive medicine; psychiatry; radiology; surgery; veterinary medicine

Environmental Sciences

Atmospheric sciences: aeronomy; extraterrestrial atmospheres; meteorology; solar; weather modification

Geological sciences: engineering geophysics; general geology; geodesy and gravity; geomagnetism; hydrology; inorganic geochemistry; isotopic geochemistry; laboratory geophysics; organic geochemistry; paleomagnetism; paleontology; physical geography and cartography; seismology; soil sciences

Oceanography: biological oceanography; chemical oceanography; marine geophysics; physical oceanography

Social Sciences include anthropology; economics; political science; and sociology.

Psychology comprises biological aspects (animal behavior; clinical psychology; comparative psychology; ethology; experimental psychology) and social aspects (development and personality; educational, personnel, and vocational psychology and testing; industrial and engineering psychology; social psychology).

dependent on high cost facilities and that funding trends in agencies that support construction exhibit fluctuations accordingly. The assessment also necessarily entails an appreciation for and articulation of how the character and orientation of research are changing.

Also, from time to time, agencies responding to the NSF survey of federal funds for research and development change their procedures for classifying research obligations by field of research. In 1996, for example, NSF changed its classification of engineering and the environmental sciences research activities so that its support of mechanical engineering appeared to be much less and its funding of oceanography much greater. Mechanical engineering funding went from about $60 million in 1995 to $6 million in 1996; oceanography funding went from about $85 million to $209 million at the same time. If NSF did not actually change what it was funding, the drop in overall federal funding of mechanical engineering was somewhat less than reported, and the apparent increase in federal support of oceanography may not be real. The impact of NSF changes is addressed in the discussion of these two fields (below). Most fine fields were not affected by such changes during the 1993-1999 period, and the broad trends documented in this report—expansion of life sciences funding relative to funding of the physical sciences and engineering—are not affected.

HISTORICAL TRENDS IN RESEARCH FUNDING

The point of departure for our analysis is 1993, the year in which research funding in most fields peaked before the effect of the end of the Cold War and consensus to reduce the budget deficit took hold. Because this or any other point of departure influences the findings regarding trends in subsequent years, we briefly examine previous funding trends in major fields of research. The NSF Federal Funds Survey began to ask federal agencies about their research allocations in 1970, early in a 5-year period of flat research funding following the lunar landing and coinciding with the budget pressures of the Vietnam War. Within the total, however, there were major shifts in shares (Figure 2-1). Engineering and the physical sciences (mainly physics) experienced reductions of 18 and 15 percent while support of the life sciences increased 26 percent and the environmental sciences increased 10 percent.

Following a 5-year period of growth in most fields, research funding overall went down in the early 1980s, a period of recession, but the drop was of shorter duration and affected fewer fields—mainly the environmental and social sciences that were less popular with a conservative administration. Support of the physical sciences actually increased 16 percent from 1980 to 1985, as did support of the life sciences. Engineering support dropped slightly. The next 7 years, 1986 to 1993, were another period of across-the-board growth in support for the most part.

Taken as a whole, the quarter century from 1970 to the early 1990s saw relatively sustained growth of the life sciences, with the exception of a slight and brief downturn in the early 1980s (and more fluctuation in support of other fields.) The U.S. emphasis on health-related research (nearly 20 percent of the nation's entire R&D investment) is of course a distinguishing characteristic in international comparisons.[4]

RECENT TRENDS IN RESEARCH FUNDING

As the STEP Board observed in its previous report, although the overall level of federal research funding in 1997 was about the same as in 1993, there were markedly divergent trends among fields of research, with 12 of the 22 fields experiencing a decline in federal funding (four of them by margins of 20 percent or more) while other fields prospered (one—computer science—by more than 20 percent). As noted above, the funding level of most federal agencies' research programs increased after 1997. This broad improvement in the budget picture raises the question of what has happened to funding by field in 1998 and 1999 and beyond. Was the decline in funding in some fields through the mid-1990s, particularly in some fields of the physical sciences and engineering, halted or even reversed? The answer is yes in a few, but by no means all, cases. Funding was greater in 1999 than in 1993 in 15 of the 22 fields, six of them by more than 20 percent (aeronautical engineering, other engineering, biological sciences, medical sciences, computer science, and oceanography). But seven fields were still below their 1993 funding levels, five of them by more than 20 percent. The seven fields with less funding included three fields of engineering (chemical, electrical, and mechanical), three fields in the physical sciences (astronomy, chemistry, and physics), and one in the environmental sciences (geology).

ENGINEERING

Total Research. Overall, engineering experienced a modest turnaround after 1997, from a 4.7 percent deficit in FY 1997 to an increase of 2.0 percent in FY 1999, but within engineering, the picture is exceedingly mixed (Figure 2-2). Aeronautical (Figure 2-3) and civil engineering (Figure 2-4) went from little or negligible growth to increases of 20.9 and 16.8 percent, respectively. Astronautical engineering (Figure 2-5) also experienced modest growth through 1999 (12.6 percent).[5] On the other hand, funding of chemical (Figure 2-6) and mechanical engineering (Figure 2-7) research was even less in 1999 than in

---

[4]National Science Board. 2001. *Science and Engineering Indicators 2000,* pp. 2-51 and Figure 2-34. Arlington, National Science Foundation.

[5]But astronautical and other engineering fields including chemical and civil engineering had higher levels of funding before 1993.

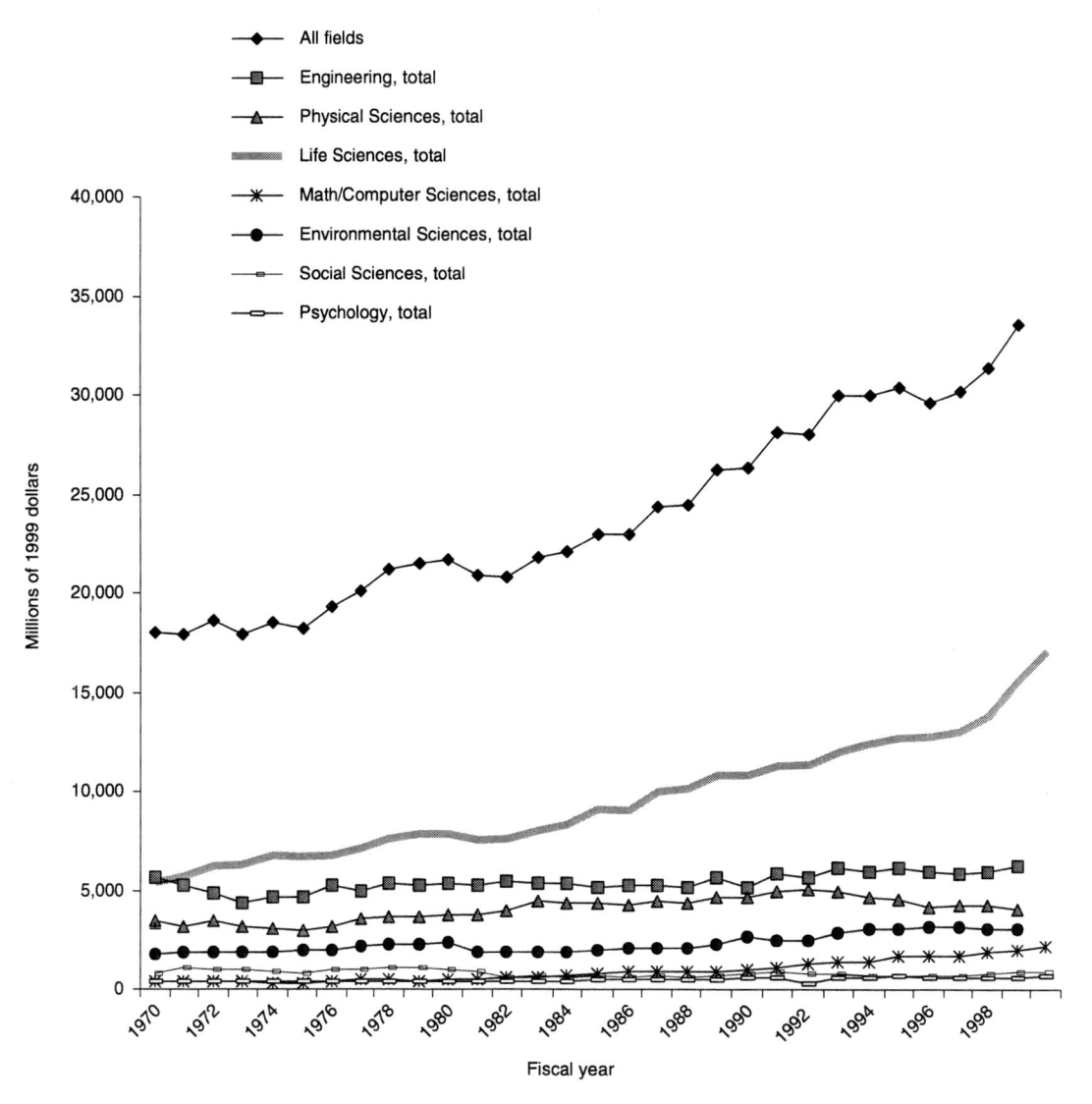

FIGURE 2-1 Federal obligations for research, total and by broad field FY 1970–FY 2000 (in constant dollars).

1997. They were down by −25.9 and −53.9 percent from 1993 to 1999, in contrast with −11.8 and −49.8 percent from 1993 to 1997, respectively.[6] Another losing field in the mid-1990s, electrical engineering (Figure 2-8), showed little improvement after 1997. In 1999, its support was still 29.0 percent less than its 1993 peak. Surprisingly, one of the mid-1990s "success stories," metallurgy/materials engineering (Figure 2-9), suffered a reversal in 1998. Its 14.0 percent increase in 1997 was shaved to a mere 1.5 percent in 1999, compared with 1993. Other engineering (Figure 2-10) also increased substantially from 1998 to 1999, by 25.1 percent.[7] The increases came at DOE, where other engineering went from $365.2 million in 1998 to 567.9 million in 1999, and DOD, where it went from $346.7 to $465.9 million, reduced by a decrease at EPA, from $138.0 million to $28.1 million.

Basic Research. Basic engineering research fared well compared with overall research in engineering. While total engineering research was just 2.0 percent more in 1999 than in 1993 in real terms, basic engineering research was 21.7 percent more. This increase took place, of course, at the expense of applied engineering research, which had 3.5

---

[6]Mechanical engineering was substantially affected by a change in NSF's criteria for classifying research in 1996. See Appendix A. NSF funding of the field dropped from $54.5 million in 1995 to $6.1 million in 1996. If NSF support is held constant at the 1995 level, assuming that only the classification of the research changed and not the nature of the research funded, then the overall decrease in federal funding is less, 44.3 instead of 53.9 percent.

[7]"Other engineering" includes agricultural, bioengineering, biomedical, industrial and management, nuclear, ocean, and systems engineering (see Box 2).

percent less funding in 1999 than in 1993. The same fields that had increases in total research also experienced increases in basic research from 1993 to 1999: aeronautical, astronautical, civil, metallurgy/materials, and other engineering. Those that had less total research funding also had less basic research funding: chemical, electrical, and mechanical engineering.

In some fields, the increase or decrease in basic research funding was about the same for total and basic research (e.g., aeronautical, astronautical, and chemical engineering). Most of the increase took place in a few fields. In metallurgy/materials engineering, total federal research funding increased 1.5 percent (from $776.5 to $788.0 million), but basic research funding increased by 78.6 percent (from $269.4 to $481.2 million). This increase of $211.8 million accounted for nearly three-quarters of the net overall increase in basic engineering research during the 1993 to 1999 period. Other fields in which basic research increased substantially more than total research included civil engineering (59.5 vs. 16.8 percent) and other engineering (50.5 vs. 25.1 percent).

In several fields, federal funding of basic research dropped less than total research funding. In electrical engineering, for example, research funding fell 29.0 percent, while basic research funding fell 18.1 percent. In mechanical engineering, support for basic research dropped 37.4 percent, less than the drop in support for total research of 53.9 percent. If we assume that the amount of total and basic research that NSF defined as mechanical engineering in 1993 has stayed at the same funding level in real terms, then support for basic research fell 24.4 percent, less than the drop of 44.3 percent in total research.

University-Performed Research. Federal obligations for engineering research at universities were $1,046 million in 1999, 5.5 percent more than the $991 million they obligated in 1993 in 1999 dollars. That increase was larger than the 2.0 percent increase in agency obligations for total engineering research during the same 6-year period. As a result, the share of federally funded engineering research performed by universities increased slightly, from 16.1 to 16.7 percent.[8]

From 1993 to 1999, federal funding of university research increased by a larger percentage than federal funding of total research or decreased by a smaller percentage in most fields of engineering: aeronautical (24.5 vs. 20.9 percent), astronautical (79.5 vs. 12.6 percent), chemical (+2.2 vs. −25.9 percent), electrical (−12.0 vs. −29.0

---

[8]Federal support of university engineering research increased to slightly more than 19 percent in 1995 and 1996, because overall funding of engineering research was stagnant. Subsequently, federal support of university engineering fell in real terms while overall federal funding began to increase again.

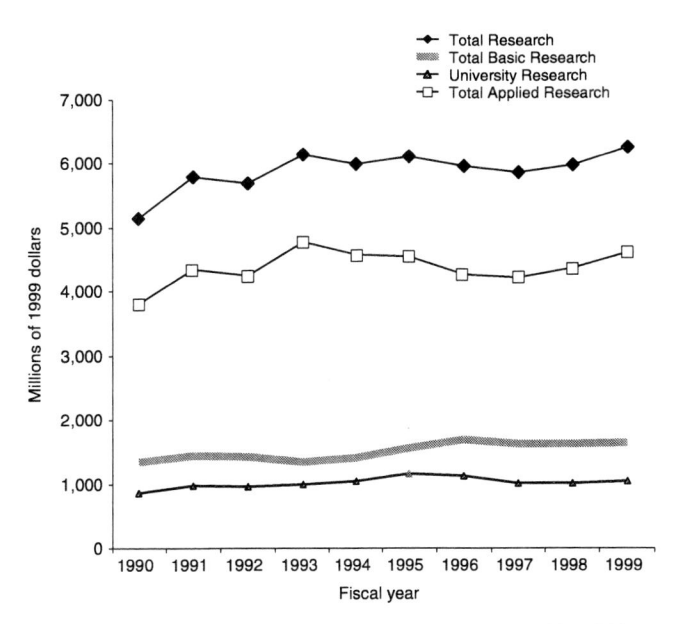

FIGURE 2-2 Federal funding of engineering research, FY 1990–FY 1999 (in constant dollars).

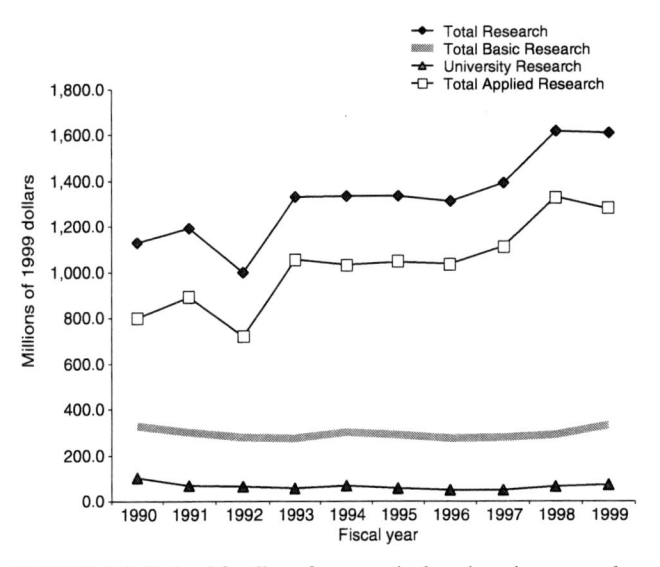

FIGURE 2-3 Federal funding of aeronautical engineering research, FY 1990–FY 1999 (in constant dollars).

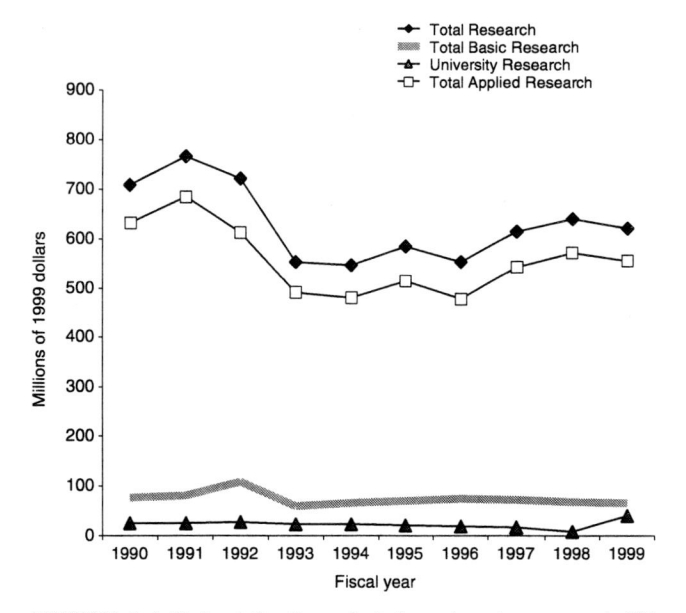

FIGURE 2-4 Federal funding of civil engineering research FY 1990–FY 1999 (in constant dollars).

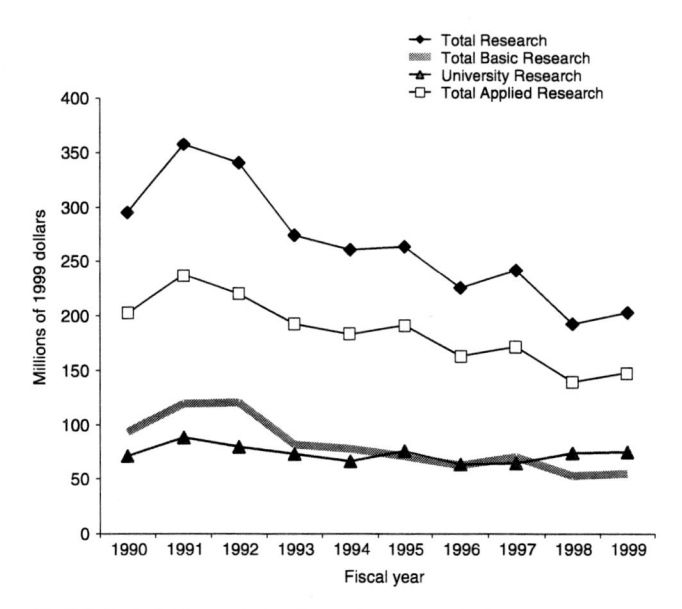

FIGURE 2-5 Federal funding of astronautical engineering research, FY 1990–FY 1999 (in constant dollars).

percent), mechanical (–40.5 vs. –53.9 percent),[9] and metallurgy/materials (7.7 vs 1.5 percent). Civil engineering was the only engineering field in which university research had a smaller increase than total research.

Because of relatively higher increases in funding (or smaller decreases) from 1993 to 1999, universities now perform a substantially higher share of federally funded engineering research in several fields. In chemical engineering, for example, federal funding of university research held steady (+2.2 percent) while overall federal funding fell (–25.9 percent), and universities increased their share of federal funding from 26.6 percent to 36.7 percent. In mechanical engineering, funding of university research was cut less than funding of total research (–40.5 vs. –53.9 percent), and universities increased their share of mechanical engineering research from 25.1 to 32.4 percent. The university share in 1999 was larger—37.6 percent—if we assume that NSF changes are a function of the 1996 reclassification and the agency supported mechanical engineering to the same extent in 1999 as in 1993.

Federal funding of basic engineering research at universities also increased, from $647.4 million in 1993 to $725.2 million in 1999, although that increase of 12.0 percent was less than the increase of 21.7 percent in overall federal funding of basic engineering. Basic research funding was larger in 1999 than in 1993 in five of the seven fields of engineering: aeronautical (2.6 percent), astronautical (114.4 percent), chemical (5.4 percent), civil (9.7 percent), metallurgy/materials (43.6 percent), and other engineering (58.9 percent). Only electrical and mechanical engineering had less funding in 1999 than in 1993 in real terms (–15.4 and –36.8 percent, respectively).[10]

Universities were responsible for performing much more federally funded basic research than total research in engineering in 1993 (48.0 vs. 16.1 percent in 1993). This role had not changed much by 1999, when universities accounted for 44.2 percent of federally funded basic engineering research vs. 16.7 percent of total engineering research. There were more complex shifts at the fine field level, however. The university share of federal funding of basic research increased sharply in two fields—astronautical and chemical engineering (from 22.1 to 42.9 percent and from 51.8 to 80.4 percent, respectively). It fell in two other fields—civil and metallurgy/materials engineering (from 67.8 to 46.7 percent and from 53.0 to 42.6 percent, respectively).

There were substantial shifts in emphasis on basic

---

[9]If NSF funding is held constant on the assumption that the reported decline in mechanical engineering reflected a reclassification of obligations, the overall declines are –6.9 percent vs. –44.3 percent.

[10]If NSF funding is held constant, the decrease in mechanical engineering was less: 24.3 percent.

versus applied research in a few fields. In astronautical and metallurgy/materials engineering, basic research expanded relative to applied research. In 1999, for example, 85.0 percent of research in metallurgy/materials engineering was basic, compared with 63.7 percent in 1993. In aeronautical research performed at universities, however, 62.8 percent was basic in 1999, compared with 76.3 percent in 1993.

In summary, universities, which play a relatively small role in performing federally funded engineering research, fared relatively well compared with other performers in most fields during the period of budget cuts and recovery, and within universities, basic research did better than applied research in most fields. Nevertheless, there is less funding in two of the seven fields in 1999 than there was in 1993 (electrical and mechanical engineering), and several other fields experienced modest growth—chemical, civil, and metallurgy/materials (2.2, 6.4, and 7.7 percent, respectively). Only two fields had substantial increases—aeronautical and astronautical engineering (24.5 percent and 79.5 percent, respectively).

Other engineering also experienced substantial growth. Federally funded engineering research in universities in this category grew 36.1 percent from 1993 to 1999 (from $221.8 million to $301.9 million, in 1999 dollars), and basic research support in this category increased by 58.9 percent (from $101.7 million to $161.6 million). If this category of funding had not increased, federal support of engineering research at universities would have been 4.9 percent less in 1999 than in 1993, rather than 5.5 percent more.

PHYSICAL SCIENCES

Total Research. The physical sciences overall continued to experience a decline in funding (Figure 2-11). Down by 13.6 percent from 1993 in 1997, they were down by 17.7 percent in 1999. That trend was reflected in the support of chemistry research, which was off by 13.4 percent from 1993 in contrast to a 7.6 percent decline from 1993 to 1997 (Figure 2-12). Astronomy, which had been up by 4.0 percent in 1997 compared with 1993, had 1.1 percent less funding in 1999 than in 1993 (Figure 2-13). Like electrical engineering, physics experienced a slight improvement in funding from 1997 to 1999, although the total federal research support of the field was still nearly one-quarter below its 1993 level (Figure 2-14).

Federal funding of research in the physical sciences was $4.1 billion in 1999, compared with $4.9 billion in 1993 (measured in 1999 dollars). The bulk of the decline occurred in physics research. Federal funding was $2.2 billion, compared with $2.9 billion in 1993. Astronomy also had less funding in 1999 than in 1993 ($757.9 vs. $766.0 million), as did chemistry ($814.9 vs. $941.1 million).

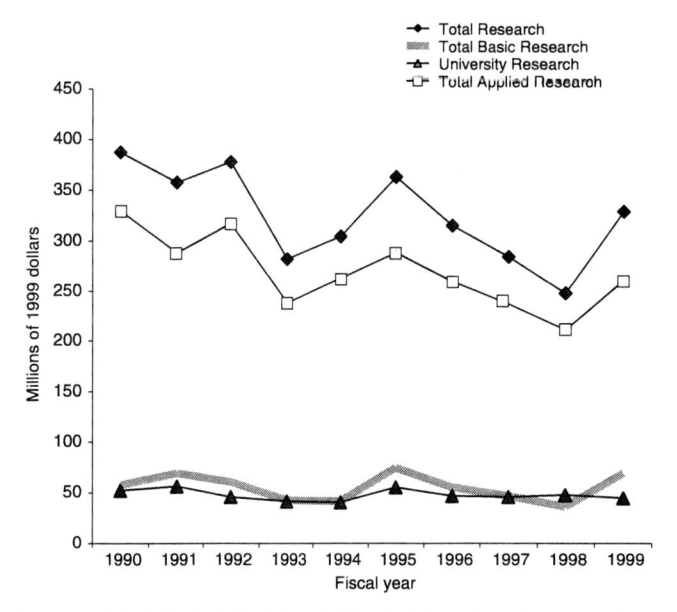

FIGURE 2-6 Federal funding of chemical engineering research, FY 1990–FY 1999 (in constant dollars).

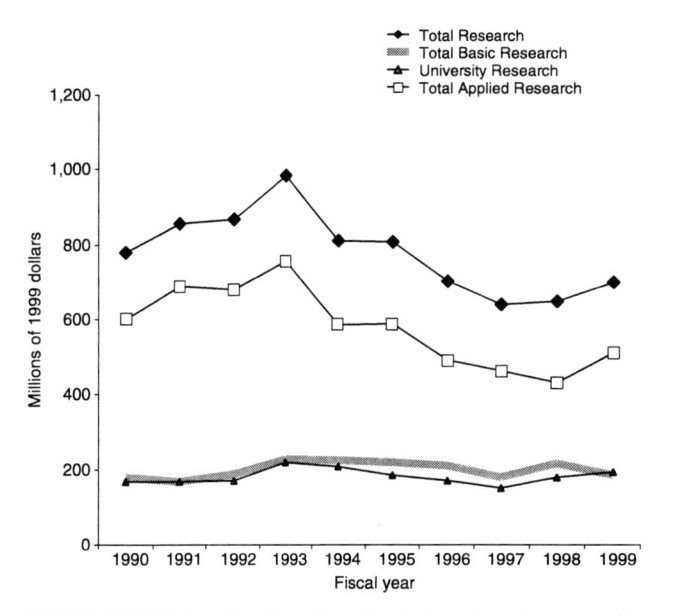

FIGURE 2-7 Federal funding of mechanical engineering research, FY 1990–FY 1999 (in constant dollars).

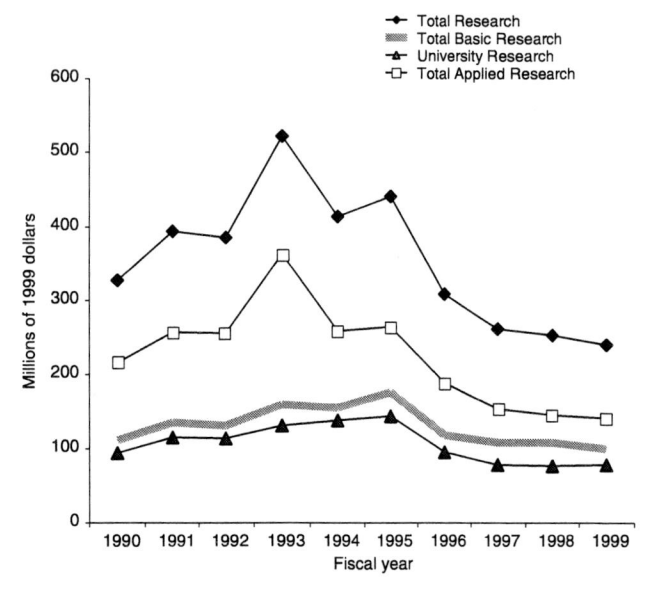

FIGURE 2-8 Federal funding of electrical engineering research, FY 1990–FY 1999 (in constant dollars).

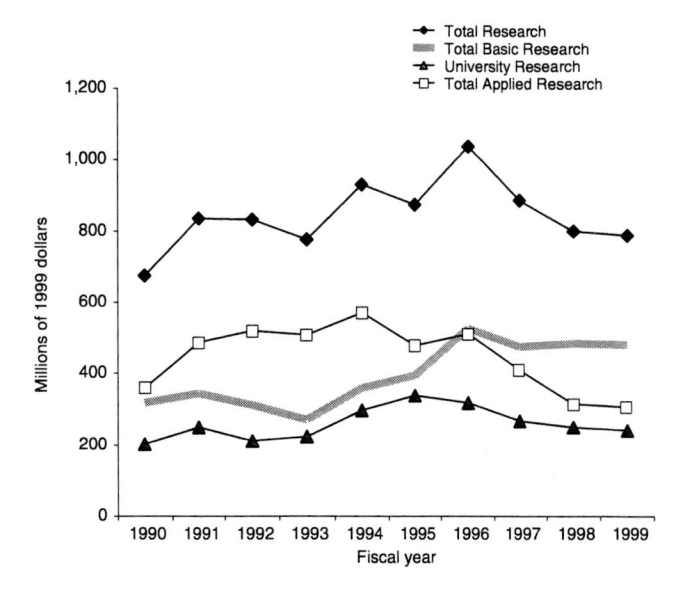

FIGURE 2-9 Federal funding of metallurgy/materials engineering research, FY 1990–FY 1999 (in constant dollars).

The major cuts in physics research were made by DOE and DOD. DOE reduced its support by $461.7 million (–25.3 percent) and DOD by $308.3 million (–57.8 percent), compared with the 1993 funding level. NSF also reduced its level of support, by 8.6 million (–4.7 percent). Some agencies (NIH, DOC, NASA, and others) increased funding, but the total of $75.4 million did little to offset the large cuts at DOE and DOD.

In astronomy, where federal funding fell slightly, from $766.0 to $757.9 million, the major factor was DOE, which dropped funding of astronomy in 1995. Although more than half that cut of $14.0 million was offset by other agencies by 1999, astronomy was still down from 1993.

In chemistry, funding declined rather than improved after 1997. Federal funding in 1999 was $814.9 million, compared with $941.1 million in 1993 (13.4 percent less). In 1997, the funding level was $869.9 million (7.6 percent less than in 1993). The major factors were cuts of $85.4 million by DOE (–31.0 percent) and $50.5 million by DOD (–32.3 percent). The Interior Department reduced its funding by $28.7 million (–98.3 percent) and USDA by $10.3 million (–10.8 percent). Small increases at DOC, NIH, Department of the Interior, EPA, and NSF offset the cuts by $55.1 million. It should be noted that Interior's level of funding of approximately $35 million a year in 1994 through 1997 fell sharply to less then $1 million in 1998 and to half a million dollars in 1999.

Basic Research. Basic research fared better than total research in the physical sciences as it did in engineering. Basic research funding was 4.8 percent less in 1999 than in 1993, while total research funding was 17.7 percent less. This was mostly due to substantial cuts in applied physics research (–54.4 percent) and to a lesser extent, in applied chemistry research (–22.1 percent).

In physics, federal agencies obligated 5.2 percent less for basic research in 1999 than they had in 1993, compared with a decrease in 24.6 percent in total research. Similarly, in chemistry, the decrease in funding for basic research was less than the decrease for total research, although the differential was not as great as in physics (–8.6 vs. –13.4 percent). In astronomy, however, the decrease in basic research was greater than that for total research (–3.0 vs. –1.1 percent), because DOD and NASA cut support of basic astronomy and increased support of applied astronomy.

University-Performed Research. Federal obligations for university research in the physical sciences increased by $14 million (1.1 percent) from 1993 to 1999 (from $1,309 million to $1,323 million, in 1999 dollars). This was much better than overall federal support of the physical sciences, which was 17.7 percent less in 1999 than in 1993. Federal support of basic research performed by universities was 6.9 percent larger in 1999, again better than overall federal support of basic research in the physical sciences, which dropped by 4.8 percent.

The funding situation for university research in the physical sciences has improved since 1997, when federal funding was $181 million, 8.5 percent less than in 1993. In 1998, it was $1,197 million, 6.7 percent less.

Two of the three fields had less federal funding for university research in 1999 than in 1993. Federal funding of university physics research decreased by 7.4 percent (from $678.6 to $628.7 million). In chemistry, funding decreased by 2.0 percent (from $388.4 to $380.7 million). These decreases were more than offset by the increase in funding of university astronomy research during the 1993-1999 period. Federal funding of astronomy research at universities increased from $134.1 to $197.0 million, or by 46.9 percent.

Because federal funding of total research decreased more than federal funding of university research in each field, universities performed a larger share of federal research in each field in 1999 compared with 1993. The university role in astronomy research increased the most, because federal funding of astronomy research at universities had increased substantially despite an overall decrease in federal support for astronomy research. Universities conducted 26.0 percent of all federally funded astronomy research in 1999, compared with 17.5 percent in 1993. In the other two fields, universities increased their share of federal support even though federal funding decreased, because federal support fell even more for other performers. In 1999, universities accounted for 46.7 percent of federal funding for chemistry research, and 28.3 percent of physics research, compared with 41.3 and 23.0 percent in 1993, respectively.

In astronomy, NASA increased support of university research by 77.6 percent. DOD reduced its support by 69.6 percent, and NSF's support stayed about the same (+1.2 percent). The same pattern held for basic research (70.5, –69.6, and 1.3 percent, respectively). NASA support was 12 times larger than DOD's to begin with, so the increase in NASA support drove the large increase in federal support of astronomy research.

In chemistry, NIH, NSF, and NASA provided more funding for university research in 1999 than in 1993 (9.8, 6.5, and 115.0 percent, respectively), but this increase was offset by decreased funding levels at DOE, USDA, and DOD (–9.6 percent, –21.2 percent, and –38.7 percent, respectively). Basic research did less well. USDA and DOD reduced support by 28.8 and 37.6 percent. Although DOE increased its funding by 7.1 percent, NIH reduced its level of support by 10.5 percent and NSF and NASA increases were modest (3.8 and 5.6 percent, respectively).

In physics, all the major agencies except NASA and USDA cut the level of funding in 1999 from 1993, especially DOD and NIH (by 31.8 and 47.1 percent, respectively). DOE, the largest funder, and NSF, the second

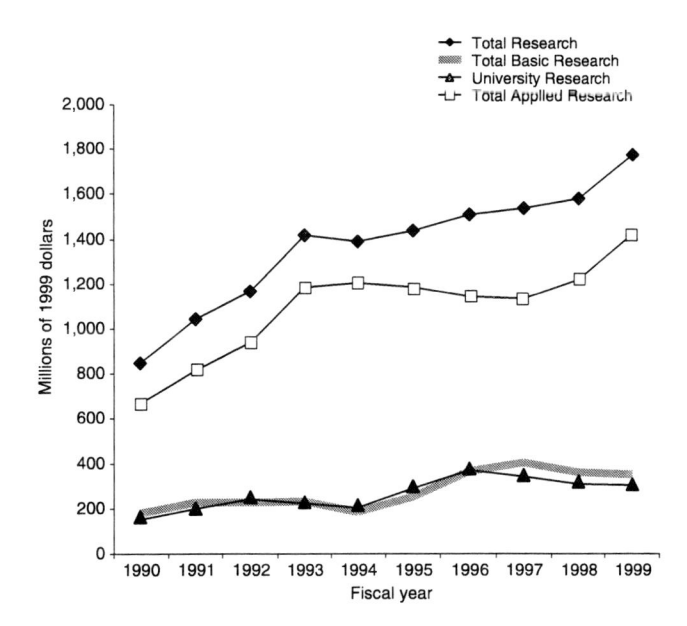

FIGURE 2-10 Federal funding of other engineering research, FY 1990–FY 1999 (in constant dollars).

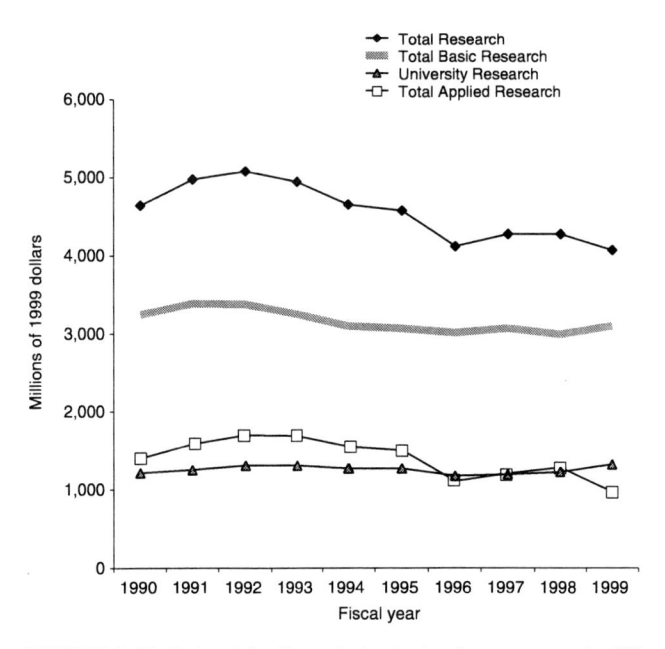

FIGURE 2-11 Federal funding of physical sciences research, FY 1990–FY 1999 (in constant dollars).

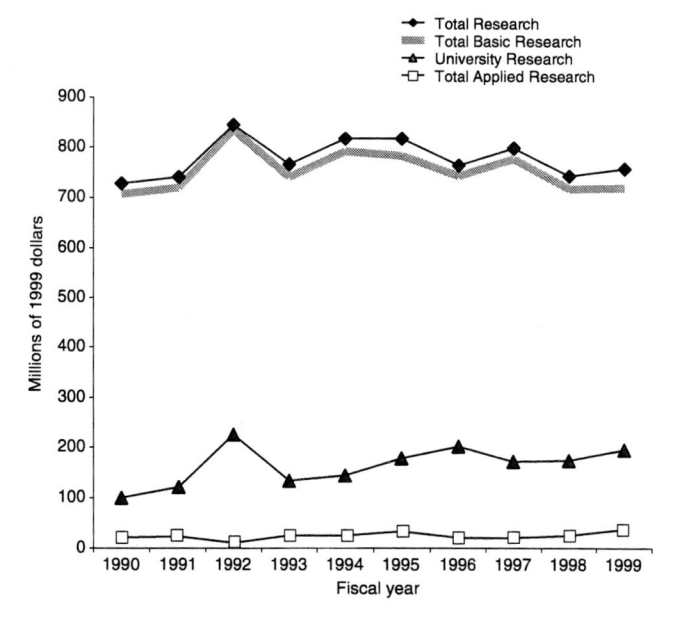

FIGURE 2-12 Federal funding of chemistry research, FY 1990–FY 1999 (in constant dollars).

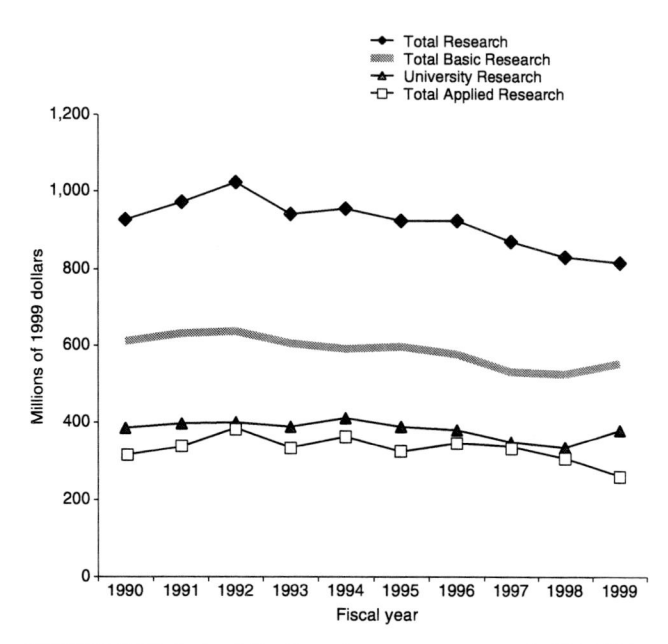

FIGURE 2-13 Federal funding of astronomy research, FY 1990–FY 1999 (in constant dollars).

largest funder, imposed relatively small decreases (–3.3 and –6.2 percent, respectively), so overall funding was reduced by only 7.4 percent. Basic research in physics at universities increased despite the cut in total university funding for physics. This occurred because DOE's contribution was 40.6 percent larger ($77.6 million), which more than offset the decreased funding by most of the other agencies, especially DOD (–28.7 percent) and NSF (–6.6 percent).

In summary, universities were less affected than other performers by the steep decrease in federal funding for research in the physical sciences in the 1993 to 1996 period. Since 1996, funding for university research increased each year while overall funding stayed flat. Thus in 1999, federal funding of university research in the physical sciences was larger than in 1993 by 1.1 percent, while overall federal funding of the physical sciences remained 17.7 percent less. The increase was not across the board, however. University research in astronomy actually increased in the 1993 to 1996 period before leveling off. Meanwhile, federal support of chemistry and physics declined after 1993 and has only recovered recently. Funding of chemistry research at universities, 2.0 percent less in 1999 than in 1993, was 13.5 percent less just a year earlier.

MATHEMATICS AND COMPUTER SCIENCE

Total Research. Mathematics funding, like that of some engineering and biological fields, experienced a modest turnaround after 1997 (Figure 2-15). By 1999, its support was up by 6.4 percent over 1993 levels whereas in 1997 it had been down by 4.4 percent from the peak year. Computer science funding continued to accelerate (Figure 2-16). By 1999, it was up 64.4 percent from the 1993 level, compared with 41.1 percent in 1997.

Federal funding of computer science research was $1.5 billion in 1999, up from $0.9 billion in 1993. The main forces in this large percentage increase were DOE, which increased its support by $390.9 million (338.7 percent), and NSF, which increased support by $155.3 million (109.5 percent). Several other agencies also increased their support, including DOD despite the substantial cut in its funding of research overall. DOD support was up by $10.0 million over 1993 (1.9 percent). There were relatively small cuts at USDA, NASA, and Department of the Interior, and among other agencies.

In 1997, federal funding of mathematics research was $310.2 million, $14.4 million less than in 1993. By 1999, it was up to $345.3 million, $20.7 million more than in 1993. In dollar terms, the main factors were a large cut at DOD and substantial increases at NIH and DOE. In 1997, DOD funding was $43.7 million less than in 1993, offset by increases at NIH, DOE, and NSF. DOD funding increased after 1997 (although it was still down by $31.3

FIELD TRENDS IN FEDERAL RESEARCH SUPPORT

million), as did support by NIH and DOE (NSF funding decreased to less than the 1993 level).

Basic Research. In these fields, basic research did not increase as much as total research funding. Overall, federal obligations for basic research in mathematics were 2.6 percent larger in 1999 than in 1993, while the increase in total research was 6.4 percent. Basic research in computer science was up 38.1 percent, compared with an increase of 64.4 percent in total research funding.

Federal agencies made relatively larger investments in applied research than in basic research in both mathematics and computer science in 1999, compared with 1993. This occurred mostly because, although cutting its overall level of support, DOD increased support of applied mathematics, while other agencies increased support of basic and applied research about the same.

Although federal funding of basic computer science research increased by 38.1 percent from 1993 to 1999 (from $317.4 million to $438.3 million), federal funding of total research in computer science increased much more: 64.4 percent (from $922.1 million to $1,516.1 million). Most of this was the result of increased investment in applied computer science research by DOD. There were substantial increases in basic computer science by NSF (119.5 percent) and, from a small base, NIH (408.4 percent), but these were offset by reductions in funding of basic computer science by DOD (–47.8 percent).

University-Performed Research. The fact that federal funding of basic research did not increase as much as total federal funding of research in math/computer science affected university research, because universities conduct a higher percentage of basic research than total research in this area. Although overall federal support of math/computer research was 44.8 percent larger in 1999 than in 1993, federal support of such research at universities was 21.2 percent larger. In 1999, federal agencies obligated $663.0 million, compared with $547.1 million in 1993. Most of this was basic research ($484.0 million, or 73 percent, in 1999). Of the two fields, however, computer science experienced a large increase and mathematics a decrease.

Federally funded computer science research at universities increased by 34.3 percent from 1993 to 1999 (from $377.1 million to $506.3 million). Mathematics research at universities decreased by 13.5 percent (from $151.7 million to $131.3 million). The divergence was even greater in basic research. Federal support of basic research in computer science in 1999 was 38.1 percent more than in 1993 ($337.9 million vs. $242.6 million), while support of basic mathematics research was 16.5 percent less ($121.5 million vs. $145.5 million). As a result, funding for computer science research went from 2.8 percent of federal funding of all research conducted at universities in 1993 to 4.0

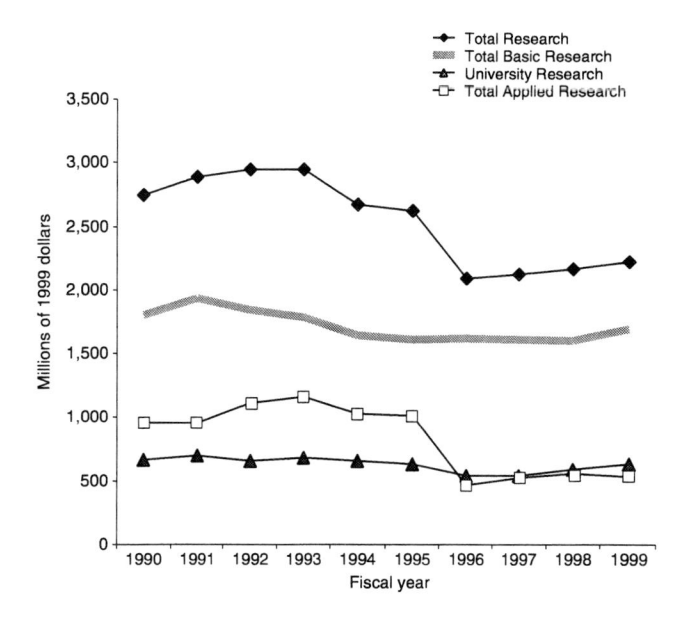

FIGURE 2-14 Federal funding of physics research, FY 1990–FY 1999 (in constant dollars).

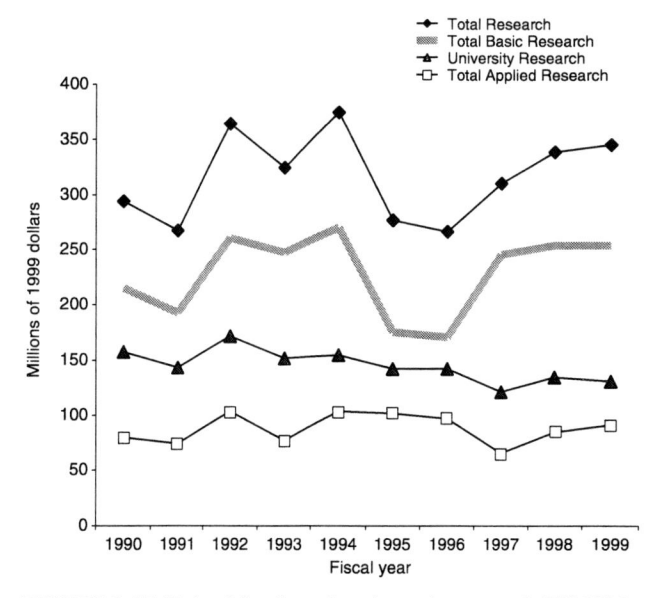

FIGURE 2-15 Federal funding of mathematics research, FY 1990–FY 1999 (in constant dollars).

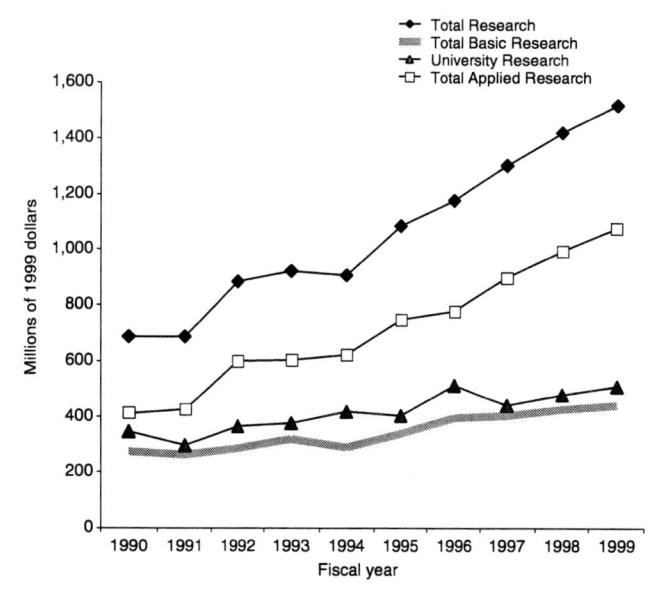

FIGURE 2-16 Federal funding of computer science research, FY 1990–FY 1999 (in constant dollars).

percent in 1999, a large increase but still a small share of overall federal investment in academic research.

LIFE SCIENCES

Total Research. In the 1990s, the life sciences as a whole experienced faster growth then other major fields (Figure 2-17). This is primarily because after 1993, when many federal agency research budgets were flat or decreasing, NIH's budget authority for R&D increased about 6 percent a year until 1999, when the increase was 14.0 percent.[11] The sustained growth in the NIH budget is reflected in the higher level of funding of the medical sciences in 1999 (up by 38.3 percent from 1993) (Figure 2-18) as well as in substantial growth in biological science support (up by 21.2 percent from 1993), although the latter had been relatively flat through 1997 (Figure 2-19). The other biological subfields, which draw most of their support from agencies other than NIH, have reversed downward trends in funding in the past 2 years. Environmental biology is up by 16.0 percent, in contrast to a decline of 3.5 percent through 1997 (Figure 2-20), and funding of agricultural biology is 6.7 percent more in 1999 than in 1993, compared with being 17.1 percent less in 1997 (Figure 2-21).

Federal obligations for medical sciences research increased from $4.9 billion in 1993 to $6.8 billion in 1999,

or 38.3 percent. Most of the net increase of $1.9 billion was accounted for by NIH and other parts of the Department of Health and Human Services. Most other agencies, in fact, scaled back support of medical research, but the amounts were comparatively small. DOD reduced its support by $24.0 million (–9.7 percent), EPA by $18.9 million (–98.7 percent), USDA by $8.2 million (–24.8 percent), DOE by $1.6 million (–2.9 percent), and other agencies (primarily VA) by $54.4 million (–16.2 percent). Accordingly, NIH's share of federal funding of medical research increased from 78.8 percent in 1993 to 82.0 percent.

The pattern in biological research was similar. Federal funding increased from $5.2 billion in 1993 to $6.5 billion in 1999, with 86.1 percent of the net increase accounted for by NIH. In contrast to medical sciences, most other agencies also increased support, including DOD by $65.4 million (67.7 percent), NSF, by 62.9 million (26.3 percent), and Department of the Interior, by $29.2 million (55.4 percent). The level of federal funding of biological sciences did not increase as much as for medical sciences (21.2 vs. 38.3 percent), primarily because NIH expanded the medical research part of its portfolio more than the biological sciences.

The reversal of fortune for agriculture research in 1999, after a period of little or no growth, resulted from a large increase in support by USDA that year. Federal funding of the field was $849.4 million in 1999, compared with $773.5 million in 1998. The increase of $75.9 million came from USDA, which jumped its funding by $91.7 million [offset by decreases elsewhere, primarily the AID].

The environmental biology story is more complicated because it has a more diverse base of support. Like agricultural sciences, federal funding increased sharply in 1999 to $720.6 million, from $612.9 million in 1998, but the increased levels of support came from several agencies. EPA, USDA, NSF, and Department of the Interior each increased funding by amounts ranging from $53.3 to $22.3 million (61.5 to 23.3 percent) and other agencies contributed smaller increases. In the longer run, from 1993 to 1999, increased support from these same agencies far outweighed reductions in funding at DOD, NIH, and other agencies (primarily AID and Smithsonian Institution). DOD support was $24.4 million in 1999, compared with $56.7 million in 1993, a reduction of 56.9 percent.

Basic Research. Basic research increased a little more than total research in the life sciences (31.0 vs. 28.3 percent), although both increased substantially. The pattern at the fine field level was a little more complicated. In the biological sciences and environmental biology, basic research did not increase quite as much as total research. This was due to relatively larger increases in applied biological research by NIH and applied environmental research by EPA and, to a lesser extent, USDA. The trend

---

[11]Most NIH R&D—87 percent in 1999—is research, not development.

FIELD TRENDS IN FEDERAL RESEARCH SUPPORT 33

in the medical sciences and agricultural sciences was toward basic research and away from applied research. This was the result of a shift toward basic medical sciences research by VA and toward basic agricultural sciences research by USDA.

University-Performed Research. Federal obligations for life sciences research at universities increased by $2.0 billion (31.8 percent) from 1993 to 1999 (from $6.1 to $8.1 billion). This percentage increase was a little more than the 28.3 percent increase in total federal funding of life sciences research in the same period. Federally funded basic research at universities was 28.5 percent more in 1999, not quite as much of an increase as the 31.0 percent increase in total basic research.

Federal funding of life sciences research was flat for several years after 1993 but began to grow again after 1995, with the largest increases occurring in the last several years (from $6.8 billion in 1997 to $7.1 billion in 1998 to $8.1 billion in 1999). The funding of basic life sciences research at universities has followed a similar trend.

Universities are the largest performers of federally funded life sciences research. They received 52.5 percent of the research funding and 58.9 percent of basic research funding in 1999. These percentages had not changed much since 1993, when they were 51.1 percent and 60.0 percent, respectively. There was some shifting at the fine field level, however. The percentage of federal funding going to universities for biology research increased from 57.3 percent in 1993 to 66.2 percent in 1999; in basic research, the increase was from 62.8 to 70.7 percent. Federal funding of medical sciences at universities decreased in the same time period, from 53.0 to 46.2 percent; federal funding of research in the basic medical sciences decreased more, from 62.7 to 51.0 percent. The role of universities in performing environmental research and agricultural research did not change appreciably.

Federal obligations for research and basic research at universities increased in every field of the life sciences from 1993 to 1999, more in some than others. In two cases, university funding increased by a greater percentage than total research funding for all performers. Research in biological sciences increased by 39.9 percent (from $3.1 to $4.3 billion), although total research funding for biological sciences increased only 21.2 percent. Similarly, in agricultural sciences, funding for research performed at universities increased by 21.7 percent (from $166.6 to $202.7 million), compared with a total increase of 6.7 percent. In the other two fields, university research funding increased, but less than for total research. In medical sciences, for example, federal funding increased by 20.5 percent (from $2.6 to $3.1 billion), compared with an overall increase of 38.3 percent. In environmental biology, the increase was 8.7 percent (from $179.1 to $194.7 million, less than the

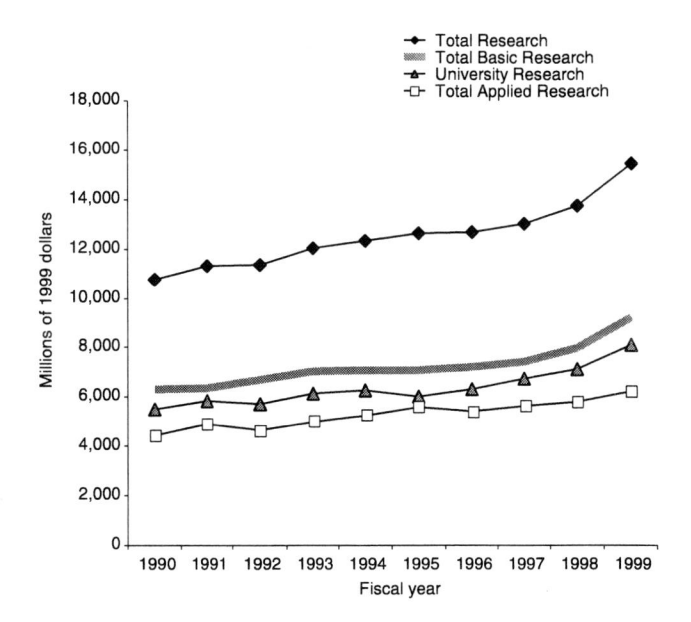

FIGURE 2-17 Federal funding of life sciences research, FY 1990–FY 1999 (in constant dollars).

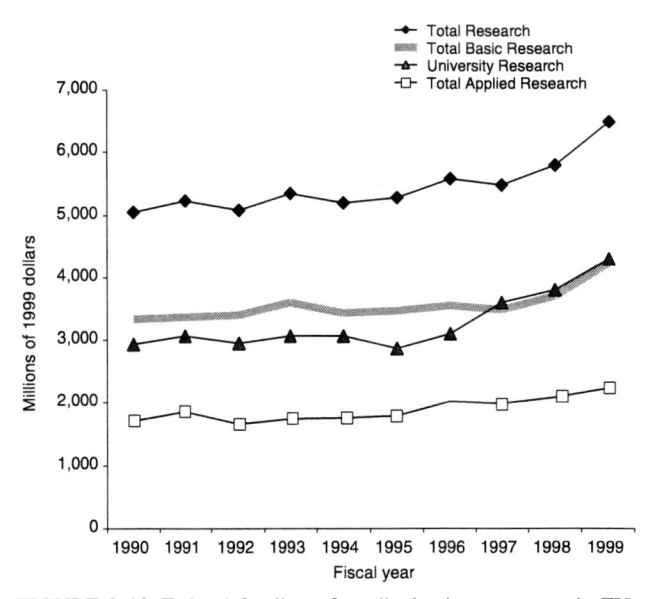

FIGURE 2-18 Federal funding of medical sciences research, FY 1990–FY 1999 (in constant dollars).

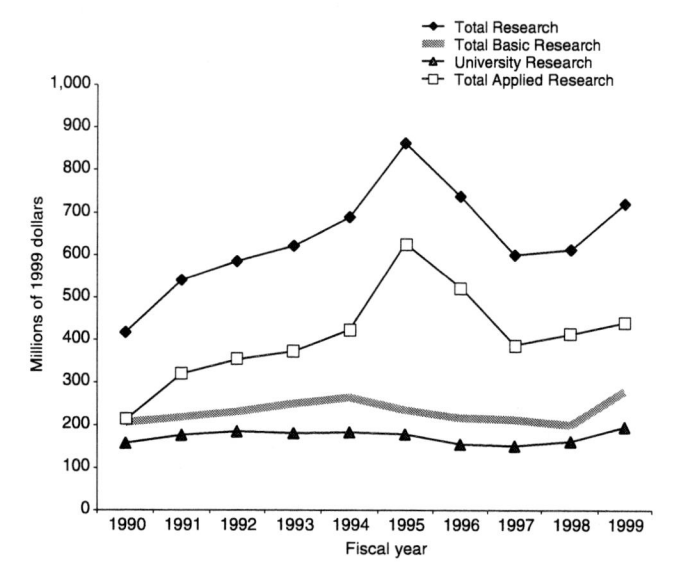

FIGURE 2-19 Federal funding of biological sciences research, FY 1990–FY 1999 (in constant dollars).

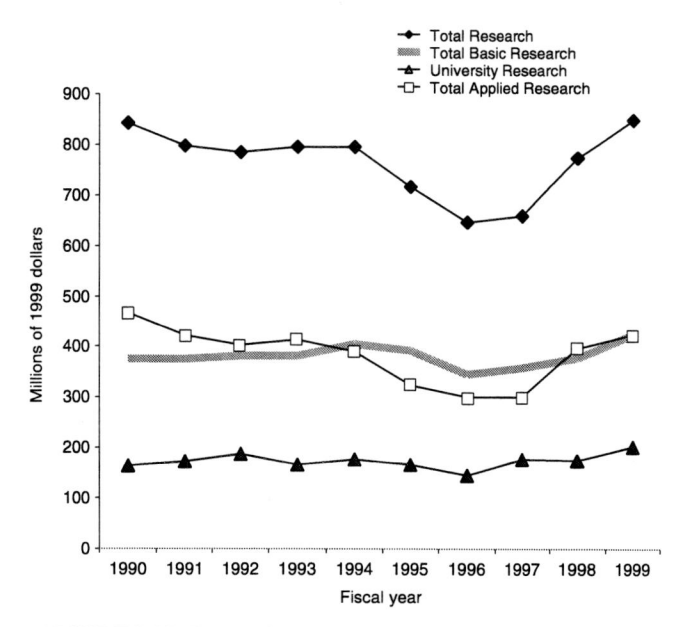

FIGURE 2-20 Federal funding of environmental biology research, FY 1990–FY 1999 (in constant dollars).

overall increase of 16.0 percent. The same pattern held in basic research funding.

In biological sciences, funding provided by NIH for research at universities increased by 44.7 percent and accounted for 95.2 percent of the net increase of $1.2 billion in 1999 over 1993. USDA and DOE provided less funding (–15.7 percent and –17.8 percent, respectively), but the amounts were relatively small (–$28.8 million together). NSF increased its funding of universities by 24.4 percent ($52.5 million) and DOD by 70.0 percent ($25.7 million). The latter increase occurred at Washington headquarters (expanded research programs on breast, prostate, and uterine cancer) and DARPA (research related to defense against biological terrorism). Basic biological research did a little less well, mostly because NIH did not provide as large a percentage increase for basic research relative to its overall increase. NIH increased its funding of universities by 38.2 percent, which accounted for 96.8 percent of the net increase of $738.6 million. DOD provided less funding for basic biological research in 1999 than in 1993 despite the larger overall increase it provided for total biological research at universities. Thus both NIH and DOD shifted support from basic to applied research at universities.

In agricultural sciences, USDA is the dominant funder, providing more than 99 percent of the federal funding in 1993 and 1999. Its increase of 22.0 percent ($36.5 million) accounted for the entire increase in federal funding. DOD and DOE zeroed out funding for agricultural research in 1999, although the amounts were very small, and NASA funding was about the same. The pattern was similar for basic research.

In medical sciences, NIH is the largest funder, accounting for 92.1 percent of all federal funding at universities. NIH funding increased by 18.1 percent ($442.2 million) from 1993 to 1999. This determined most of the increase in federal funding of 20.5 percent. Other DHHS agencies [Agency for Healthcare Research and Quality (AHRQ), Centers for Disease Control and Prevention (CDC), and Health Resources and Services Administration (HRSA)] provided an increase of 85.5 percent ($66.2 million). Funding from DOD and DOE was also larger by about 50 percent ($31.1 million), offset slightly by small decreases from USDA and NASA. The basic research picture was a little more complicated. DOE and DHHS agencies other than NIH do not support basic medical research. NIH's increase of 22.4 percent ($362.8 million) accounted for the entire federal increase. DOD cut its support of basic medical research by 20.6 percent ($7.1 million) although DOD funding of total medical research at universities was up.

In environmental biology, NSF and USDA provided more funding for university research in 1999 than in 1993 (26.0 percent and 19.7 percent, respectively), but DOD offset half the increase with a reduction of 68.0 percent. Other agencies also provided less funding although the amounts were small. It was the same pattern for basic research.

ENVIRONMENTAL SCIENCES

Total Research. The 1993 to 1997 pattern in the environmental sciences more or less continued in the subsequent two fiscal years (Figure 2-22). Atmospheric research held its single-digit growth (Figure 2-23) and oceanography its double-digit growth (Figure 2-24), while geology continued its steep decline (down by 25.9 percent in FY 1999 in contrast to 20.1 percent in 1997) (Figure 2-25).

In atmospheric sciences, EPA reduced its level of support from $113.2 million in 1993 to $56.5 million in 1999 (–50.1 percent), and there were smaller cuts at DOD, DOE, USDA, and DOI totaling $29.2 million. But the majority funder, NASA, increased its support from $574.1 million in 1993 to $657.9 million in 1999, joined by DOC, NSF, and smaller agencies, and federal funding of the field increased by $78.0 million (7.1 percent). In fact, unlike most other fields of research, funding of atmospheric sciences has declined somewhat in the past few years. In 1997, funding was 9.0 percent more than in 1993; in 1998, it was 8.4 percent more. This trend results from declining support by NASA during those years.

Oceanography appears to have done well compared with most other fields. Federal obligations increased from $521.7 million in 1993 to $656.6 million in 1999. Much of the increase of $134.9 million came from NSF, which obligated $126.4 million more in 1999 than in 1993. DOD also increased its level of support by $86 million (to $182.8 million), despite the substantial overall reduction in its annual budget for research. These increases, along with a smaller increase at EPA, overcame cuts at DOC, DOI, and NASA by a wide margin, making oceanography one of the six fields to register an increase of 20 percent or more from 1993 to 1999. However, oceanography is another field substantially affected by a change in NSF's criteria for classifying research in 1996.[12] NSF funding of the field increased from $84.5 million in 1995 to $209.4 million in 1996. If NSF support is held constant at the 1995 level, assuming that only the classification of the research changed and not the nature of the research funded, there was no change in the overall level of federal funding (+0.1 percent).

Geology did not fare as well as the other environmental sciences. It lost support by most agencies and went from $890.6 million in 1993 to $660.2 million in 1999, making it one of the five fields with a loss of funding of 20 percent

---

[12]See Appendix.

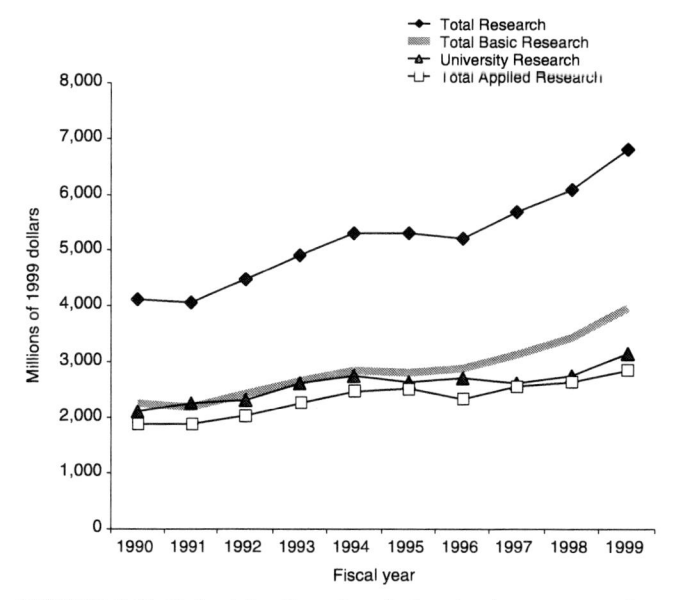

FIGURE 2-21 Federal funding of agricultural sciences research, FY 1990–FY 1999 (in constant dollars).

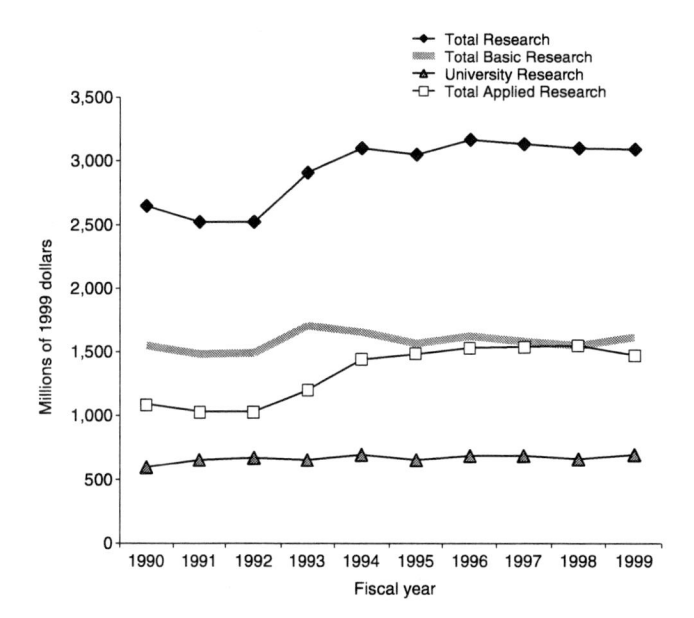

FIGURE 2-22 Federal funding of environmental sciences research, FY 1990–FY 1999 (in constant dollars).

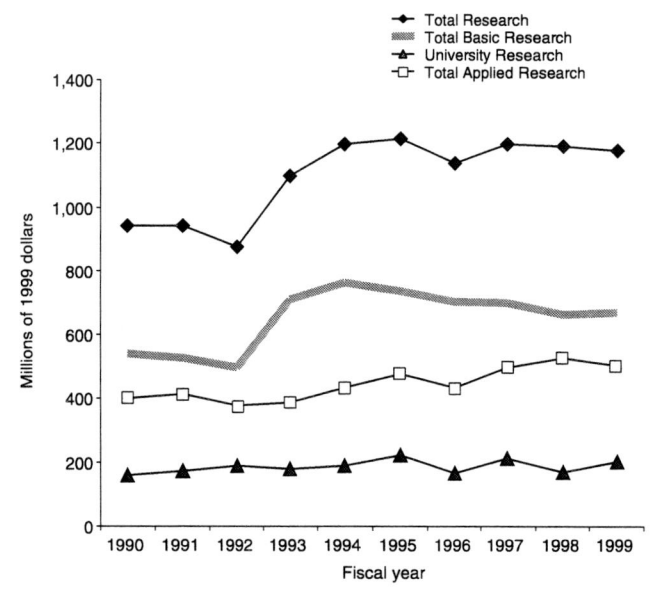

FIGURE 2-23 Federal funding of atmospheric sciences research, FY 1990–FY 1999 (in constant dollars).

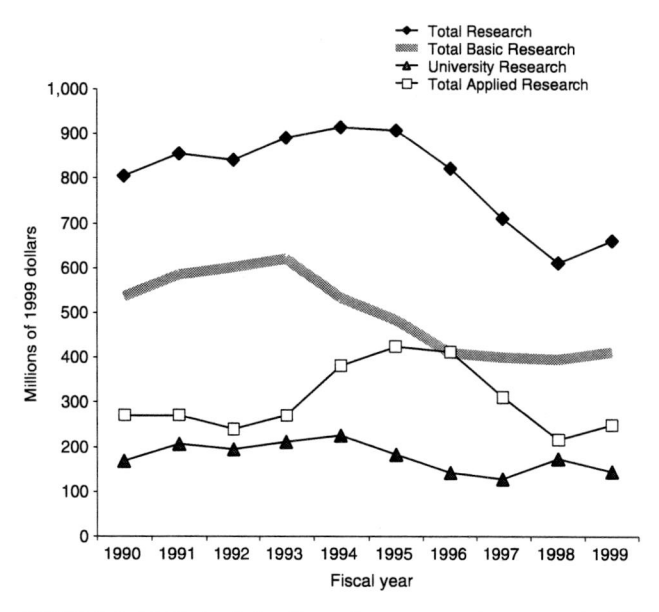

FIGURE 2-24 Federal funding of oceanography research, FY 1990–FY 1999 (in constant dollars).

or more. The largest reduction was at DOD ($87.4 million), which cut its funding by more than 90 percent, but there were also substantial cuts at DOI (–$50.1 million), NSF (–$43.4 million), and DOE (–$43.1 million). These were cuts of 17.1, 28.4, and 33.1 percent, respectively. It should be noted that geology was one of the fields affected by NSF's decision to reclassify the research fields of some of its activities in 1996. NSF funding of geology went from $160.0 million in 1995 to $98.5 million in 1996, a level it has maintained since. If we assume that NSF only changed its definition of geology and not the actual types of projects it funds, and we therefore hold NSF funding constant at the 1995 level, then the cut in geology was closer to 21.4 percent than 25.9 percent.

Basic Research. Federal obligations for basic research in the environmental sciences totaled 5.6 percent less in 1999 than in 1993 even though obligations for total research increased by 6.3 percent. That is, federal agencies spent $96.0 million less on basic research but $279.6 million more on applied research in the environmental sciences. Most ($204.1 million) of the increase in applied research came in the unclassified environmental sciences category. The rest came from increases in federal funding of applied atmospheric research.

Oceanography was the only field in which support for basic research was larger in 1999 than in 1993 (but see below). In basic atmospheric research, federal funding decreased by 5.3 percent ($37.9 million). Although NSF increased its support by $15.0 million (10.4 percent), EPA and DOD reduced support by $27.9 million (–100.0 percent) and $24.3 million (–61.8 percent), respectively. In basic geological research, federal funding decreased by 33.5 percent ($207.7 million). Most agencies reduced funding, with Interior making the largest cut in absolute terms (–$125.9 million). DOD and NSF also reduced support substantially, by $57.2 million (–94.7 percent) and $40.8 million (–27.2 percent), respectively. Only DOE increased funding of basic geology, by $25.1 million (40.4 percent).

Oceanography was a different story. Federal agencies obligated 25.9 percent more in total research dollars but 66.0 percent more in basic research. The main driver was NSF, which increased funding of basic oceanography by 149.0 percent ($127.6 million) from 1993 to 1999. DOD also increased its investment in basic oceanography in 1999 (47.2 percent more than in 1993 and 105.4 percent more than in 1998). However, oceanography is another field affected by the change in NSF field definitions in 1996. NSF funding of basic oceanography research jumped from $83.1 million in 1995 to $207.5 million in 1996. At the same time, NSF funding of basic geology research dropped by $60.7 million and basic atmospheric research by $8.6 million. If we assume that NSF changed its classification criteria rather than what it funded, and hold its investment constant at the 1995 level, then the increase in funding of basic oceanography research since 1993 is a much more modest 7.4 percent.

University-Performed Research. Federal funding of university research in the environmental sciences presents a very mixed picture. Overall, funding of university research from 1993 to 1999 did not increase by quite as much as total research (5.6 percent vs. 6.3 percent), but the increase in funding of basic research at universities was much larger than that for basic research overall. In fact, overall basic research was 5.6 percent less while university basic research was 5.6 percent more. These trends, however, mask very different situations at the detailed field level. Federal support for university research in atmospheric sciences is up moderately, for oceanography it is up substantially, and for geological sciences it is much less than in 1993. The trends in university basic research were basically the same in each detailed subfield.

In 1999, federal funding of atmospheric research at universities increased by 13.7 percent over 1993 ($202.6 compared with $178.1 million). Basic research was 11.1 percent more ($188.0 compared with $169.1 million). In the same time period, federal funding of oceanography research at universities increased by 46.9 percent (from $163.8 to $240.6 million). Since this was almost all basic research, funding of basic research increased by nearly the same percentage: 44.1 percent. The gains in atmospheric and, especially, oceanography research funding at universities were offset by a large decrease in geology research at universities of 31.6 percent (from $210.4 to $143.9 million). Similarly, basic geology research was 26.5 percent less. The trends in funding of university research in geology and oceanography are affected not only by NSF's change in classification procedures in 1996 but also by the fact that only the six largest R&D agencies are included in the survey of federal funding of university research. That excludes funding from agencies that are large supporters of geology (U.S. Geological Survey in the Department of the Interior) and oceanography (National Oceanographic and Atmospheric Administration in the Department of Commerce).

SOCIAL SCIENCES

Total Research. For most of the period after 1993, federal funding of social sciences was reduced (Figure 2-26). As recently as 1997, it was 4.9 percent less than in 1993 ($716.2 million vs. $753.3 million). Federal support increased in 1998 and again in 1999, when it was $854.9 million, 13.5 percent larger than in 1993. The increases came from NSF and a number of smaller agencies (primarily the Social Security Administration, Department of Justice, and the Agency of International Development). Funding was 15.1 percent less from USDA (–$20.7 mil-

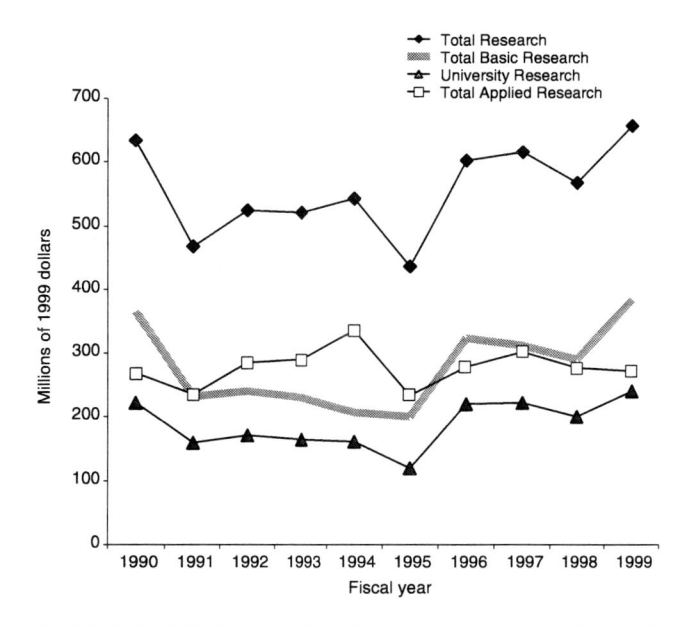

FIGURE 2-25 Federal funding of geology research, FY 1990–FY 1999 (in constant dollars).

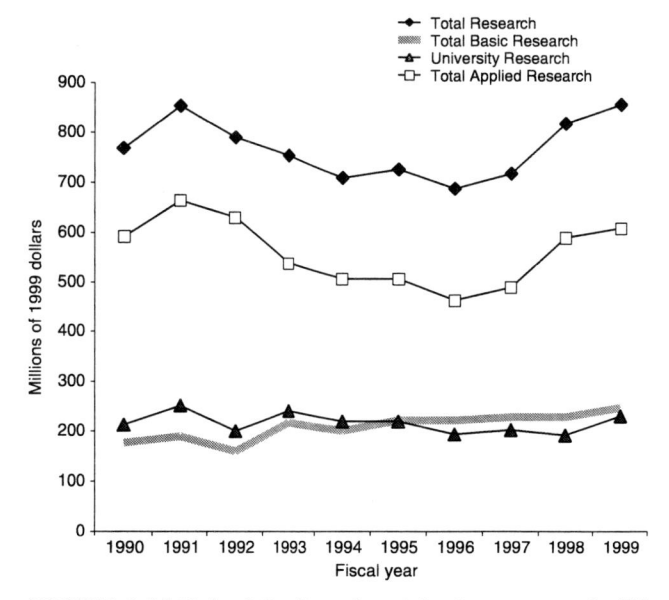

FIGURE 2-26 Federal funding of social sciences research, FY 1990–FY 1999 (in constant dollars).

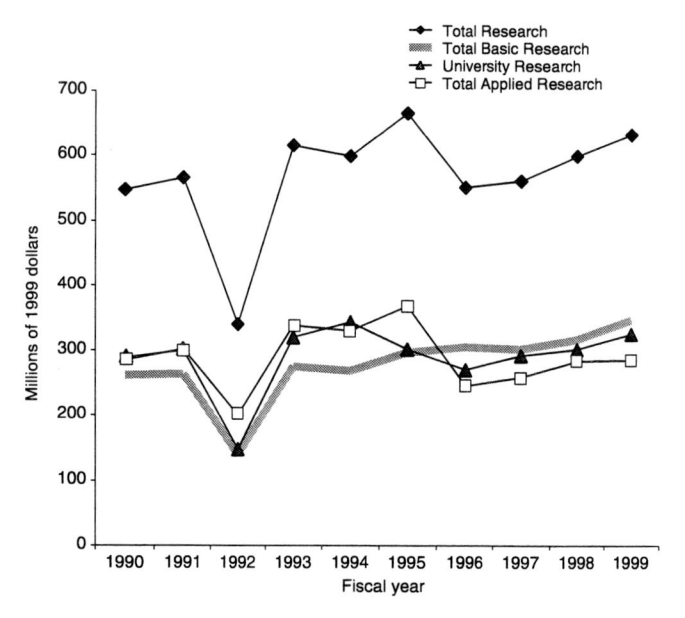

FIGURE 2-27 Federal funding of psychology research, FY 1990–FY 1999 (in constant dollars).

lion), 100 percent less from DOD (–$22.3 million), and 11.1 percent less from DHHS (–$23.0 million) despite an increase from NIH.[13]

Basic Research. The increase in support of the social sciences in 1999 over 1993 was about the same for basic as for total research (13.8 percent vs. 13.5 percent). This increase resulted from increased investment in basic research by NSF (by 82.5 percent) and DHHS (all from NIH) (by 29.7 percent). These increases, which totaled $62.2 million, were offset in part by reduced support by DOD (–100.0 percent) and USDA (–38.8 percent), which totaled $32.7 million. The large increase in total research from small agencies was mostly for applied research, as was the cut in total research by NIH.

University-Performed Research. Although federal funding of social sciences research at universities increased substantially from 1998 to 1999, it was still 4.0 percent less than in 1993. It had been 20.3 percent less in 1998. As with overall federal funding, USDA, DOD, and DHHS reduced their support, in DOD's case to zero. NSF was the only agency that provided more funding in 1999 than 1993 (79.9 percent more). The increased funding of total research by SSA, IRS, and AID was mostly for applied research and did not go to universities. Basic research in the social sciences did better than total research. Although USDA and DOD reduced support of basic research, DHHS maintained its support while NSF increased its by 89.6 percent. As a result, university basic research funding increased by 15.7 percent. Like total university research in the social sciences, however, basic research was in negative territory until 1999, although not down as much as total university research.

PSYCHOLOGY

Total Research. Funding of psychology research was $632.6 million in 1999, 2.9 percent more than in 1993 (Figure 2-27). The low point in funding was 1996. Although funding resumed growth after 1996, it was still 8.7 percent less in 1997 than in 1993, and 2.5 percent less in 1998. DOD, which provided $111.2 million for psychology research in 1993, had reduced its investment by 58.8 percent in 1999 (–$45.8 million). NSF also reduced its funding by 73.3 percent (–11.7 million). But NIH maintained its support from 1993 to 1997, then increased it in 1998 and 1999. NIH funding was $479.1 million in 1999, 18.6 percent more than in 1993. The Department of Veterans Affairs (in the "All Others" category) almost doubled its funding of psychology, from $17.4 to $32.9 million, which also helped put psychology in positive territory in 1999.

Basic Research. The increase in federal obligations for basic psychology research was much larger than the increase in total psychology research in 1999 compared with 1993, because federal agencies not only increased their support of basic research (by 26.1 percent) but also reduced their funding of applied research substantially (by –15.9 percent). NIH stepped up funding of psychology by 41.6 percent ($94.4 million), which more than offset the decreases by DOD of $25.8 million (–81.9 percent) and NSF of $6.5 million (–60.5 percent). There was also an increase of $8.9 million in the "Other Agency" category, mostly due to increases in basic psychology research by VA.

University-Performed Research. The trends were similar in federal support of university research in psychology. Although DOD and NSF provided less funding in 1999 than in 1993 (86.8 percent and 70.4 percent, respectively), NIH increased its support enough in 1999 to give psychology a net increase over 1993 of 1.5 percent. The trend was more favorable in basic research, largely because DOD was not a major funder in 1993, so a reduction of 84.6 percent by DOD did not have a large impact on the total. With the major funder, NIH, increasing its funding by 40.2 percent, federal funding of university basic research in psychology increased from $186.0 million in 1993 to $223.8 million in 1999, or 20.3 percent.

---

[13] The apparent decrease in social sciences funding by DHS occurred because the Social Security Administration (SSA) became independent in 1995. If SSA were counted with DHHS in 1993 and 1999, then funding by DHHS would have increased by 14.6 percent instead of declining by 11.1 percent and funding by "all other" agencies would have increased by 17.8 percent, not 35.6 percent.

CHANGING FUNDING BASE OF SOME FIELDS

In addition to the changing distribution of funding among fields, there were major changes in the funding base or support structure of some fields but virtually no change in the funding base of other fields. By funding base, we mean the set of agencies that are major supporters of a field. In 1993, for example, some fields had a single dominant support agency. DOD provided most of the funding for research in electrical engineering (82 percent), mechanical engineering (75 percent), and metallurgy/materials engineering (73 percent). DOE funded most research in physics (62 percent) and NASA was the principal supporter of research in aeronautical engineering (81 percent), astronautical engineering (79 percent), and astronomy (76 percent). NIH was the dominant funder of research in biological sciences (82 percent) and medical sciences (84 percent), and USDA funded most agricultural research (82 percent).[14]

Several patterns emerged in the post-1993 period. Some fields primarily funded by an agency that had flat or decreased research budgets in the 1993-1997 period or after have experienced substantial cuts. These include DOE physics support and DOD electrical engineering support. But other fields whose dominant funder had less research funding overall nevertheless have enjoyed increased funding, e.g., DOD computer science support and DOD metallurgy/materials engineering support. Unlike physics and electrical engineering, these fields also prospered by diversifying their base of support. Having a major funder with a growing budget did not guarantee increases, however. Although both biological and medical sciences research receive most of their funding from NIH, NIH's funding increases in the 1993-1997 period went mostly to medical sciences. Some fields had a broad base of support in 1993. In some cases such as oceanography that worked to their advantage, but in other cases such as chemical engineering it did not insulate them from budget cuts.

Fields With a Shrinking Dominant Funder That Experienced Cuts

In 1993, physics research received 62 percent of its funding from DOE and 18 percent from DOD (Figure 2-28). Both DOE and DOD reduced funding, by 28 and 63 percent ($506 and $335 million), respectively, in 1997 compared with 1993. The next largest funder, NSF, also cut funding of physics research, by 27 percent ($49 mil-

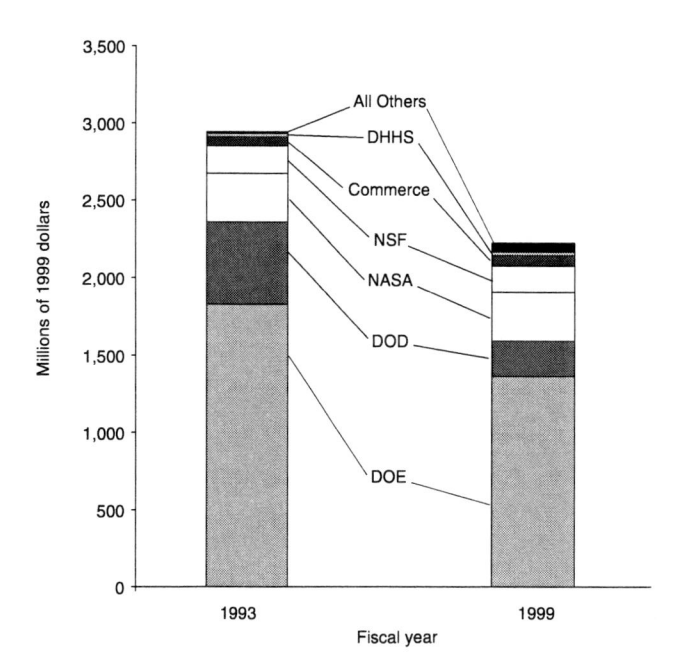

FIGURE 2-28 Agency funding of physics research, FY 1993 and FY 1999 (in constant dollars).

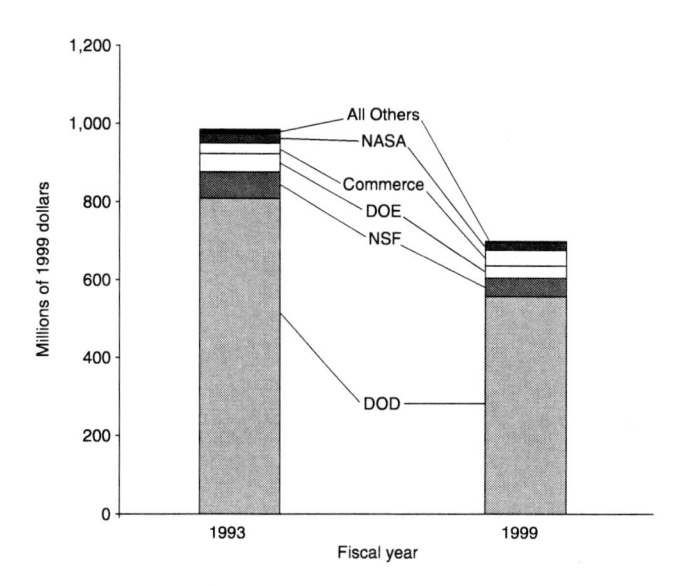

FIGURE 2-29 Agency funding of electrical engineering research, FY 1993 and FY 1999 (in constant dollars).

---

[14]Michael McGeary and Stephen A. Merrill. 1999. "Recent Trends in Federal Spending on Scientific and Engineering Research: Impacts on Research Fields and Graduate Training," Appendix A, Table A-2, National Research Council, *Securing America's Industrial Strength*, Washington, D.C.: National Academy Press.

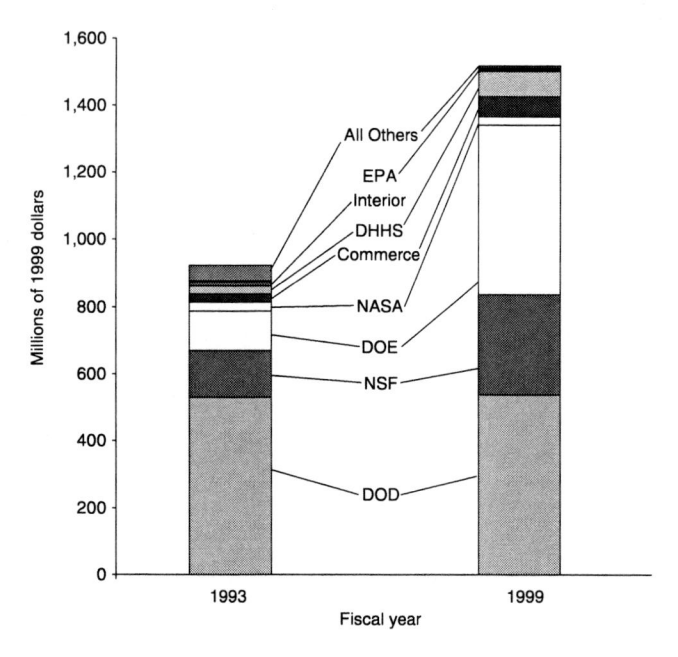

FIGURE 2-30 Agency funding of computer science research, FY 1993 and FY 1999 (in constant dollars).

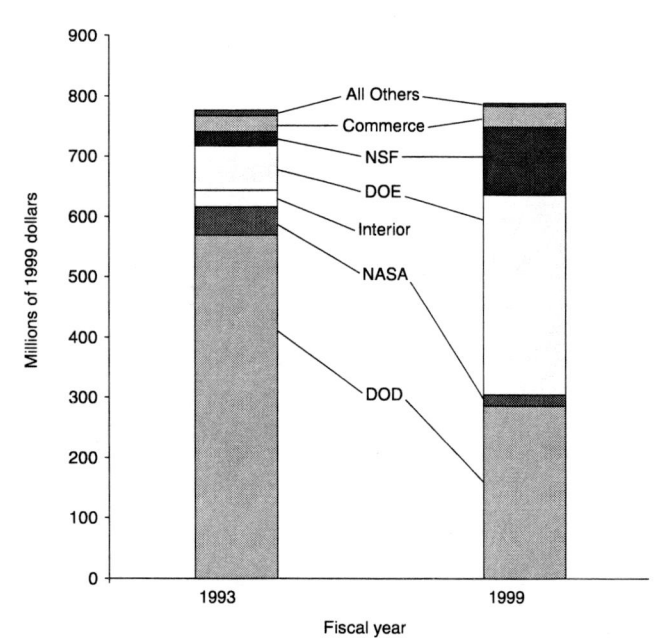

FIGURE 2-31 Agency funding of materials/metallurgy research, FY 1993 and FY 1999 (in constant dollars).

lion). There were small increases from NASA, DOC, NIH, and other agencies, but overall there was 28 percent less funding ($818 million) in 1997 compared with 1993. DOE, DOD, and NSF increased their support some after 1997, but physics research funding was still 25 percent less in 1999 than in 1993. DOE still accounted for most of the federal funding of physics research (61 percent in 1999 compared with 62 percent in 1993), indicating that physics was not able to change its base of support.

Electrical engineering was another field whose base did not change as its principal source of funds, DOD, was reducing its support (Figure 2-29). DOD support of electrical engineering was 31 percent ($252 million) less in 1999 than in 1993 in real terms. Support by most other agencies, notably DOE, NSF, and NASA, also fell. Only the Department of Commerce increased its level of funding, by 55 percent, but only $15 million. The percentage distribution of funding by agency thus barely changed between 1993 and 1999. DOD accounted for 82 percent of the federal support of electrical engineering research in 1993, 80 percent in 1999.

Fields With a Shrinking Dominant Funder That Experienced Growth

In computer science DOD was the majority federal funder of research in 1993, accounting for 57 percent (Figure 2-30). Despite funding cuts, DOD maintained its support of computer science research (2 percent more in 1999 than in 1993 in real terms); but more important, a number of other agencies increased their support substantially. In 1999, federal funding of the field was 64 percent larger than in 1993. As a result, DOD's share of federal funding fell to 36 percent in 1999 ($538 million), while DOE's stake increased from 13 percent to 33 percent and NSF's from 15 percent to 20 percent.

Materials/metallurgy engineering research was another field that was able to change its base of support even though DOD funding dropped by half from 1993 to 1999 in real terms (Figure 2-31). NASA reduced its funding by 61 percent, and Interior almost eliminated its support. As a result, the DOD percentage of federal funding of materials research went from 73 percent in 1993 to 36 percent in 1999 and NASA's from 6 percent to 2 percent. But these reductions were more than offset by increases at DOE (343 percent) and NSF (370 percent). The Department of Commerce also increased its support (by 33 percent), although the amount was relatively small. DOE accounted for 42 percent of federal support of materials engineering research in 1999, compared with 10 percent in 1993. The comparable percentages for NSF were 14 percent, compared with 3 percent. As a result, the field, which was 73 percent funded by DOD in 1993, now has a different and more distributed funding base: 36 percent DOD but also 42 percent DOE and 14 percent NSF.

Fields With a Growing Dominant Funder

Despite the sustained increases in its research budget, NIH's shares of federal funding of research in the biological sciences and medical sciences (Figure 2-32) have not changed much, in large part because other agencies also have tended to maintain and even increase their support of those fields. NIH provided 81 percent of the federal funding of biology research in 1999, compared with 80 percent in 1993. It did increase somewhat its share of federal funding of research in medical sciences, to 82 percent in 1999, compared with 79 percent in 1993. Although both fields received most of their support from NIH, it should be noted that the two fields did not prosper equally from NIH's substantial budget growth. From 1993 to 1999, NIH increased its support of medical science research more than of biological sciences research (43.8 vs. 22.9 percent), which explained nearly all of the change in federal funding of these fields (increases of 38.3 and 21.2 percent, respectively).

Fields With a Diversified Base of Support

Funding of oceanography research was more distributed at the outset of the 1990s (Figure 2-33). In 1993, the Department of Commerce accounted for one-third, NASA for nearly one-quarter, DOD for one-fifth, and NSF for a slightly smaller fraction. By 1999, Commerce had reduced its level of support by 35 percent, but other agencies had increased their support. NSF increased its funding by 145 percent and DOD by 89 percent. Funding of oceanography research was 26 percent larger in 1999 than in 1993. As a result, NSF became the largest federal funder of oceanography (33 percent), followed by DOD (28 percent) and NASA (17 percent). Commerce (16 percent) ended up just behind NASA. If the NASA increase was an artifact of a change in classification procedures the agency distribution would be different, still diversified but with Commerce still displaced as the primary funder. DOD would be the largest funder (35 percent), followed by NASA (21 percent), Commerce (21 percent), and NSF (15 percent).

Mathematics is another field with diversified support that was able to increase its level of funding (Figure 2-34). From 1993 to 1999, DOD support fell substantially (by 35 percent) and there were small reductions by a number of other agencies (USDA, Interior, NSF, Commerce, and NASA), but several other agencies increased funding, which offset the DOD loss. Federal funding of research in mathematics was 6 percent more in 1999 than in 1993, because of substantial increases in support by NIH (120 percent), DOE (33 percent), and EPA, which did not fund mathematics research in 1993. Accordingly, DOD's share of federal support went from 28 percent to 17 percent, while DOE went from 24 percent to 30 percent, NIH from

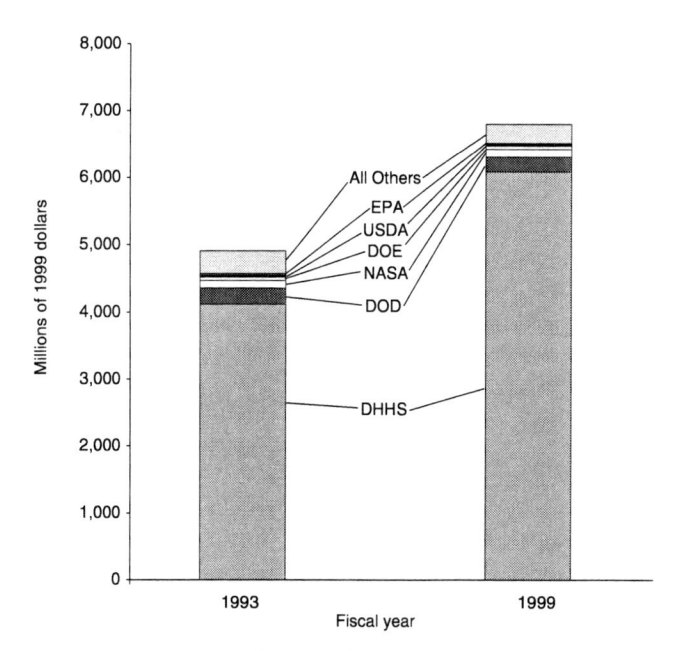

FIGURE 2-32 Agency funding of medical sciences research, FY 1993 and FY 1999 (in constant dollars).

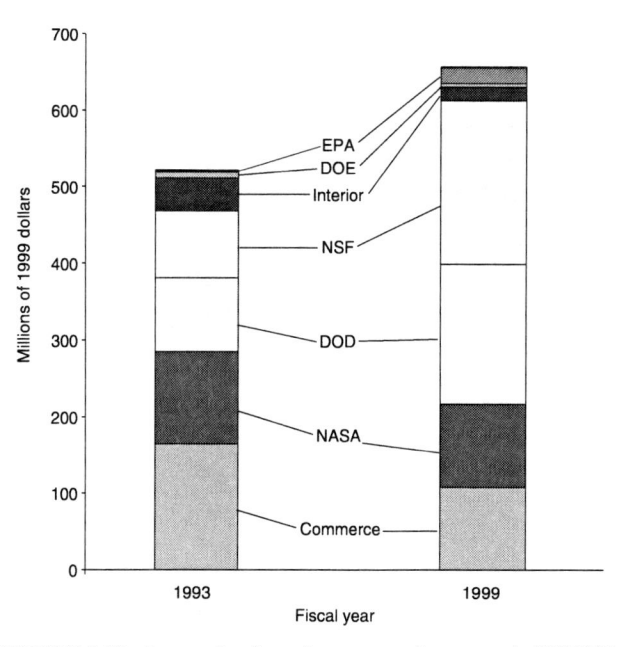

FIGURE 2-33 Agency funding of oceanography research, FY 1993 and FY 1999 (in constant dollars).

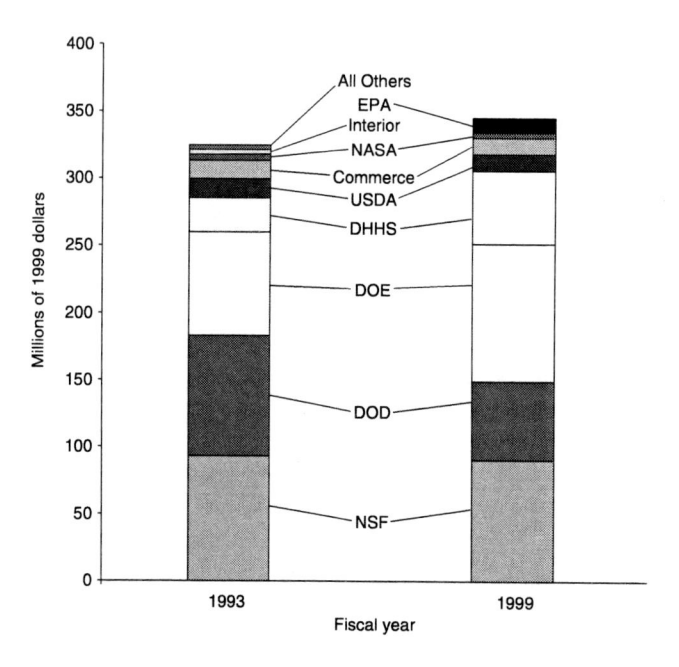

FIGURE 2-34 Agency funding of mathematical sciences research, FY 1993 and FY 1999 (in constant dollars).

8 percent to 16 percent, and EPA from 0 percent to 3 percent.

Not all fields with a broad base of support were able to weather funding reductions, however. Chemical engineering, for example, received funding from a number of agencies in 1993, including DOE (42 percent), DOD (28 percent), NSF (16 percent), DOI (4 percent), DOC (3 percent), and smaller amounts from other agencies (USDA, EPA, NASA) (Figure 2-35). Although the percentages did not change much in 1999, overall research funding was 26 percent less in 1999 than in 1993 because all the funders but EPA and USDA reduced their support, including DOD (–55 percent), DOE (–19 percent), DOI (–50 percent), DOC (–34 percent), NASA (–6 percent), and NSF (–4 percent).

In summary, there were major shifts in the funding base of some fields. They included some but not all of the fields whose principal source of support was DOD or another agency, such as DOE or DOI, that cut research funding in the mid-1990s. The fields that grew despite reliance on a shrinking agency—e.g., computer science, metallurgy/materials engineering—diversification of support explains their success in large part. For the fields such as electrical engineering and physics that were dependent mainly on an agency with a shrinking budget and that were not able to diversify saw their funding decline significantly.

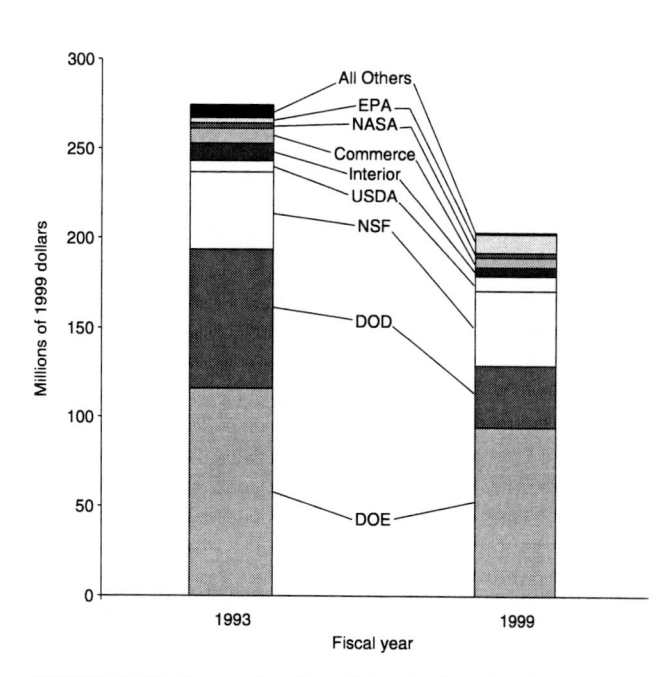

FIGURE 2-35 Agency funding of chemical engineering research, FY 1993 and FY 1999 (in constant dollars).

ANNEX

TABLE 2-1 Percent Change in Federal Funding for Research, by Field, FY 1993–1999 (in constant dollars)

	All Performers			Universities		
Total	Total	Basic	Applied	Total	Basic	Applied
All fields	11.7%	16.6%	6.8%	19.9%	19.8%	20.2%
Engineering, total	2.0%	21.7%	–3.5%	5.5%	12.0%	–6.6%
Aeronautical	20.9%	20.7%	20.9%	24.5%	2.6%	94.8%
Astronautical	12.6%	10.6%	12.8%	79.5%	114.4%	31.3%
Chemical	–25.9%	–32.1%	–23.2%	2.2%	5.4%	–2.2%
Civil	16.8%	59.5%	9.1%	6.4%	9.7%	–1.2%
Electrical	–29.0%	–18.1%	–32.2%	–12.0%	–15.4%	–2.0%
Mechanical*	–53.9%	–37.4%	–61.1%	–40.5%	–36.8%	–60.8%
Metallurgy/materials	1.5%	78.6%	–39.5%	7.7%	43.6%	–55.3%
Engineering other	25.1%	50.5%	20.1%	36.1%	58.9%	16.8%
Physical Sciences, total	–17.7%	–4.8%	–42.4%	1.1%	6.9%	–22.9%
Astronomy	–1.1%	–3.0%	54.7%	46.9%	39.9%	126.8%
Chemistry	–13.4%	–8.6%	–22.1%	–2.0%	–7.5%	33.1%
Physics	–24.6%	–5.2%	–54.4%	–7.4%	8.4%	–50.4%
Life Sciences, total	28.3%	31.0%	24.4%	31.8%	28.5%	39.0%
Biological Sciences	21.2%	17.8%	28.1%	39.9%	32.7%	60.2%
Environmental Biology	16.0%	12.5%	18.4%	8.7%	4.7%	17.0%
Agricultural Sciences	6.7%	11.1%	2.7%	21.7%	18.7%	24.6%
Medical Sciences	38.3%	48.9%	25.9%	20.5%	21.0%	19.5%
Math/Computer science, total	44.8%	28.8%	56.3%	21.2%	23.2%	16.1%
Mathematics	6.4%	2.6%	18.6%	–13.5%	–16.5%	58.9%
Computer science	64.4%	38.1%	78.2%	34.3%	39.3%	25.2%
Environmental Sciences, total	6.3%	–5.6%	23.3%	5.6%	4.6%	23.5%
Atmospheric	7.1%	–5.3%	29.8%	13.7%	11.1%	62.7%
Geological	–25.9%	–33.5%	–8.4%	–31.6%	–26.5%	–95.1%
Oceanography*	25.9%	66.0%	–6.1%	46.9%	44.1%	238.4%
Social Sciences, total	13.5%	13.8%	13.4%	–4.0%	15.7%	–24.3%
Psychology, total	2.9%	26.1%	–15.9%	1.5%	20.3%	–24.6%

NOTE: Constant dollar conversions were made using the GDP deflators in OMB, Historical Tables: Budget of the United States Government, FY 2002, Table 10.1. Washington, D.C.: U.S. Government Printing Office, 2001.

*Mechanical engineering and oceanography are among the fields for which NSF changed the classification criteria in reporting funding for FY 1996. In these cases, NSF was a principal funding agency, and therefore the amounts reported in 1993 and 1999 are not strictly comparable.

SOURCE: National Science Foundation/SRS, Survey of Federal Funds for Research and Development, Fiscal Years 1999, 2000, and 2001.

TABLE 2-2 Trends by Field and Character of Research, 1990–1999 (millions of 1999 dollars)

	1990	1991	1992	1993	1994	1995	1996	1997	1998	1999	1993–1997	1993–1999
All Fields												
Total Research	26,346.2	28,112.1	27,989.3	30,015.1	29,951.1	30,407.9	29,631.7	30,201.9	31,355.0	33,527.5	0.6%	11.7%
Total Basic Research	13,751.2	14,274.9	14,274.1	14,956.0	14,776.5	14,840.2	15,166.2	15,367.6	15,831.5	17,443.7	2.8%	16.6%
Total Applied Research	12,595.1	13,837.2	13,715.1	15,059.0	15,174.5	15,567.7	14,465.5	14,834.3	15,523.5	16,083.9	-1.5%	6.8%
University Research	9,488.2	10,008.4	9,880.8	10,653.3	10,836.8	10,648.1	10,845.5	11,087.1	11,471.0	12,776.1	4.1%	19.9%
Engineering, total												
Total Research	5,150.0	5,799.3	5,688.0	6,138.4	5,987.1	6,104.6	5,956.7	5,852.4	5,977.9	6,263.4	-4.7%	2.0%
Total Basic Research	1,342.2	1,447.0	1,428.4	1,347.7	1,410.0	1,549.5	1,690.3	1,628.1	1,616.8	1,639.7	20.8%	21.7%
Total Applied Research	3,807.9	4,352.3	4,259.6	4,790.7	4,577.1	4,555.1	4,266.4	4,224.3	4,361.2	4,623.7	-11.8%	-3.5%
University Research	868.4	972.1	955.5	991.2	1,043.0	1,166.5	1,132.0	1,016.2	1,007.6	1,046.1	2.5%	5.5%
Aeronautical engineering												
Total Research	1,129.6	1,191.9	999.5	1,331.7	1,336.0	1,334.9	1,310.0	1,391.3	1,618.8	1,609.7	4.5%	20.9%
Total Basic Research	328.6	300.5	280.1	274.8	301.4	289.9	274.4	276.7	289.2	331.7	0.7%	20.7%
Total Applied Research	801.1	891.4	719.5	1,056.9	1,034.6	1,045.0	1,035.6	1,114.5	1,329.5	1,278.0	5.5%	20.9%
University Research	102.4	68.3	65.1	58.2	69.1	56.2	48.8	50.7	63.0	72.5	-12.8%	24.5%
Astronautical engineering												
Total Research	707.7	766.0	720.5	551.4	545.3	584.5	552.1	613.3	639.9	620.6	11.2%	12.6%
Total Basic Research	75.9	81.7	107.9	59.8	65.4	70.9	75.3	71.8	68.9	66.2	20.0%	10.6%
Total Applied Research	631.8	684.3	612.6	491.6	480.0	513.5	476.8	541.5	571.0	554.4	10.2%	12.8%
University Research	24.6	25.7	28.7	22.8	22.6	21.1	18.8	18.1	8.9	41.0	-20.8%	79.5%
Chemical engineering												
Total Research	294.7	356.9	340.0	274.1	260.3	263.2	225.6	241.7	192.8	203.2	-11.8%	-25.9%
Total Basic Research	92.4	119.2	119.9	81.2	77.5	71.4	62.7	70.0	53.0	55.2	-13.9%	-32.1%
Total Applied Research	202.3	237.7	220.0	192.8	182.8	191.8	162.9	171.7	139.8	148.0	-11.0%	-23.2%
University Research	71.3	88.6	79.7	73.0	66.0	75.5	63.6	64.5	74.4	74.6	-11.6%	2.2%
Civil engineering												
Total Research	387.1	357.7	377.4	281.3	303.7	363.0	314.7	283.5	247.5	328.5	0.8%	16.8%
Total Basic Research	57.6	69.5	61.0	43.2	41.7	75.0	55.4	46.7	36.4	68.8	8.2%	59.5%
Total Applied Research	329.5	288.2	316.4	238.1	262.0	288.0	259.3	236.8	211.2	259.7	-0.6%	9.1%
University Research	52.3	56.5	45.5	42.1	40.8	55.3	47.1	46.4	48.1	44.8	10.1%	6.4%
Electrical engineering												
Total Research	779.9	856.1	867.4	983.9	810.5	808.8	702.2	639.9	648.3	698.7	-35.0%	-29.0%
Total Basic Research	179.0	167.1	189.0	226.7	224.8	218.8	211.2	177.8	216.9	185.6	-21.6%	-18.1%
Total Applied Research	600.8	689.0	678.4	757.2	585.8	590.0	491.0	462.1	431.4	513.1	-39.0%	-32.2%
University Research	168.3	167.5	169.8	218.4	207.7	185.7	171.8	150.5	179.8	192.2	-31.1%	-12.0%
Mechanical engineering												
Total Research	327.0	393.5	385.4	521.1	413.1	441.1	308.3	261.8	253.0	240.4	-49.8%	-53.9%
Total Basic Research	111.4	135.5	130.1	159.2	154.7	176.1	118.7	107.8	108.2	99.6	-32.3%	-37.4%
Total Applied Research	215.6	258.0	255.3	361.9	258.4	265.0	189.6	154.0	144.9	140.8	-57.4%	-61.1%
University Research	94.4	115.5	113.2	131.0	137.4	143.7	95.0	78.4	77.5	78.0	-40.2%	-40.5%

Metallurgy and materials engineering											
Total Research	675.7	833.5	831.1	776.5	930.3	871.9	1,037.0	885.2	800.1	788.0	14.0%	1.5%
Total Basic Research	317.0	345.5	312.7	269.4	360.7	394.0	526.2	475.8	484.9	481.2	76.6%	78.6%
Total Applied Research	358.6	488.0	518.4	507.1	569.5	477.9	510.8	409.4	315.2	306.9	-19.3%	-39.5%
University Research	201.7	250.7	209.6	223.9	298.1	340.0	318.5	268.6	250.1	241.2	20.0%	7.7%
Other engineering											
Total Research	848.4	1,043.6	1,166.6	1,418.6	1,387.9	1,437.3	1,506.8	1,535.7	1,577.4	1,774.3	8.3%	25.1%
Total Basic Research	180.2	227.9	227.7	233.4	183.9	253.3	366.4	401.5	359.3	351.4	72.0%	50.6%
Total Applied Research	668.2	815.6	939.0	1,185.1	1,204.1	1,183.9	1,140.4	1,134.2	1,218.1	1,422.9	-4.3%	20.1%
University Research	153.4	199.4	244.0	221.8	201.5	288.8	367.5	339.0	305.9	301.9	52.8%	36.1%
Physical sciences, total											
Total Research	4,640.8	4,967.6	5,073.3	4,941.4	4,647.6	4,575.3	4,113.4	4,267.4	4,268.6	4,066.2	-13.6%	-17.7%
Total Basic Research	3,243.0	3,379.6	3,373.1	3,244.9	3,088.9	3,063.6	3,001.5	3,061.2	2,982.5	3,089.8	-5.7%	-4.8%
Total Applied Research	1,397.8	1,587.9	1,700.3	1,696.4	1,558.7	1,511.6	1,111.9	1,206.2	1,286.0	976.4	-28.9%	-42.4%
University Research	1,220.3	1,255.9	1,315.0	1,308.9	1,276.7	1,276.8	1,181.4	1,197.0	1,221.0	1,322.8	-8.5%	1.1%
Astronomy											
Total Research	727.6	740.9	844.6	766.0	816.9	817.5	764.3	796.8	742.4	757.9	4.0%	-1.1%
Total Basic Research	706.6	718.2	833.9	740.5	792.0	782.3	743.2	775.7	716.8	718.4	4.7%	-3.0%
Total Applied Research	21.0	22.7	10.7	25.5	24.9	35.2	21.1	21.1	25.6	39.4	-17.1%	54.7%
University Research	100.1	122.4	225.2	134.1	144.9	178.5	201.9	172.8	175.8	197.0	28.9%	46.9%
Chemistry											
Total Research	928.1	971.6	1,024.2	941.1	955.5	923.4	923.9	869.9	830.5	814.9	-7.6%	-13.4%
Total Basic Research	611.8	631.9	636.1	606.9	590.3	598.2	577.5	532.6	524.8	554.6	-12.2%	-8.6%
Total Applied Research	316.3	339.8	388.1	334.3	365.2	325.2	346.4	337.3	305.7	260.3	0.9%	-22.1%
University Research	386.7	398.3	402.1	388.4	411.6	388.2	381.7	350.6	336.0	380.7	-9.7%	-2.0%
Physics											
Total Research	2,747.6	2,886.4	2,946.5	2,944.9	2,669.5	2,621.3	2,088.0	2,126.5	2,161.6	2,221.9	-27.8%	-24.6%
Total Basic Research	1,796.4	1,929.3	1,837.1	1,786.6	1,641.5	1,612.0	1,620.7	1,606.2	1,601.9	1,693.8	-10.1%	-5.2%
Total Applied Research	951.1	957.1	1,109.4	1,158.3	1,028.1	1,009.3	467.3	520.3	559.7	528.1	-55.1%	-54.4%
University Research	665.6	693.1	655.5	678.6	656.5	630.8	536.5	536.9	585.2	628.7	-20.9%	-7.4%
Life sciences, total											
Total Research	10,758.9	11,285.5	11,326.3	12,023.8	12,329.9	12,630.8	12,650.0	13,022.0	13,747.3	15,422.5	8.3%	28.3%
Total Basic Research	6,308.7	6,372.9	6,676.2	7,019.5	7,071.8	7,059.4	7,213.0	7,409.0	7,963.3	9,197.1	5.5%	31.0%
Total Applied Research	4,450.2	4,912.5	4,650.0	5,004.2	5,258.1	5,571.3	5,437.1	5,613.1	5,784.0	6,225.3	12.2%	24.4%
University Research	5,521.8	5,826.1	5,727.0	6,139.6	6,275.9	6,034.1	6,310.8	6,753.1	7,103.4	8,091.1	10.0%	31.8%
Biological sciences											
Total Research	5,050.1	5,228.5	5,068.6	5,346.5	5,185.5	5,267.2	5,567.7	5,471.8	5,786.4	6,477.6	2.3%	21.2%
Total Basic Research	3,341.2	3,364.4	3,407.8	3,596.9	3,430.1	3,473.8	3,551.6	3,487.6	3,704.1	4,236.9	-3.0%	17.8%
Total Applied Research	1,708.9	1,864.1	1,660.8	1,749.6	1,755.5	1,793.5	2,016.1	1,984.2	2,082.3	2,240.7	13.4%	28.1%
University Research	2,932.7	3,061.9	2,945.7	3,064.5	3,076.5	2,862.0	3,096.9	3,600.3	3,791.4	4,288.3	17.5%	39.9%

continues

45

TABLE 2-2 Continued

	1990	1991	1992	1993	1994	1995	1996	1997	1998	1999	1993–1997	1993–1999
Environmental Biology												
Total Research	417.1	539.2	584.0	621.2	688.3	862.8	738.1	599.1	612.9	720.6	-3.5%	16.0%
Total Basic Research	205.1	219.3	230.4	249.1	264.6	236.0	215.7	211.9	199.6	280.2	-14.9%	12.5%
Total Applied Research	212.0	320.0	353.6	372.1	423.7	626.9	522.5	387.2	413.3	440.4	4.1%	18.4%
University Research	155.9	175.1	185.2	179.1	182.3	178.3	155.2	150.8	160.5	194.7	-15.8%	8.7%
Agricultural sciences												
Total Research	842.5	797.9	785.8	795.8	794.6	716.8	645.9	659.6	773.5	849.4	-17.1%	6.7%
Total Basic Research	375.9	374.6	381.9	381.9	404.9	393.0	345.5	358.0	377.7	424.5	-6.3%	11.1%
Total Applied Research	466.5	423.3	403.9	413.8	389.7	323.8	300.4	301.6	395.7	424.9	-27.1%	2.7%
University Research	163.3	173.1	187.6	166.9	176.9	167.2	145.8	178.0	174.4	202.7	6.9%	21.7%
Medical sciences												
Total Research	4,121.3	4,058.5	4,468.5	4,916.2	5,312.6	5,317.3	5,214.8	5,690.4	6,080.2	6,801.2	15.7%	38.3%
Total Basic Research	2,253.7	2,178.9	2,435.5	2,657.5	2,852.2	2,797.4	2,873.8	3,121.6	3,439.9	3,956.5	17.5%	48.9%
Total Applied Research	1,867.6	1,879.6	2,033.0	2,258.7	2,460.5	2,519.9	2,341.0	2,568.7	2,640.3	2,844.7	13.7%	25.9%
University Research	2,106.3	2,263.3	2,312.9	2,607.9	2,740.2	2,640.3	2,708.7	2,609.6	2,752.4	3,141.6	0.1%	20.5%
Math/Computer science, total												
Total Research	1,024.4	1,059.9	1,326.1	1,367.8	1,422.2	1,688.6	1,647.9	1,719.5	1,862.5	1,980.6	25.7%	44.8%
Total Basic Research	495.8	499.8	550.2	570.7	570.1	644.8	670.6	680.2	715.4	734.9	19.2%	28.8%
Total Applied Research	528.6	560.2	775.9	797.1	852.1	1,043.8	977.3	1,039.3	1,147.2	1,245.7	30.4%	56.3%
University Research	505.6	467.6	545.9	547.1	590.2	572.3	682.2	587.9	632.8	663.0	7.5%	21.2%
Mathematics												
Total Research	294.1	267.0	364.2	324.6	374.0	276.6	266.8	310.2	338.7	345.3	-4.4%	6.4%
Total Basic Research	214.9	192.8	260.8	247.6	270.6	175.3	170.5	245.0	254.2	254.0	-1.0%	2.6%
Total Applied Research	79.2	74.2	103.4	77.0	103.4	101.2	96.3	65.2	84.5	91.3	-15.3%	18.6%
University Research	157.4	143.0	171.9	151.7	154.1	142.4	142.6	121.5	134.4	131.3	-19.9%	-13.5%
Computer science												
Total Research	684.9	686.1	882.0	922.1	907.1	1,084.2	1,174.2	1,300.7	1,418.3	1,516.1	41.1%	64.4%
Total Basic Research	274.4	262.2	283.1	317.4	286.6	339.1	395.1	400.6	425.0	438.3	26.2%	38.1%
Total Applied Research	410.5	423.9	598.9	604.7	620.5	745.1	779.1	900.1	993.3	1,077.8	48.8%	78.2%
University Research	343.5	295.2	365.6	377.1	415.6	402.3	512.0	441.6	477.0	506.3	17.1%	34.3%
Environmental sciences, total												
Total Research	2,649.1	2,521.4	2,523.0	2,911.6	3,101.2	3,052.5	3,166.3	3,132.4	3,104.8	3,095.3	7.6%	6.3%
Total Basic Research	1,553.3	1,482.0	1,489.9	1,711.7	1,657.0	1,569.3	1,629.5	1,587.5	1,550.1	1,615.7	-7.3%	-5.6%
Total Applied Research	1,095.7	1,039.5	1,033.1	1,199.9	1,444.2	1,483.2	1,536.8	1,545.0	1,554.7	1,479.5	28.8%	23.3%
University Research	595.5	655.2	668.2	659.0	696.3	657.7	688.7	691.2	662.0	696.1	4.9%	5.6%
Atmospheric sciences												
Total Research	942.4	941.5	876.9	1,098.5	1,196.5	1,214.4	1,138.4	1,197.5	1,190.9	1,176.5	9.0%	7.1%
Total Basic Research	540.7	526.6	497.4	708.9	763.0	736.0	703.7	698.9	664.4	671.0	-1.4%	-5.3%
Total Applied Research	401.7	414.9	379.5	389.5	433.5	478.4	434.7	498.6	526.5	505.5	28.0%	29.8%
University Research	158.3	172.5	189.7	178.1	190.2	223.4	165.8	211.6	167.9	202.6	18.8%	13.7%

Geological sciences										
Total Research	805.5	854.7	840.8	890.6	915.6	907.2	822.3	711.5	611.8	660.2	−20.1%	−25.9%
Total Basic Research	535.8	585.3	601.7	619.8	533.0	483.1	408.9	399.3	396.6	412.1	−35.6%	−33.5%
Total Applied Research	269.8	269.5	239.1	270.7	382.6	424.1	413.4	312.2	215.1	248.1	15.3%	−8.4%
University Research	168.5	207.2	195.3	210.4	224.5	183.1	143.3	127.7	173.8	143.9	−39.3%	−31.6%
Oceanography										
Total Research	633.8	467.5	524.5	521.7	542.8	435.6	602.2	614.7	567.6	656.6	17.8%	25.9%
Total Basic Research	365.2	231.7	240.0	231.2	207.8	201.3	324.1	312.2	290.0	383.9	35.0%	66.0%
Total Applied Research	268.5	235.8	284.5	290.4	335.0	234.3	278.0	302.6	277.6	272.7	4.2%	−6.1%
University Research	221.7	159.0	170.6	163.8	161.6	118.7	220.0	221.5	200.0	240.6	35.3%	46.9%
Social sciences, total										
Total Research	767.6	853.0	788.2	753.3	707.4	725.8	686.3	716.2	817.4	854.9	−4.9%	13.5%
Total Basic Research	177.9	189.2	159.8	216.7	201.1	221.0	222.8	227.3	227.9	246.5	4.9%	13.8%
Total Applied Research	589.7	663.9	628.4	536.7	506.3	504.8	463.5	488.8	589.5	608.3	−8.9%	13.4%
University Research	213.6	250.6	199.6	241.1	219.1	218.7	193.6	203.1	192.2	231.4	−15.8%	−4.0%
Psychology, total										
Total Research	546.6	565.8	340.7	614.7	599.2	665.8	550.5	560.9	599.2	632.6	−8.7%	2.9%
Total Basic Research	262.0	264.5	140.1	275.5	268.9	297.3	305.7	302.2	316.4	347.3	9.7%	26.1%
Total Applied Research	284.6	301.3	200.7	339.2	330.3	368.5	244.8	258.7	282.9	285.3	−23.7%	−15.9%
University Research	289.4	300.4	147.5	320.9	344.0	301.1	270.0	291.5	301.5	325.6	−9.2%	1.5%

NOTE: Constant dollar conversions were made using the fiscal year GDP deflators used by OMB in preparing the FY 2002 budget request. FY1990=.8207, FY1991=.8526, FY1992=.8750, FY1993=.8959, FY1994=.9152, FY1995=.9351, FY1996=.9537, FY1997=.9723, FY1998=.9862, FY1999=1.0000. See Budget of the United States Government, Fiscal Year 2002. Washington, D.C.: U.S. Government.

SOURCE: National Science Foundation/SRS, Survey of Federal Funds for Research and Development, Fiscal Years 1999, 2000, and 2001.

3

Field Trends in Graduate Education Support

Since World War II, graduate education in science and engineering in the United States has been closely linked to university-based research.[1] Trends in federal obligations for university research directly affect graduate enrollment because research funding supports graduate research assistantships. Moreover, trends in federal obligations for university-based research also indirectly affect graduate enrollment by shaping the job market in given research fields. Students become aware of whether research funding opportunities in a field, and therefore academic job prospects, are increasing or decreasing and choose fields of study at least in part based on those prospects.

Yet there are many other factors that influence enrollment in graduate education programs. The flow of students through secondary school science and mathematics courses and undergraduate science and engineering majors determines the number of domestic students qualified to pursue graduate degrees in science and engineering. Higher education institutions may allocate funding, including graduate student assistance, to sustain competence in research and training in a wide range of fields. And investigators have a variety of options for staffing their laboratories—not only graduate student assistants and students on fellowships and traineeships but also postdoctoral fellows, non-faculty research scientists, and trained laboratory technicians. In part this is an economic decision, and in some fields such as the biological sciences the number of recent Ph.D.'s available for postdoctoral fellowships at costs similar to those of graduate research assistants has increased in recent years.

Student preferences, influenced by the intrinsic interest of particular subjects, perceived job opportunities, and other factors, also affect graduate enrollment trends. Federal research funding plays a role in this equation by affecting the prospects for future academic employment of Ph.D.'s. Nevertheless, an increasing majority of students in science and engineering—many of whom will leave school with master's degrees rather than doctorates—eventually pursue careers outside of academia. In the latter half of the 1990s an important factor in the job market for people with advanced technical training was the high demand on the part of industry as well as the public and non-profit sectors for expertise in information technology (IT). The tight job market for IT workers contributed to rising salaries and other compensation that attracted students to computer science and engineering, perhaps away from other fields, and lured other students out of graduate school altogether or away from completing any advanced degree or progressing from a master's degree to a Ph.D. program.[2]

As the most highly regarded system for advanced technical training in the world, U.S. science and engineering graduate education attracts large number of students

---

[1] For reasons articulated by The National Academies' Committee on Science, Engineering, and Public Policy (COSEPUP), the close linkage between research funding and training support is not necessarily desirable, especially in a world in which most new scientists and engineers with advanced degrees do not pursue academic careers. First, the research assistantship is a product of the needs of a particular investigator and a particular project rather than a reflection of the student's educational needs. It may limit students' flexibility to design graduate programs better suited to employment in industry or other non-university settings. Second, the prevalence of research assistantships tends to hold graduate enrollments hostage to shifts in government agency missions and research budgets independent of the market for people with advanced technical degrees. In short, the United States has "no clear human resources policy for advanced scientists and engineers."

COSEPUP recommended less reliance on research assistantships and increased use of education/training grants to institutions and departments. National Academy of Sciences, National Academy of Engineering, Institute of Medicine. 1995. *Reshaping the Graduate Education of Scientists and Engineers*, pp. 3–4, Washington, D.C.: National Academy Press.

[2] National Research Council. 2001. *Building a Workforce for the Information Economy*, Washington, D.C.: National Academy Press.

from abroad.[3] Trends in the enrollment of foreign graduate students—a substantial portion of students in many fields and a majority in some—are also affected by many factors, including home country political conditions and employment and training opportunities, the availability of home country financial support for graduate education abroad, and opportunities for permanent residence and eventual employment in the United States.

While acknowledging that a host of factors influences trends in graduate enrollment in different disciplines, this chapter seeks to relate trends in federal obligations for university research to graduate enrollments in subfields of science, engineering, and health, and to anticipate what recent increases and reductions in research support mean for the production of people with advanced technical degrees. To the extent that graduate enrollment is affected by changes in research funding, changes in enrollment should appear within a year or two. Analyzing trends in awarded doctoral degrees is more complicated because of the substantial time lag between initial enrollment and completion of Ph.D. degree requirements—on average between 6.6 and 7.5 years in the natural sciences, engineering, and social sciences.[4] Thus, it may take 7 years for enrollment increases in a field to show up in doctoral award data, although the effect of declining enrollment on doctorates may show up earlier as students drop out of degree programs or switch fields.

The analysis that follows draws principally on data from the National Science Foundation's Survey of Graduate Students and Postdoctorates in Science and Engineering (GSPSE), which allows us to examine trends in graduate enrollment by field, by mechanism of support (i.e., research assistantship, teaching assistantship, traineeship or fellowship) and by source of support (i.e., federal government agency, nonfederal sources, institutional support, and self-support). Federal support is in the form of research assistantships, fellowships, and traineeships. Research assistantships (RAships) now account for a large majority of students with federal support in most fields except for the medical sciences, where traineeships and fellowships are the dominant mode of government support. RAships are typically the only form of federal government support for which non-U.S. citizens are eligible. Self-support includes loans (including federal loans), personal and family contributions, and foreign government grants for foreign nationals' study in the United States. The analysis also draws on data gathered on doctorate awards by field for U.S. and non-U.S. citizens from the Survey of Earned Doctorates (SED). The field classification used in both surveys is similar but not identical to the classification of research fields used in the Federal Funds Survey and in Chapter II. Here aeronautical and astronautical engineering are combined as "aerospace engineering." Environmental biology is combined with biological sciences, and "health sciences" encompasses most of the clinical fields that comprise "medical sciences."[5]

In general we find a high but not perfect correlation between declining research funding in the mid-1990s and declining graduate student enrollment and Ph.D. production through 1999.[6] Fields that experienced increasing federal research support show a mixed pattern of enrollment and Ph.D. output. The anomalies—fields with rising research funding and declining enrollment (aeronautical, astronautical, chemical, civil, and materials engineering; astronomy, agricultural sciences, atmospheric and ocean sciences and psychology)[7]—underscore that there are other factors at work and demonstrate the complexity of any causal analysis or, to the extent that the decreases are of concern, of any attempt to boost enrollment and Ph.D. awards.

The data may be misleading in one respect. Although the role of federally funded research assistantships, fellowships, and traineeships varies greatly among fields, in general less than one-third of graduate students are reported to be supported principally by federal funds and in some cases—e.g., much of engineering, computer science, and agriculture—the share is closer to 20 percent. This might lead one to conclude that federal research funding is a relatively small factor in enrollment trends. Yet the data on sources of support reflect students' principal funding at a snapshot in time. Over the typical 6 to 7 year graduate education career leading to the Ph.D., students are likely to receive support from different sources. Thus, the proportion of students who during their tenure receive some support from federal research grants and contracts is undoubtedly higher than one third. Moreover, the availability of research assistantships enables institutions to allocate resources to other purposes and thus has powerful indirect effects on enrollment and institutional operations generally.

---

[3]William G. Bowen and Neil L. Rudenstine. 1992. *In Pursuit of the Ph.D.*, Princeton, N.J.: Princeton University Press. National Academy of Sciences, National Academy of Engineering, and Institute of Medicine, Committee on Science, Engineering, and Public Policy. 1995. *Reshaping the Graduate Education of Scientists and Engineers*, Washington, D.C.: National Academy Press.

[4]Allen R. Sanderson, Bernard L. Guoni, et al. 2000. *Doctorate Recipients from United States Universities: Summary Report, 1999*, pp. 54. Chicago: National Opinion Research Center.

[5]See Appendix.

[6]The decline in graduate enrollment in science and engineering is not explained by an overall decline in the number of students graduating from U.S. institutions with appropriate bachelor's degrees. In fact, that number increased by 12.9 percent from 1992 to 1997, the last year for which NSF data are available, although there may have been declines in bachelor's degrees in certain fields and in certain years during the decade.

[7]Of these ten fields, four had declining research funding through 1997. There are no cases of declining research funding and rising enrollments.

PHYSICAL, ENVIRONMENTAL, AND MATHEMATICAL SCIENCES

Federal funding for physical, environmental, and mathematical sciences declined for most, though not all, fields from 1993 to 1999. In a number of these fields, including three cases where federal research funding actually increased, there is a uniform pattern of decline in graduate student enrollment in the 1990s. The drop in the number of students whose primary source of support was the federal government was larger than the overall decline in numbers of graduate students. The number of students with federally funded graduate research assistantships declined in each case, although typically by smaller percentages than the numbers of students with other kinds of federal support (e.g., fellowships and traineeships).

Federal funding for university physics research declined by 7.4 percent from 1993 to 1999. During this period, the number of full-time physics graduate students declined steadily and substantially, by 22.1 percent (Figure 3-1). Federally supported graduate students declined by 22.6 percent and federally supported graduate research assistants (RAs) declined by 20.8 percent. The average annual decrease for federally supported physics graduate students was 4.2 percent and for those with nonfederal funding was 4.0 percent.

In 1999, federal funding for university chemistry (Figure 3-2) was 2.0 percent lower than in 1993. During this period, the number of full-time chemistry graduate students declined by 7.2 percent, federally supported graduate students declined 13.2 percent, and federally supported RAs declined by 7.9 percent. The average annual decline in federally supported graduate students was 2.3 percent and in those with nonfederal funding was 0.7 percent.

By contrast, federal funding for university astronomy research increased by 46.9 percent from 1993 to 1999 (Figure 3-3). Full-time graduate enrollment in astronomy nevertheless dropped 4.7 percent during this period. This was largely due to a decrease of 7.6 percent in the number of graduate students supported by the federal government. The number of federally supported RAs declined slightly by 1.2 percent. The average annual decline in federally supported graduate students was 1.3 percent. The average annual decline in those with nonfederal funding was negligible.

Federal funding for university research in mathematical sciences declined by 13.5 percent from 1993 to 1999 (Figure 3-4). The number of full-time mathematics graduate students declined by 18.8 percent and the number of mathematics graduate students with federal support declined by 25.1 percent in the same period. Federally supported RAs in mathematics decreased by 19.3 percent. The average annual decline in federally supported graduate students was 4.7 percent and among those whose primary

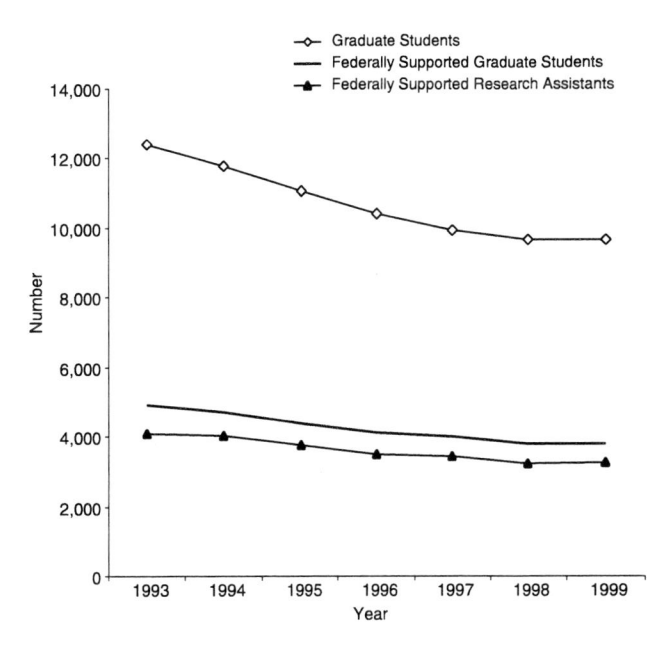

FIGURE 3-1 Full-time graduate enrollment in physics, 1993–1999.

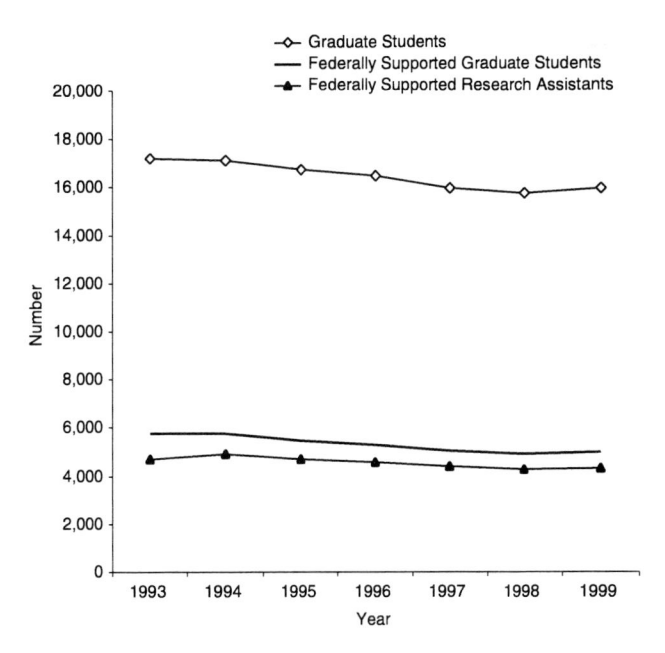

FIGURE 3-2 Full-time graduate enrollment in chemistry, 1993–1999.

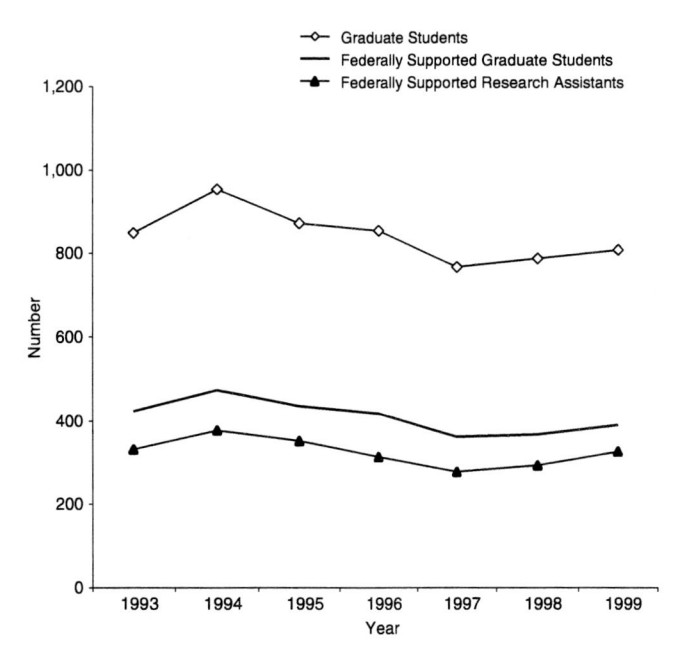

FIGURE 3-3 Full-time graduate enrollment in astronomy, 1993–1999.

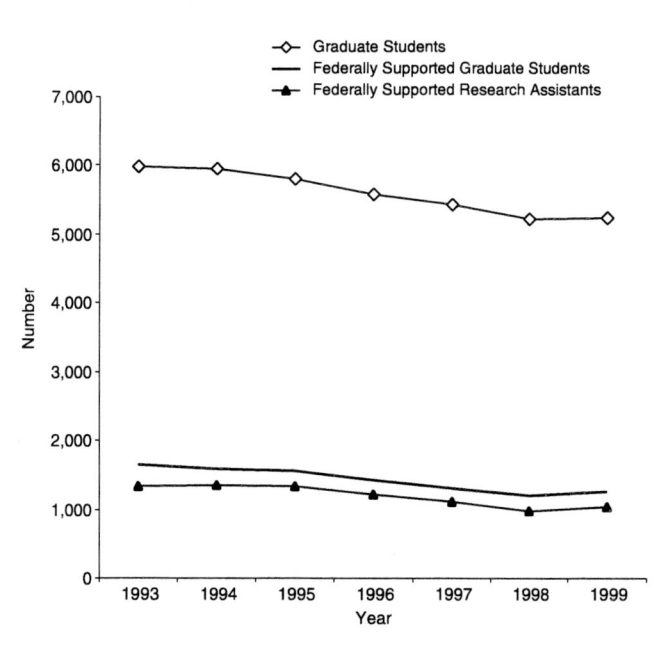

FIGURE 3-5 Full-time graduate enrollment in geosciences, 1993–1999.

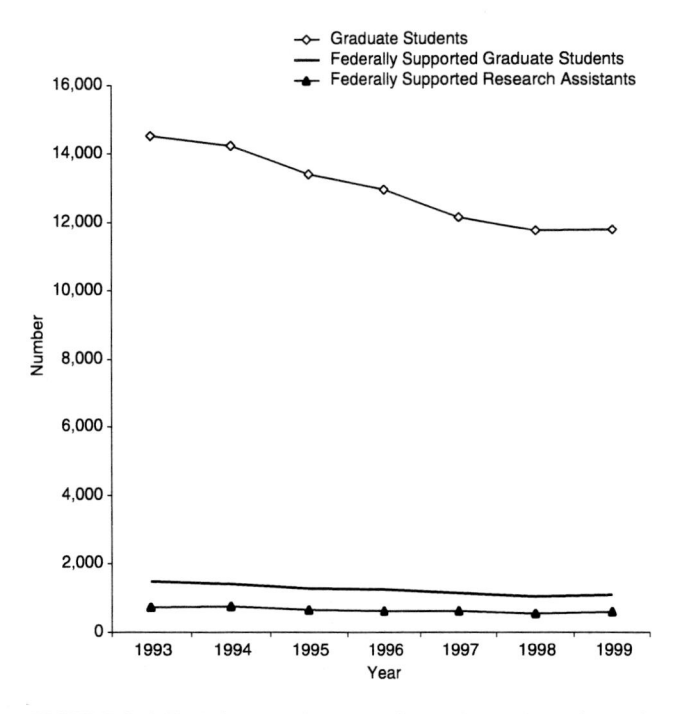

FIGURE 3-4 Full-time graduate enrollment in mathematical sciences, 1993–1999.

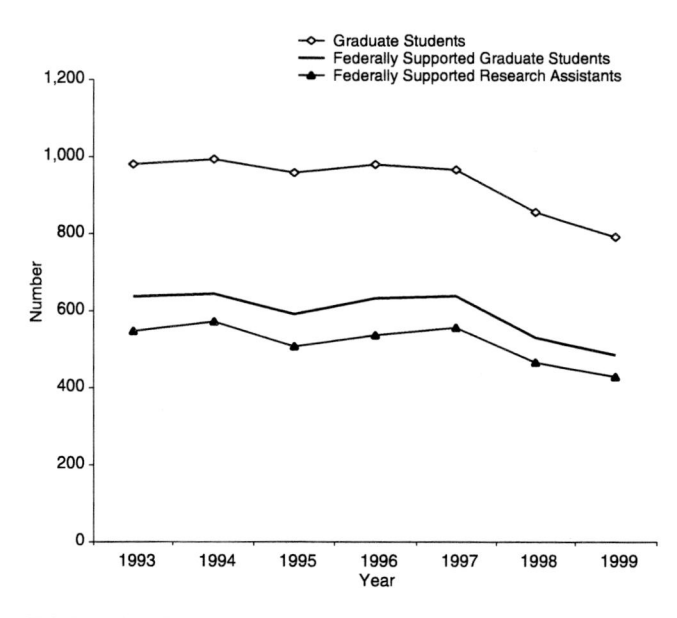

FIGURE 3-6 Full-time graduate enrollment in atmospheric sciences, 1993–1999.

support was from a nonfederal source the average decrease was 3.3 percent.

Federal funding for university research in geology decreased sharply, by 31.6 percent, from 1993 to 1999 (Figure 3-5). The number of full-time graduate students in the geosciences decreased by 12.2 percent and those who were federally supported decreased by 23.3 percent during this period. Federally supported RAs decreased by a similar margin of 22.3 percent. The average annual decline in federally supported graduate students was 4.3 percent and in those whose primary support was from a nonfederal source was 1.4 percent.

Federal funding for atmospheric research in universities increased by 13.7 percent from 1993 to 1999 (Figure 3-6). Full-time graduate enrollment in atmospheric sciences nevertheless decreased 19.1 percent during this period and federally supported graduate students decreased by 23.7 percent. Federally supported RAs decreased by a similar margin of 21.4 percent. The average annual decline in federally supported graduate students was 4.4 percent and among those whose primary support was from a nonfederal source the decline was 1.8 percent.

Federal funding for university research in oceanography increased by 46.9 percent from 1993 to 1999 (Figure 3-7). Full-time graduate enrollment in ocean sciences decreased by 2.2 percent during this period anyway and federally supported graduate students declined by 10.1 percent. Federally supported RAs were down by 8.9 percent. The average annual decrease in graduate students with federal support was 1.8 percent and for those with nonfederal funding was 0.8 percent.

Institutions may have stepped in to pick up support of students in the pipeline who previously received federal support. This may account for the slower decline in graduate enrollment supported by nonfederal funds. Institutional support of graduate students in the geological and atmospheric sciences actually increased from 1993 to 1999.

At the same time the number of self-supported students in these fields declined even more rapidly than the numbers receiving federal support, suggesting that students do not readily invest their resources in fields that are not growing. The exception was ocean sciences, a field with rising federal research expenditures, an increase in self-supporting students, and a drop in students with institutional support.

ENGINEERING

It is more difficult to generalize about trends in engineering fields. Changes in federal funding for university research between 1993 and 1999 range from large gains to flat funding to deep cuts. Nevertheless, full-time graduate enrollment in every engineering field is down. In two cases—aerospace and civil engineering—graduate students with federal support declined more rapidly than other

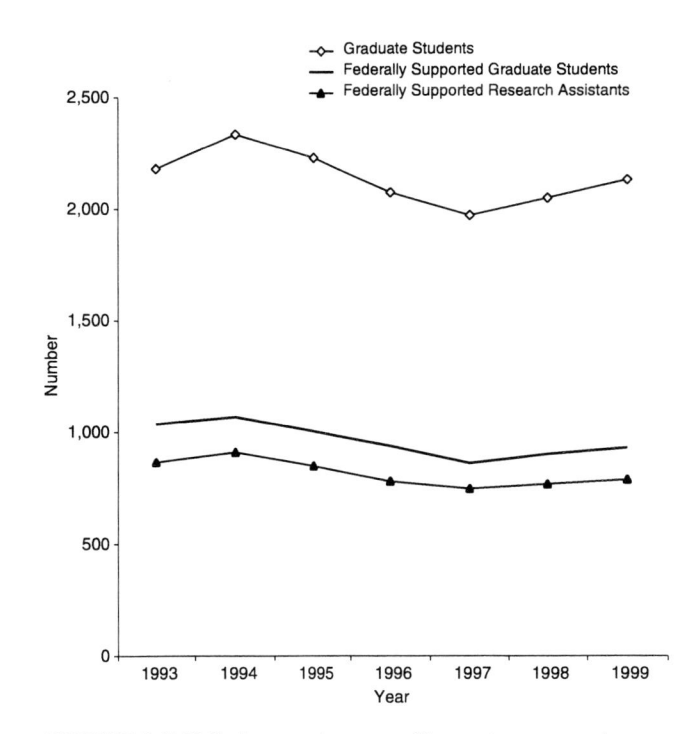

FIGURE 3-7 Full-time graduate enrollment in ocean sciences, 1993–1999.

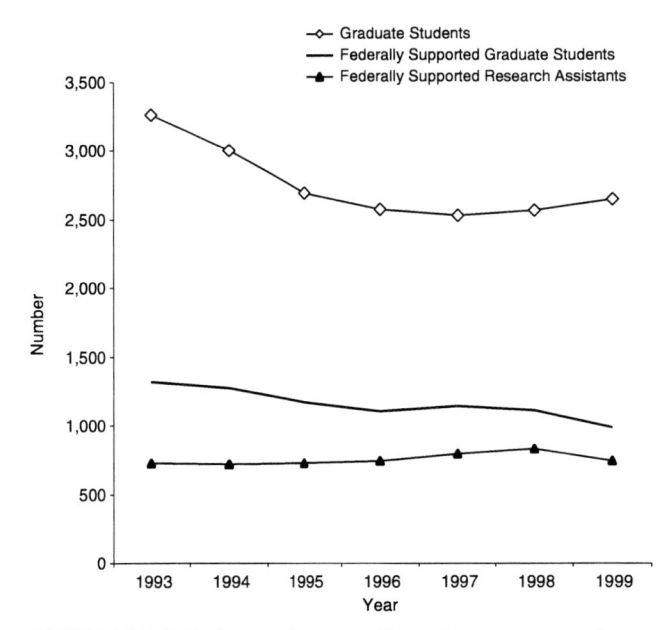

FIGURE 3-8 Full-time graduate enrollment in aerospace engineering, 1993–1999.

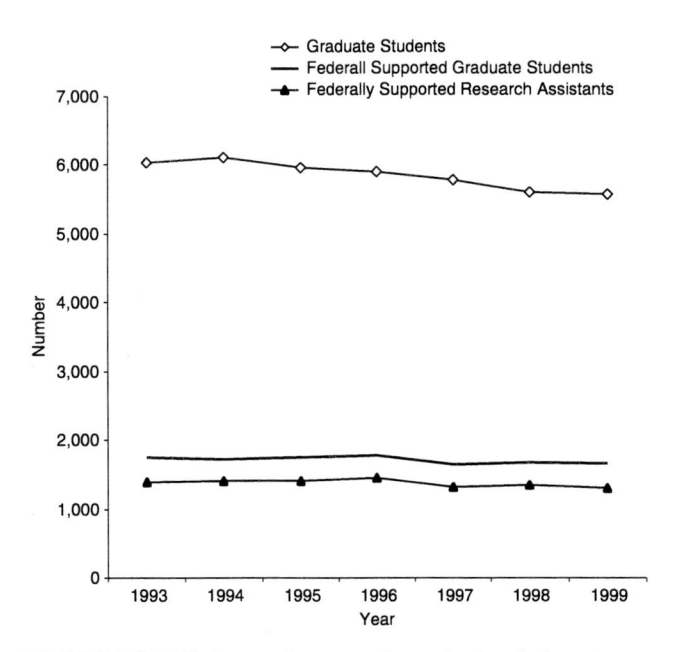

FIGURE 3-9 Full-time graduate enrollment in chemical engineering, 1993–1999.

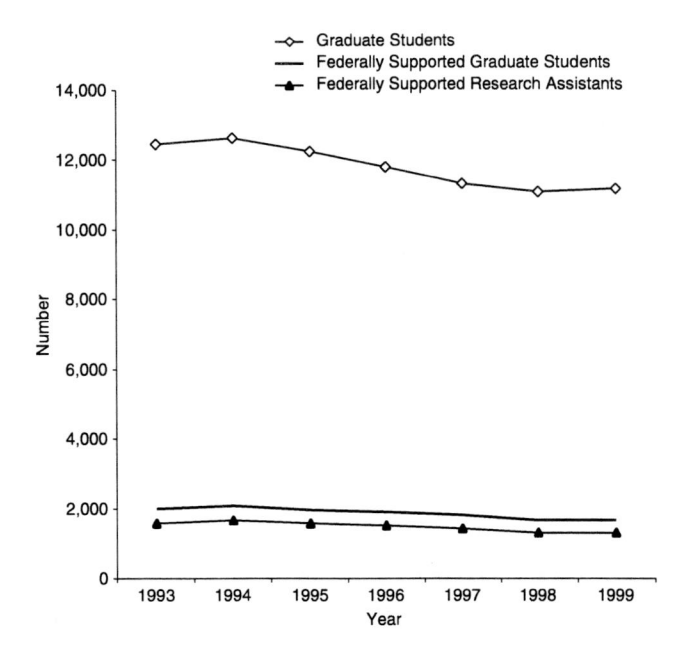

FIGURE 3-10 Full-time graduate enrollment in civil engineering, 1993–1999.

categories, but the reverse was the case in other fields. Overall, the number of engineering graduate students with institutional support has increased very slightly, but the number of self-supported students has dropped precipitously. The drop in self-supported students accounts for almost 85 percent of the overall enrollment decline in engineering.

Federal funding for aeronautical engineering research in universities is 24.5 percent higher in 1999 relative to 1993 and for astronautical research it is 79.5 percent higher in 1999. But these gains were the result of a late turnaround, from 1998 to 1999. Earlier research funding was down significantly from 1993. The downward trend in full-time graduate enrollment in aerospace engineering of 18.9 percent from 1993 to 1999 is consistent with the deep cuts in spending in the early part of this period (Figure 3-8). Moreover, the number of graduate students in this field who are federally supported dropped by 25.5 percent during this period. On the other hand, the number of federally supported RAs in aerospace engineering increased by 2.2 percent during this period, increasing from 55 to 75 percent of federally supported students over this period. The average annual decline in federally supported graduate students was 4.8 percent and in those whose primary support was from a nonfederal source was 2.6 percent.

Federal funding for university research in chemical engineering was also down from 1993 to 1997, by 11.6 percent, before increasing in 1998 and 1999. Funding in 1999 is up 2.2 percent from 1993 (Figure 3-9). During this period, the number of full-time graduate students in the field declined by 7.8 percent. The number of graduate students with federal support declined by 5.2 percent and the number of federally supported RAs declined 6.3 percent. Federally supported graduate students had an average annual decline of 0.9 percent, while those with nonfederal support declined 1.5 percent annually.

Federal funding for university research in civil engineering increased by 6.4 percent from 1993 to 1999, but full-time graduate enrollment fell by 10.3 percent during this period (Figure 3-10). Federally supported graduate students decreased by 15.6 percent and federally supported RAs by 17.2 percent. RAs supported by nonfederal sources increased 13.0 percent generating an overall increase in civil engineering RAs. The average annual decrease in the number of federally supported graduate students was 2.8 percent and that for those with nonfederal support declined 1.6 percent annually.

By contrast, full-time graduate enrollment in electrical engineering declined by only 0.6 percent from 1993 to 1999, despite a decrease of 12.0 percent in federal funding for university research in this field (Figure 3-11). Indeed, the number of full-time graduate students with federal support increased by 12.3 percent during this period, largely due to an increase of 15.1 percent in the number of graduate students in electrical engineering supported by NSF. Federally supported RAs increased 33.6 percent. Institutional support increased 5.8 percent, but students who are self-supporting decreased 15.9 percent. The average annual change in federally supported students was 2.0 percent and for nonfederally supported students –0.7 percent.

Mechanical engineering has experienced declines in both funding and enrollment (Figure 3-12). Federal funding of university research in this field decreased more than 40 percent from 1993 to 1999. Full-time graduate enrollment decreased 16.6 percent. Despite an increase of 9.1 percent in the number of graduate students with support from NSF, the total number of graduate students with federal support declined 13.4 percent during this period and federally supported RAs decreased 8.7 percent. Students with institutional support declined 4.6 percent. Students supporting themselves declined 41.8 percent. The average annual decrease in the number of federally supported graduate students was 2.4 percent and that for those with nonfederal support declined 3.2 percent annually.

Federal funding for university-based research in metallurgical and materials engineering increased 7.7 percent from 1993 to 1999 (Figure 3-13). Nonetheless, both full-time graduate enrollment and federally supported graduate enrollment in the field decreased 16.8 percent during this period, an average annual decrease of 3.0 percent. Federally supported RAs were down 13.7 percent.

Graduate students in other engineering fields not represented in the survey of federal research obligations—agricultural, biomedical, industrial, mining, nuclear, and petroleum engineering and engineering science and physics—make up about 20 percent of full-time graduate enrollment in engineering. The number of students in these fields decreased 4.5 percent from 1993 to 1999, at an average annual rate of –0.8 percent. Federally supported graduate students were down 2.3 percent and federally supported RAs were down 2.4 percent.

COMPUTER SCIENCE

In the computer sciences, both federal funding for university research and full-time graduate enrollment are increasing rapidly. The number of students with nonfederal support, however, is growing faster than the number with federal support, as seen in Figure 3-14. Federal funding for university research in computer science grew by 34.3 percent from 1993 to 1999. During this period, the number of full-time graduate students in computer science whose primary source of support is the federal government grew by 15.1 percent (annual average of 2.4 percent), whereas, the number whose main source of support was nonfederal grew 33.6 percent (annual average growth of 4.9 percent) (Figure 3-14). The number of federally supported research assistants grew 15.6 percent and the number of research

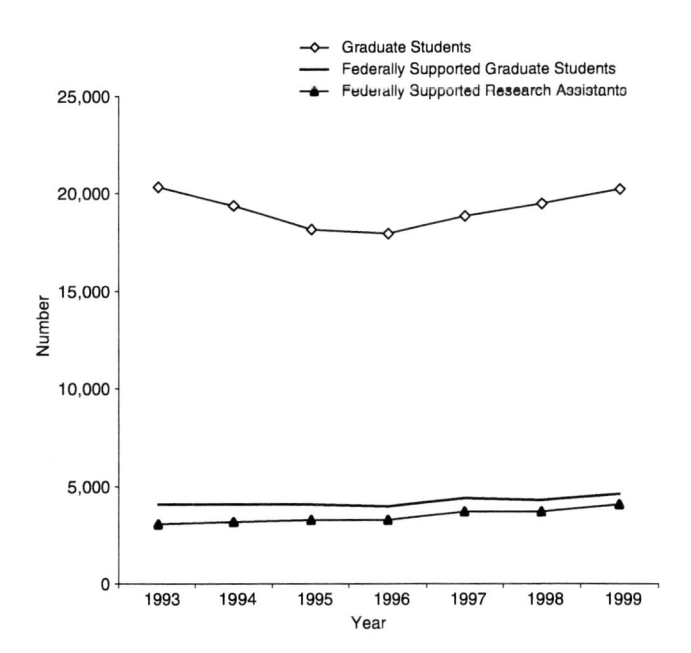

FIGURE 3-11 Full-time graduate enrollment in electrical engineering, 1993–1999.

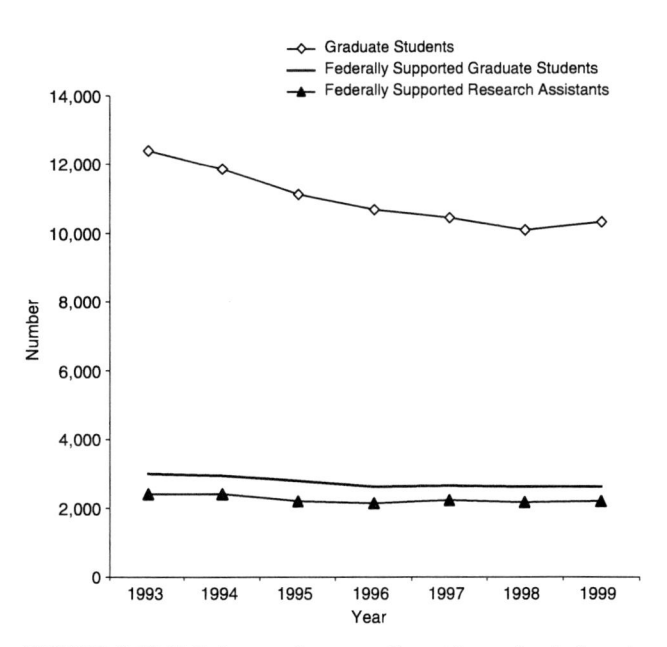

FIGURE 3-12 Full-time graduate enrollment in mechanical engineering, 1993–1999.

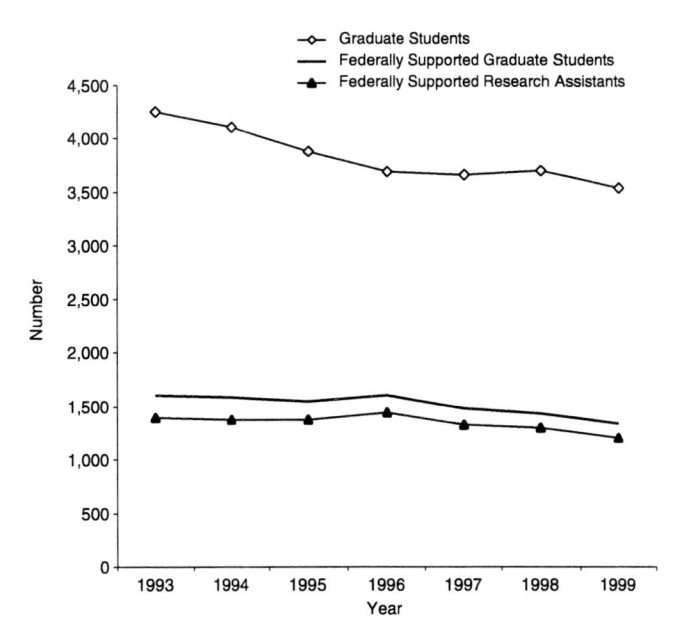

FIGURE 3-13 Full-time graduate enrollment in metallurgical and materials engineering, 1993–1999.

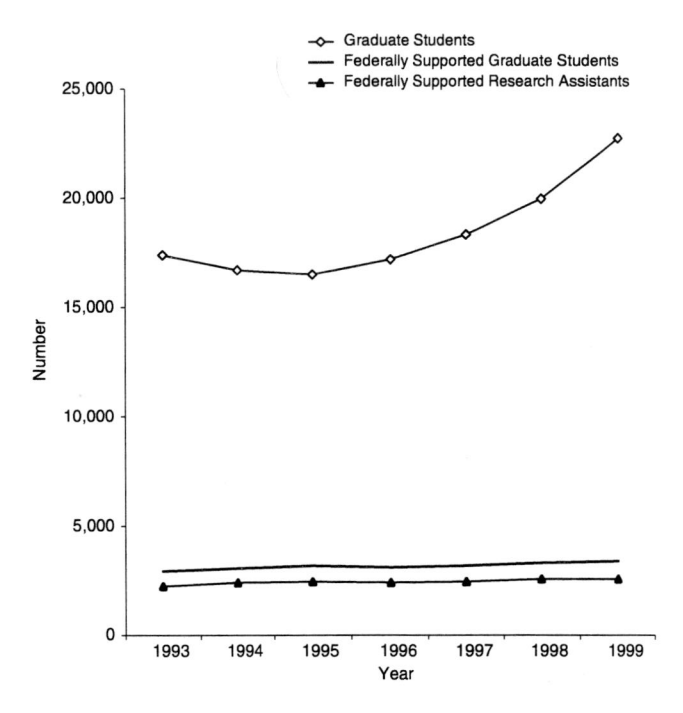

FIGURE 3-14 Full-time graduate enrollment in computer science, 1993–1999.

assistants supported by other sources of funding grew 47.3 percent. That the number of institutionally supported graduate students grew 25.8 percent and the number of self-supporting students increased 34.3 percent in the 1990s is probably a testament to how promising these fields were or were perceived to be in terms of employment opportunities by both institutions and individuals.

LIFE SCIENCES

Although funding for university research in the life sciences increased from 1993 to 1999, graduate enrollment changes differed significantly among subfields. In agricultural sciences the number of graduate students fell. In biological sciences enrollment grew only modestly, while in medical sciences enrollment grew at an even faster rate than the growth in research spending.

Federal funding for university agricultural sciences research increased 21.7 percent from 1993 to 1999 (Figure 3-15). Despite this increase in research obligations, the number of full-time graduate students in the agricultural sciences decreased 2.9 percent and the number of federally supported graduate students decreased 2.7 percent during this period. Federally supported RAs decreased 4.1 percent. The average annual decrease in the number of both federally and nonfederally supported graduate students was 0.5 percent.

Given that federal funding for university research in the biological sciences increased 39.9 percent from 1993 to 1999, it is somewhat surprising that graduate enrollment in the biological sciences has grown only modestly during this time (Figure 3-16). Total graduate enrollment in the biological sciences grew only 1.7 percent and the number of graduate students supported by federal funds grew only 2.0 percent, an average annual change of 0.3 percent. The number of federally supported RAs actually dropped 4.5 percent during this period. It is important to note, however, that the number of postdoctorates in the biological sciences increased 15.4 percent. This trend is consistent with anecdotal evidence that the troubled job market in the biological sciences not only dampens potential growth in graduate enrollment but also funnels recent Ph.D.'s into a series of postdoctoral appointments.

Meanwhile federal support for university research in the medical sciences increased 20.5 percent from 1993 to 1999 and graduate enrollment in health fields increased 41.5 percent during this time (Figure 3-17). Those who were supported by federal sources grew just 14.1 percent, an average annual increase of 2.2 percent, but a disproportionate share of the additional students supported by the federal government were RAs. Federally supported RAs grew 39.7 percent. Still, the number of students supported by nonfederal sources increased 48.5 percent, an average annual increase of 6.8 percent. As with computer science, the number of students whose primary source of support was institutional support grew 33.8 percent and the number who were self-supporting increased by an extraordinary 56.3 percent. Again, this trend is probably attributable to perceived growth and superior career opportunities in these fields.

SOCIAL AND BEHAVIORAL SCIENCES

Federal funding for university research in the social and behavioral sciences declined after 1993, turning up again in only the last few years. The upturn in university-based social science research appears not to have affected graduate enrollment trends yet. The upturn in federal—especially NIH—funding for university psychology research may have helped lift enrollments in that field.

Although federal funding for university research in the social sciences was up in 1999 over 1998, it was still 4.0 percent lower than in 1993 (Figure 3-18). In 1998, funding for university research had been 20.3 percent lower than in 1993. Graduate enrollment in the social sciences decreased 4.2 percent from 1993 to 1999 and the number of federally supported graduate students decreased 10.2 percent, an average annual decline of 1.8 percent. Federally supported RAs dropped about 1.7 percent per annum.

Federal funding of university-based psychology research, boosted by increases from NIH, was up 1.5 percent from 1993 to 1999 (Figure 3-19). Such funding of basic psychology research in universities, however, was 20.3 percent higher in 1999 than 1993. Federal funding may have made much of the difference in graduate enrollment in psychology. Federally supported graduate students in psychology were up 22.7 percent, an average annual increase of 3.5 percent. Students supported by nonfederal sources decreased by 2.1 percent, an average annual decline of 0.4 percent. Thus, overall, graduate enrollment in psychology was down 0.2 percent from 1993 to 1999. It is interesting to note that trends in number of RAs were reversed. Federally supported RAs were down 7.0 percent, while nonfederally supported RAs increased by 11.5 percent.

RECENT TRENDS IN DOCTORAL AWARDS

To supplement trends in graduate enrollment, it is useful to examine trends in the number of new doctorates by field during the period 1993 to 1999. Analyzing the trends in doctoral degrees awarded is somewhat more complicated because of the time lag between enrollment and degree award, which is often seven or more years. Thus, it may take 7 years for enrollment increases in a field to show up in doctoral award data, though the effect of enrollment decreases on doctoral degrees awarded may show up much sooner as students drop out of degree

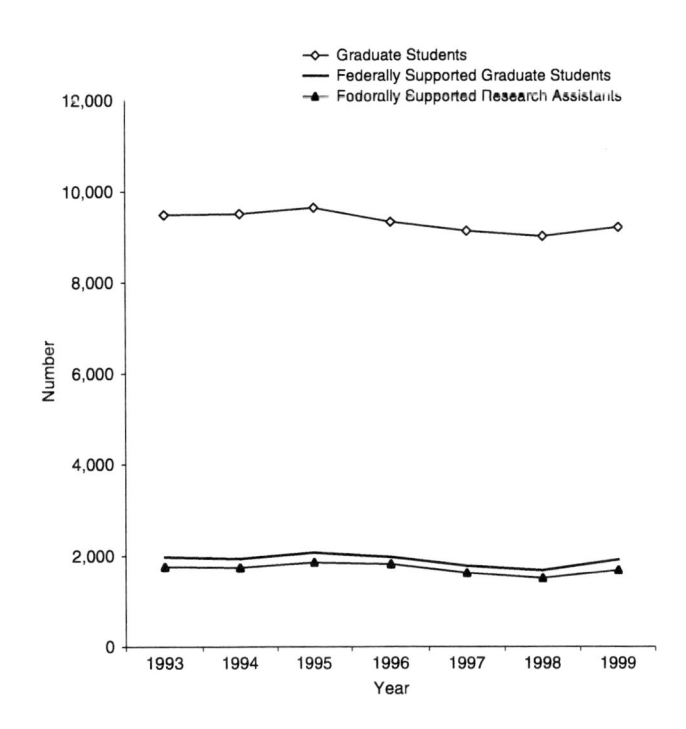

FIGURE 3-15 Full-time graduate enrollment in agricultural sciences, 1993–1999.

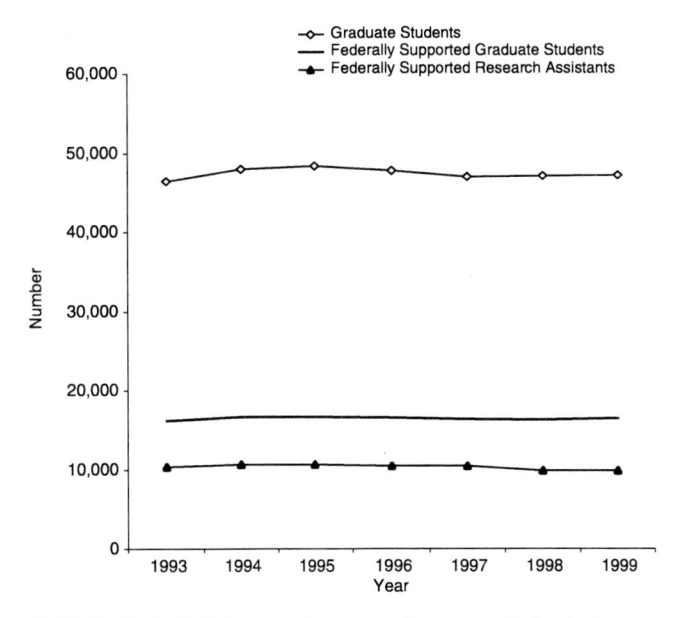

FIGURE 3-16 Full-time graduate enrollment in biological sciences, 1993–1999.

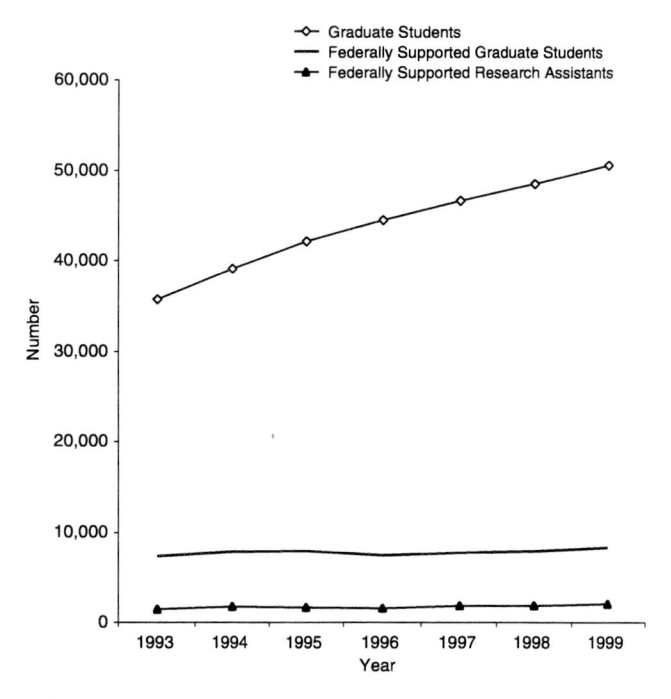

FIGURE 3-17 Full-time graduate enrollment in health fields, 1993–1999.

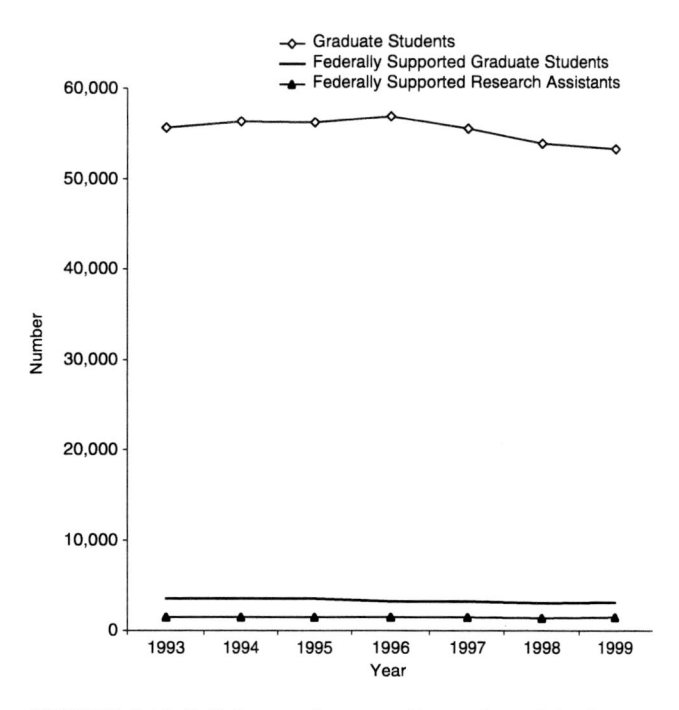

FIGURE 3-18 Full-time graduate enrollment in social sciences, 1993–1999.

programs or switch fields. Indeed, the data shown below reveal that fields in which federal funding for R&D decreased from 1993 to 1997 almost universally had decreases in doctoral awards from 1993 to 1999. Fields with increases in federal funding from 1993 to 1997, however, had mixed results in doctoral awards, which may be accounted for, in part, by time to degree for Ph.D.'s.

During this period the number of individuals earning science and engineering doctorates from U.S. institutions peaked at 27,309 in 1998 and then declined by 5.0 percent from 1998 to 1999. There are, however, important differences in trends by field that correspond to trends in federal funding for university research and graduate education. Moreover, there are important differences in trends for U.S. and non-U.S. citizens that contribute to overall trends. For engineering fields, the number of new doctorates was 6.3 percent lower in 1999 than in 1993. As seen in Table 3-1, the decreases in new Ph.D.'s were seen across almost all engineering fields. The one exception to this trend was "other" engineering in which new doctorates increased 12.2 percent from 1993 to 1999.

There were key differences in trends among new engineering doctorates by citizenship status. While the number of new U.S. citizen engineering doctorates was down by 3.6 percent in 1999 compared to 1998, it was nevertheless up by 11.0 percent in 1999 compared to 1993. Here there were major differences by field. From 1993 to 1999, new U.S. doctorates increased 54.2 percent in civil engineering, 32.6 percent in "other" engineering, and 14.1 percent in mechanical engineering. In the same period, new U.S. doctorates declined 9.6 percent in aeronautical/astronautical engineering, 3.4 percent in industrial engineering, and 2.2 percent in metallurgical and materials engineering. By contrast, the number of new non-U.S. citizen engineering doctorates was down over 20 percent from 1993 to 1999 and this drop occurred across engineering fields. The largest numerical and percentage drop from 1993 to 1999 was in mechanical engineering (–34.9 percent). There was also a major drop of 30.8 percent in non-U.S. citizens earning civil engineering Ph.D.'s.

For science fields, the story is somewhat different. The number of new doctorates in the sciences decreased 3.6 percent from 1998 to 1999, but the number in 1999 was still 4.4 percent higher than in 1993. This masks important differences by field. From 1993 to 1999, the number of new Ph.D.'s decreased 9.1 percent in physics, 5.3 percent in mathematics, and 3.4 percent in computer science. Meanwhile, there were increases in astronomy (10.3 percent), biological sciences (10.0 percent), social sciences (7.7 percent), psychology (7.2 percent), and earth, atmospheric, and ocean sciences (4.7 percent).

For U.S. citizens, trends in new doctorates are generally in the same direction as for all new Ph.D.'s. The one exception is in mathematics where the number of U.S.

citizen Ph.D.'s is 8.5 percent higher in 1999 compared to 1993, while the overall number of Ph.D.'s in that field has decreased by 5.3 percent. For non-U.S. citizens, trends in new doctorate recipients are in the same direction as for Ph.D.'s overall, although the changes are pronounced. For example, non-U.S. citizens earning physics Ph.D.'s decreased 16.3 percent from 1993 to 1999 compared with an overall decline of 9.1 percent and non-U.S. citizens earning mathematics Ph.D.'s decreased 16.4 percent from 1993 to 1999 compared to an overall decrease of 5.3 percent. Similarly, non-U.S. citizens earning biological sciences Ph.D. have increased 13.0 percent from 1993 to 1999 compared to an overall increase of 10.0 percent. There is a similar trend for health fields, in which non-U.S. citizens earning doctorates increased 32.8 percent from 1993 to 1999 compared to a 17.8 percent increase in all doctorates in health fields.

Trends for non-U.S. citizen Ph.D.'s have clearly affected overall trends in the number of new Ph.D.'s. The drop in non-U.S. citizens earning Ph.D.'s from 1993 to 1999 accounts for much or all of the overall decline in physics, mathematics, computer science, and nearly every engineering field that experienced a decrease in Ph.D.'s. Non-U.S. citizens also account for a significant share of the increase in such fields as astronomy, earth, atmospheric, and ocean sciences, biological sciences, and health fields. Fields that do not fit this pattern are agricultural sciences, in which non-U.S. citizen Ph.D.'s increased while overall Ph.D.'s decreased, and psychology and social sciences, in which non-U.S. citizen Ph.D.'s decreased despite substantial overall increases in new Ph.D.'s.

TRENDS ACROSS FIELDS

The data in Table 3-1, summarizing data in federal funding for university research, full-time graduate enrollment, and doctorate recipients from 1993 to 1999, reveal two divergent patterns among science and engineering fields. First, fields in which federal funding for university research was down from 1993 to 1997 have almost all had declines in both graduate enrollments and doctorate recipients from 1993 to 1999. Second, fields with increasing federal funding for university research have a range of divergent trends in graduate enrollment and doctorate production.

Fields With Decreased Federal Funding

Seven fields experienced substantial cuts in both federal funding for university research from 1993 to 1997 and full-time graduate enrollment from 1993 to 1999—mechanical engineering, aerospace engineering, chemical engineering, mathematics, physics, chemistry, and social sciences.

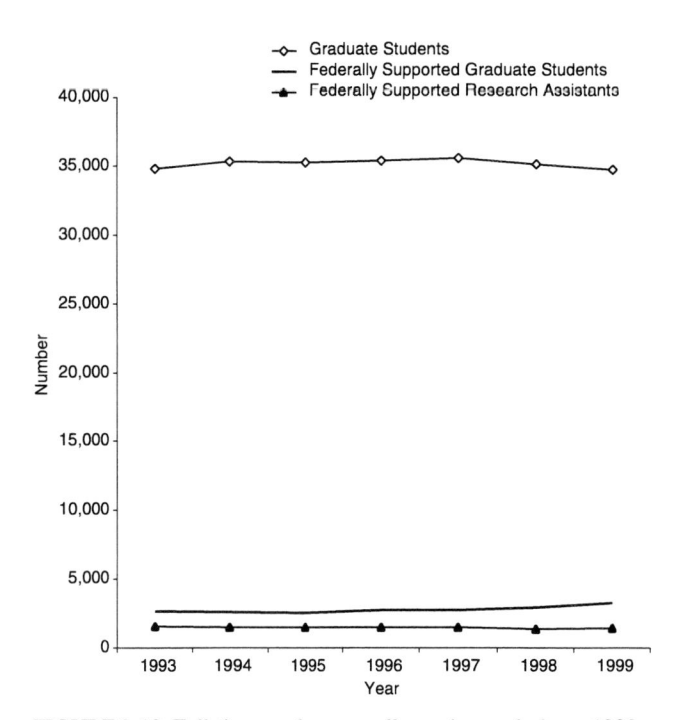

FIGURE 3-19 Full-time graduate enrollment in psychology, 1993–1999.

These fields have had cuts in federal funding for university research ranging from 9.7 percent to 40.2 percent from 1993 to 1997 and the majority of them are still substantially below their 1993 funding levels in 1999. These fields have also experienced decreases in full-time graduate students, graduate students who are supported by the federal government, and graduate research assistants supported by the federal government. The declines in federally supported RAs have typically not been as deep as for all students who are federally supported.

Electrical engineering and psychology are exceptions. Electrical engineering also had deep cuts in federal funding for university research (31.1 percent from 1993 to 1997 and was still down 12.0 percent by 1999), but had only a very minor drop in graduate enrollment from 1993 to 1999 of 0.6 percent. Moreover, federally supported graduate students increased 12.3 percent and federally supported RAs, in particular, increased 33.6 percent. As noted above, this increase in federally supported graduate students in electrical engineering can be accounted for in large part by a 15.1 percent increase in graduate students whose primary source of support is NSF. Psychology meanwhile had a decrease of 9.2 percent in federal funding for university research from 1993 to 1997, but recent increases in federal funding resulted in an overall increase of 1.5 percent from 1993 to 1999. Perhaps because of the recent increase, the field had almost no change in graduate enrollment and a substantial increase in federally supported graduate students.

The number of doctorate awards from 1993 to 1999 was also generally down for these seven fields by 0.1 to 17.2 percent, although there were divergent trends for U.S. and non-U.S. citizens. For seven of these eight fields, doctorate awards decreased between 0.1 and 17.2 percent during this time. The exception to this trend was the social sciences, a field less dependent on federal research dollars, which experienced a 7.7 percent increase during this period. There were, however, differences among the seven fields based on citizenship status. Non-U.S. Ph.D.-earners declined across all nine fields, from 3.7 to 34.9 percent, accounting for most or all of the decline in doctorates awarded. U.S. citizens earning Ph.D.'s, by contrast, have increased for six of the nine fields and declined in only three.

Federal funding for university research may have played a key role in determining graduate enrollment patterns for most of these fields, particularly in engineering and the physical sciences, but institutions and students also played an important role. Students with institutional support in these fields also generally declined in number from 1993 to 1999 but not as rapidly as the number of students with federal support. The number of self-supported students in these fields, however, has generally declined even more sharply than the number supported by federal funding. This suggests that students do not invest their own funds in fields that are not perceived as growing. In effect, institutions may act to mitigate the effects of cuts in federal research funding, but students may work to further ratify federal cuts by opting for training in growth fields.

Fields With Increased Federal Funding

Compared to the clear downward direction in graduate enrollments and new doctorates for fields with decreased federal funding for university research, the direction of change in graduate students and doctorates in those fields with increased federal funding for university research in both 1997 and 1999 relative to 1993 is highly varied. This variability suggests that many factors in addition to federal funding play a role in determining trends in graduate enrollment and doctorates in these fields.

In only two fields with increased federal funding, health and biological sciences, have graduate enrollments and doctorate awards increased from 1993 to 1999 but even here there are other factors at play. Funding for research in the medical sciences is up 20.5 percent, graduate enrollment in the field has increased 41.5 percent, and doctorates are up 17.8 percent. Federally funded graduate students, however, have increased only 14.1 percent, while self-supporting students have increased 54 percent during this period suggesting that when a field is perceived as growing it attracts not only research funding but also students. Funding in the biological sciences is up even more, at 39.9 percent. Yet, while graduate enrollment grew, it was up only 1.7 percent and federally funded research assistants decreased 4.5 percent. Here, it appears, faculties have relied principally on postdoctorates (up 15.4 percent from 1993 to 1999 in this field) rather than graduate students to staff their laboratories.

The remaining fields exhibit a wide array of trends, influenced by various factors including the industrial job market. In computer science, graduate enrollment is up, but doctorate awards are down, reflecting the strong pull of the late 1990s information technology (IT) job market away from completing a Ph.D. degree. In astronomy and earth, atmospheric, and ocean sciences, by contrast, graduate enrollment was down but doctorate awards were up. The agricultural sciences, chemical engineering, and metallurgical and materials engineering had declining enrollments and doctorate awards, suggesting that these fields are having trouble attracting students even when funding increases. There were increases in non-U.S. citizens earning Ph.D.'s in agricultural sciences and in U.S. citizens earning Ph.D.'s in chemical engineering. Finally, psychology, which had only a modest increase in federal research funding from 1993 to 1999, had a substantial increase in federally supported graduate students and a modest increase in doctorates due to increased support from NIH.

Doctorate Awards

Trends in the number of non-U.S. citizens earning Ph.D.'s tend to mirror trends in federal funding for university research. The decrease in non-U.S. citizens earning Ph.D.'s in fields with decreased federal funding accounts for much or all of the overall decrease in doctorate awards in these fields. Meanwhile, in four of the five fields with both increased federal funding and increased numbers of doctorates—astronomy, biological sciences, medical sciences (health fields), and earth, atmospheric, and ocean sciences—the rate of growth among non-U.S. citizens has been far higher than the rate of growth among U.S. citizens.

The exception to this trend may prove the rule. In psychology, the number of U.S. citizens earning doctorates has increased 2.9 percent and the number of non-U.S. citizens has decreased 6.3 percent. Since federally supported graduate students have increased while federally supported research assistants has decreased, this suggests that the increase in federal support to graduate students has been provided in the form of traineeships. While both U.S. and non-U.S. citizens may be supported on research assistantships, only U.S. citizens are eligible to receive traineeships.

ANNEX

TABLE 3-1 Percent Change in Federal Funding for University Research, Full-time Graduate Enrollment, and Doctorate Degrees Awarded, by field, 1993–1999

	Percent Change in Federal Funding for University Research 1993–1997	1993–1999	Percent Change in Full-time Graduate Enrollment, 1993–1999 Total	Total students federally supported	Federally supported research assistants	Percent Change in Ph.D.'s, 1993–1999 Total	U.S. Citizens	Non-U.S. Citizens
Mechanical engineering	−40.2%	−40.5%	−16.6	−13.4	−8.7	−17.2	14.1	−34.9
Mathematics	−19.9%	−13.5%	−18.8	−25.1	−19.3	−5.3	8.5	−16.4
Electrical engineering	−31.1%	−12.0%	−0.6	12.3	33.6	−4.3	1.1	−12.3
Physics	−20.9%	−7.4%	−22.1	−22.6	−20.8	−9.1	−7.5	−16.3
Social sciences, total	−15.8%	−4.0%	−4.2	−10.2	−1.7	7.7	16.0	−11.7
Chemistry	−9.7%	−2.0%	−7.2	−13.2	−7.9	−0.1	−1.7	−3.7
Aeronautical engineering	−12.8%	24.5%	−18.9	−25.5	2.2	−9.2	−9.6	−13.3
Astronautical engineering	−20.8%	79.5%						
Chemical engineering	−11.6%	2.2%	−7.8	−5.2	−6.3	−8.0	3.4	−17.0
Astronomy	28.9%	46.9%	−4.7	−7.6	−1.2	10.3	3.8	15.4
Biological sciences	17.5%	39.9%	1.5	2.0	−4.5	10.0	5.9	13.0
Computer science	17.1%	34.3%	30.5	15.1	15.6	−3.4	−3.1	−7.2
Agricultural sciences	6.9%	21.7%	−2.9	−2.7	−4.1	−0.3	−3.7	2.8
Medical sciences	0.1%	20.5%	41.5	14.1	39.7	17.8	9.9	32.8
Civil engineering	10.1%	6.4%	−10.3	−15.6	−17.2	−6.3	54.2	−30.8
Metallurgy and materials engineering	20.0%	7.7%	−16.8	−16.8	−14.8	−12.1	−2.2	−20.5
Earth, atmospheric, and ocean sciences	4.9%	5.6%	−7.6	−18.2	−17.3	4.7	1.5	6.2
Psychology, total	−9.2%	1.5%	−0.2	22.7	−7.0	7.2	2.9	−6.3

SOURCES: NSF, Survey of Federal Funds for Research and Development; NSF, Survey of Graduate Students and Postdoctorates in Science and Engineering; NSF/NIH/USED/NEH/USDA/NASA, Survey of Earned Doctorates.

TABLE 3-2 Full-time Graduate Enrollment in Science and Engineering, by Field and by Selected Source and Mechanism of Support, 1993–1999

	1993	1994	1995	1996	1997	1998	1999	Change Number	Change Percent 93–99
Aerospace Engineering									
Graduate Students	3,262	3,000	2,693	2,576	2,529	2,565	2,645	−617	−18.9%
Federally Supported Graduate Students	1,320	1,279	1,168	1,104	1,143	1,109	983	−337	−25.5%
Federally Supported Research Assistants	727	719	727	740	793	833	743	16	2.2%
Chemical Engineering									
Graduate Students	6,041	6,105	5,957	5,909	5,784	5,601	5,569	−472	−7.8%
Federally Supported Graduate Students	1,748	1,716	1,752	1,786	1,649	1,683	1,657	−91	−5.2%
Federally Supported Research Assistants	1,393	1,405	1,415	1,459	1,317	1,348	1,305	−88	−6.3%
Civil Engineering									
Graduate Students	12,458	12,641	12,248	11,791	11,331	11,079	11,178	−1,280	−10.3%
Federally Supported Graduate Students	1,982	2,090	1,970	1,886	1,807	1,670	1,672	−310	−15.6%
Federally Supported Research Assistants	1,580	1,657	1,581	1,503	1,435	1,291	1,309	−271	−17.2%
Electrical Engineering									
Graduate Students	20,343	19,385	18,167	17,967	18,854	19,470	20,224	−119	−0.6%
Federally Supported Graduate Students	4,104	4,085	4,056	3,984	4,389	4,316	4,610	506	12.3%
Federally Supported Research Assistants	3,068	3,199	3,287	3,277	3,722	3,694	4,100	1,032	33.6%
Mechanical Engineering									
Graduate Students	12,395	11,875	11,128	10,690	10,432	10,073	10,333	−2,062	−16.6%
Federally Supported Graduate Students	2,999	2,946	2,777	2,602	2,626	2,607	2,596	−403	−13.4%
Federally Supported Research Assistants	2,406	2,403	2,205	2,122	2,237	2,178	2,197	−209	−8.7%
Metallurgy and Materials Engineering									
Graduate Students	4,249	4,108	3,880	3,693	3,661	3,702	3,537	−712	−16.8%
Federally Supported Graduate Students	1,605	1,578	1,544	1,597	1,473	1,431	1,336	−269	−16.8%
Federally Supported Research Assistants	1,393	1,373	1,373	1,437	1,328	1,297	1,202	−191	−13.7%
Engineering, Other									
Graduate Students	15,022	14,425	13,681	13,203	12,985	12,841	14346	−676	−4.5%
Federally Supported Graduate Students	3,130	3,160	3,093	2,873	2,780	2,687	3059	−71	−2.3%
Federally Supported Research Assistants	2,158	2,230	2,092	1,914	1,885	1,885	2106	−52	−2.4%
Physics									
Graduate Students	12,397	11,766	11,052	10,400	9,923	9,661	9,661	−2,736	−22.1%
Federally Supported Graduate Students	4,916	4,716	4,397	4,130	4,008	3,810	3,807	−1,109	−22.6%
Federally Supported Research Assistants	4,103	4,042	3,764	3,504	3,437	3,223	3,248	−855	−20.8%
Chemistry									
Graduate Students	17,204	17,104	16,736	16,479	15,992	15,777	15,963	−1,241	−7.2%
Federally Supported Graduate Students	5,751	5,775	5,469	5,278	5,031	4,909	4,994	−757	−13.2%
Federally Supported Research Assistants	4,713	4,936	4,719	4,588	4,393	4,291	4,340	−373	−7.9%
Astronomy									
Graduate Students	848	953	871	854	768	787	808	−40	−4.7%
Federally Supported Graduate Students	421	472	434	418	362	366	389	−32	−7.6%
Federally Supported Research Assistants	330	376	351	313	278	293	326	−4	−1.2%

continues

TABLE 3-2 Continued

	1993	1994	1995	1996	1997	1998	1999	Change Number	Change Percent
Geosciences									
Graduate Students	5,970	5,946	5,796	5,579	5,432	5,214	5,239	−731	−12.2%
Federally Supported Graduate Students	1,647	1,587	1,556	1,425	1,305	1,205	1,263	−384	−23.3%
Federally Supported Research Assistants	1,338	1,348	1,339	1,214	1,108	973	1,040	−298	−22.3%
Atmospheric Sciences									
Graduate Students	980	993	959	980	966	856	793	−187	−19.1%
Federally Supported Graduate Students	636	644	592	633	639	531	485	−151	−23.7%
Federally Supported Research Assistants	547	572	507	537	556	466	430	−117	−21.4%
Ocean Sciences									
Graduate Students	2,177	2,333	2,228	2,074	1,971	2,047	2,130	−47	−2.2%
Federally Supported Graduate Students	1,037	1,070	1,003	940	860	904	932	−105	−10.1%
Federally Supported Research Assistants	865	911	849	780	748	769	788	−77	−8.9%
Mathematical Sciences									
Graduate Students	14,530	14,226	13,410	12,966	12,144	11,751	11,792	−2,738	−18.8%
Federally Supported Graduate Students	1,474	1,397	1,287	1,237	1,152	1,044	1,104	−370	−25.1%
Federally Supported Research Assistants	736	743	659	615	625	541	594	−142	−19.3%
Computer Science									
Graduate Students	17,401	16,701	16,510	17,195	18,335	19,972	22,708	5,307	30.5%
Federally Supported Graduate Students	2,920	3,067	3,176	3,106	3,173	3,309	3,361	441	15.1%
Federally Supported Research Assistants	2,226	2,380	2,435	2,380	2,435	2,548	2,573	347	15.6%
Agricultural Sciences									
Graduate Students	9,484	9,510	9,633	9,327	9,133	9,015	9,210	−274	−2.9%
Federally Supported Graduate Students	1,965	1,922	2,061	1,973	1,783	1,683	1,911	−54	−2.7%
Federally Supported Research Assistants	1,752	1,739	1,851	1,811	1,624	1,505	1,680	−72	−4.1%
Biological Sciences									
Graduate Students	46,487	48,026	48,366	47,782	47,011	47,105	47,268	781	1.7%
Federally Supported Graduate Students	16,210	16,725	16,649	16,564	16,365	16,251	16,531	321	2.0%
Federally Supported Research Assistants	10,369	10,642	10,593	10,448	10,399	9,816	9,899	−470	−4.5%
Health Fields									
Graduate Students	35,679	39,109	42,111	44,497	46,633	48,468	50,490	14,811	41.5%
Federally Supported Graduate Students	7,295	7,776	7,900	7,392	7,723	7,931	8,326	1,031	14.1%
Federally Supported Research Assistants	1,473	1,725	1,659	1,542	1,850	1,857	2,058	585	39.7%
Social Sciences									
Graduate Students	55,606	56,255	56,212	56,894	55,535	53,822	53,258	−2,348	−4.2%
Federally Supported Graduate Students	3,491	3,529	3,523	3,247	3,177	3,029	3,135	−356	−10.2%
Federally Supported Research Assistants	1,487	1,437	1,454	1,448	1,424	1,391	1,462	−25	−1.7%
Psychology									
Graduate Students	34,782	35,288	35,222	35,412	35,551	35,148	34,715	−67	−0.2%
Federally Supported Graduate Students	2,653	2,634	2,543	2,752	2,720	2,927	3,255	602	22.7%
Federally Supported Research Assistants	1,549	1,473	1,467	1,499	1,491	1,359	1,440	−109	−7.0%

SOURCE: National Science Foundation, Survey of Graduate Students and Postdoctorates in Science and Engineering.

4

Agency Trends in Research and Graduate Education Support

In this chapter we examine the data presented in Chapters 2 and 3 from the perspective of the principal federal agencies supporting research. How did agencies with shrinking, growing, or steady research budgets treat their research portfolios in the 1990s, and how did these decisions affect the composition of the federal research portfolio overall? Did they change or maintain the mix of research they were funding? Did agencies that were dominant funders of particular fields attempt to protect those fields from budget cuts? Did agencies with growing budgets diversify their research portfolios? Did they step in to increase their investments in research fields whose support from other agencies was declining or to pick up slack in graduate student support? Finally, once growth resumed, as it did to varying degrees in all but one agency by 1999, have agencies moved to restore funding of fields that they previously had cut?

A variety of factors, many of them specific to agencies, their missions, and their political environments and much too complex to examine here, determine how agencies treated their research portfolios during this period. We are simply interested in whether, in a period of budget contraction, adjustments occur across agencies or across time that reflect concern about reductions in investment in particular research fields. The answer is that in most agencies, both those experiencing tight budgets and those benefiting from increasing congressional appropriations, there were substantial changes in research priorities but little evidence of adjustments across agencies.

PORTFOLIO CHANGES IN AGENCIES WITH REDUCED RESEARCH FUNDING

Department of Defense

As of 1999, two agencies had less funding for research than in 1993—Department of Defense (DOD) and Department of the Interior. Others, including the DOE and USDA, surpassed their 1993 level of spending with the budget gains in 1998 and 1999. DOD funding of research fell by 13.2 percent from 1993 to 1994 and continued to decline through 1997, when it was 26.6 percent less than in 1993. Despite some budget growth in 1998 and 1999, DOD's funding of research was still 22.4 percent less than it was in 1993.

Did the substantial cuts in research funding at DOD negatively affect fields that received most of their funding from DOD in 1993? At that time, for example, DOD accounted for 82 percent of federal funding of electrical engineering, 75 percent of mechanical engineering, 73 percent of metallurgy/materials engineering, and 57 percent of computer science research.[1]

As Annex Table 4-1 indicates, DOD did not impose across-the-board cuts on the research fields it was supporting in 1993. Those cut more than average (22.4 percent) were environmental biology, psychology, chemistry, physics, atmospheric sciences, geology, mathematics, social sciences and most fields of engineering—astronautical, chemical, civil, electrical, mechanical, and metallurgy/materials. DOD was far and away the dominant funder of the latter three fields in 1993. Medical sciences were cut, but less than average (Figure 4-1).

Despite the strong downward pressure on DOD's research spending in the mid-1990s, several fields received increased although not necessarily substantially increased DOD support—biology, astronomy, oceanography, computer science, and aeronautical engineering.

In the case of oceanography, increased funding from DOD helped offset a decrease of more than a third by the Department of Commerce, the field's largest single federal

---

[1] Michael McGeary and Stephen A. Merrill. 1999. "Recent Trends in Federal Spending on Scientific and Engineering Research: Impacts on Research Fields and Graduate Training," Appendix A, Table A-2 in National Research Council, *Securing America's Industrial Strength*. Washington, D.C.: National Academy Press.

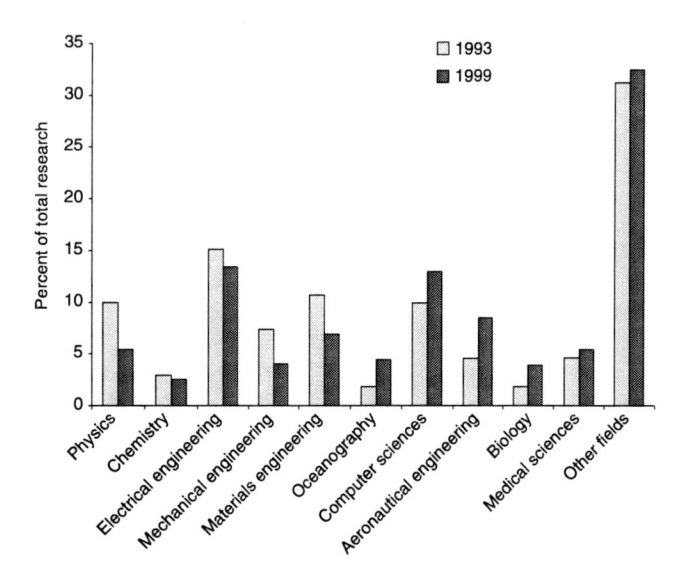

FIGURE 4-1 Research funding by field, Department of Defense, FY 1993 vs. FY 1999.

source of support in 1993 through its agency, the National Oceanographic and Atmospheric Administration. In aeronautical engineering, in which NASA is the major funder, DOD funding went from being about 7 percent less in 1997 than in 1993 to being 44 percent more in 1999. That increase helped put overall federal funding of aeronautical engineering research 21 percent higher than in 1993. DOD funding of life sciences (primarily biological and medical sciences) fell from 1993 to 1997, when it was 28 percent less than the 1993 level. But it began to increase again in 1998 (by 48 percent over 1997). In 1999, it was 14 percent more in 1999 than in 1993, and it was expected to be 43 percent more in 2000. The largest boost after 1997 was in the biological sciences, reflecting in part the growth in the congressionally mandated research programs on breast, prostate, and ovarian cancers and also increased attention to biological threats to national security.

As shares of DOD's research budgets, the life sciences increased from 7.8 percent to 11.4 percent, computer science from 9.9 percent to 13.0 percent, and environmental sciences from 5.5 percent to 7.9 percent because of increased funding of oceanography (Annex Table 4-1). The physical sciences dropped from 14.1 percent to 9.8 percent and engineering from 51.2 percent to 47.1 percent. Thus, there was a shift in DOD's portfolio of about 9 percentage points from the physical sciences and engineering to the life sciences (up 3.6 percentage points), computer science (up 3.1 percentage points), and oceanography (up 2.6 percentage points).

The fields that DOD favored—biological and medical sciences, computer science, oceanography, aeronautical engineering, and metallurgy/materials engineering—were fields receiving increases from other agencies. In fact, all but metallurgy/materials engineering had at least 20 percent more funding in 1999 than in 1993. Some fields cut at DOD—mathematics, astronautical and civil engineering, psychology, and social science—have ended up with increased funding overall because other agencies stepped up their support. But other fields with less DOD support—chemistry, physics, geology, and chemical, electrical, and mechanical engineering—did not pick up increases from other agencies and were down compared with 1993, all but chemistry by at least 20 percent.

Trends in the number of full-time graduate students supported by the DOD are generally consistent with the changes in funding levels of research. Overall, the number of DOD-supported full-time graduate students decreased by 17.6 percent, from 1993 to 1999 (Annex Table 4-2). The decreases occurred in almost all fields. Among engineering fields with the largest decreases were civil engineering, down by 52.1 percent, aerospace engineering, down by 41.5 percent, and metallurgy and materials engineering, down by 38.2 percent. Among graduate students in the sciences, those in mathematical science decreased by 43.1 percent, those in social sciences decreased by 37.4 percent, those in earth, atmospheric and ocean sciences decreased by 34.4 percent, and those in physical sciences decreased by 25.6 percent. DOD-supported students in the health fields were down by 16.6 percent, but students in the biological science were up by 23.4 percent. Also increasing were the numbers of graduate students in electrical engineering, up by 4.4 percent, and in chemical engineering, up by 17.3 percent.

Department of Energy

Although DOE's funding of research was 2.1 percent higher in 1999 than in 1993, the DOE research budget took a 7 percent cut from 1993 to 1994, bottomed out in 1996, and did not reach its 1993 level until 1998. Some fields were cut more than others were, and although research is growing, the allocation of funds among fields has been changed (Figure 4-2, Annex Table 4-3).

Despite increases in research funding since 1996, the physical sciences were cut by more than a quarter from 1993 to 1999 (26.8 percent, from $2.2 to $1.7 billion). As a share of the DOE research portfolio they declined from 58 percent to 42 percent. Environmental science research support also was reduced after 1997. These fields were up by 6 percent over 1993 in 1997 but down by 8 percent two years later. From 1993 to 1999, oceanography was down by 36 percent, geology by 33 percent, and atmospheric sciences by 8 percent.

Life sciences were also down (by 7 percent, from $275 to $255 million), but not as much as in 1997 when they were 17 percent less than in 1993. The big hits were in biology (down by $13 million) and n.e.c. (down $11 million). Environmental biology nearly quadrupled, but from a small base (280 percent, from $2.2 to $8.5 million).

Meanwhile, computer science gained relative advantage. In 1999, computer science funding was 339 percent greater than in 1993, and the field went from 3 to 13 percent of the DOE research portfolio. Engineering also increased its support, absolutely—rising 46 percent—and relatively, going from 19 to 28 percent of the portfolio. Chemical, electrical, and mechanical engineering were down substantially (19, 36, and 61 percent, respectively), but these reductions were swamped by tremendous growth in materials engineering (343 percent, from $75 million to $331 million). Engineering other (up 33 percent, from $427 million to $568 million) and civil engineering (up 27 percent, from $36 million to $46 million) also received increased funding.

In dollar terms, from 1993 to 1999 there was a substantial shift toward computer science (+$391 million) and materials engineering (+$256 million) and away from physics (–$461 million), chemistry (–$85 million), and to a lesser amount, other fields in engineering and environmental sciences (–$20 million to –$40 million each). Computer science and materials engineering went from a combined 5 percent to 21 percent of DOE's portfolio. In the case of computer science, several other agencies also increased funding although DOE accounted for 66 percent of the net increase. DOE's increase of $256 million in metallurgy/materials engineering offset most of the DOD reduction of $283 million. DOE increases for environmental biology, mathematics, and civil engineering helped offset cuts elsewhere.

DOE was the majority funder of physics in 1993, and the large reductions in funding after 1993 have not been offset by other agencies. In fact, as shown above, DOD, the second largest funder, also reduced its funding substantially, and funding for physics research is 25 percent less in 1999 than in 1993, about the same level it has been since 1996. Some other fields with reduced DOE funding have also been those cut overall—astronomy, chemistry, geology, and chemical, electrical, and mechanical engineering. It is not possible to relate these research funding trends to DOE graduate student support because the latter data were not available by field until very recently.

PORTFOLIO CHANGES IN AGENCIES WITH INCREASED RESEARCH FUNDING

National Institutes of Health

NIH has received steady annual increases during the 1993 to 1999 period, resulting in an annual compound growth rate of 4.9 percent. Those increases accounted for most of the net increase in all federal spending on research from 1993 to 1999. Where were these increases invested?

NIH increased the allocation of its research funding to the life sciences by a percentage point, to 86.8 percent, from 1993 to 1999 (Annex Table 4-4). Within the life

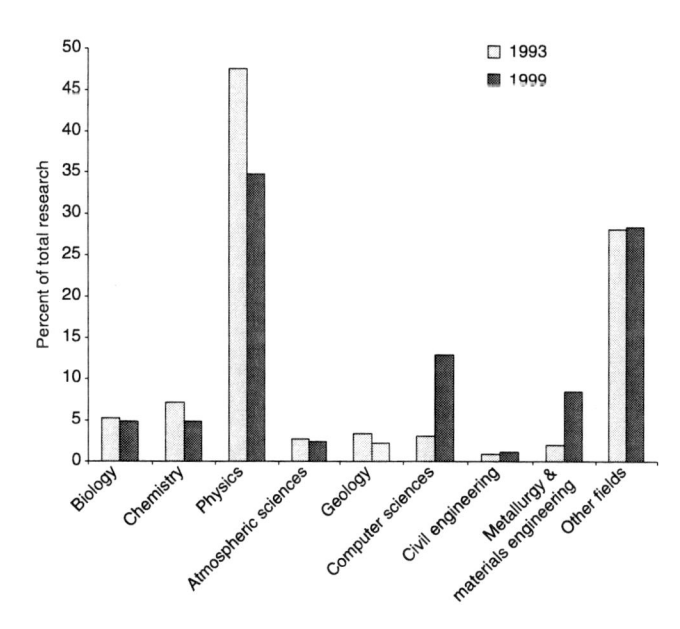

FIGURE 4-2 Research funding by field, Department of Energy, FY 1993 vs. FY 1999.

sciences, however, there was a modest shift toward medical sciences and away from biological sciences (Figure 4-3). Biological sciences went from 44.1 percent to 40.6 percent of all spending by NIH on research while medical sciences went from 40.2 percent to 43.3 percent. The greater emphasis on medical sciences was especially evident in the period between 1993 and 1997. Since 1997, the annual increases for biological sciences have been about the same as those for medical sciences.

Chemistry, physics, psychology, and social sciences received more funding in absolute terms but declined as a percentage of all NIH research funding. The increases occurred mainly after 1997. NIH accounted for 22 percent of all federal funding of chemistry research in 1999, and if it had not increased its level of support by $22 million over 1993, federal funding of chemistry would have been 15.7 percent less than in 1993 instead of 13.4 percent less. The amount of NIH funding for physics research was small, $23 million, just 1 percent of all federal funding in 1999, so the NIH increase had little effect on the reduction of 24.6 percent in funding of physics research.

Math and computer science received large percentage increases between 1993 and 1999—1,201 percent and 209 percent, respectively—but the amounts were small ($45 million in 1993, $116 million in 1999). Together, they constituted 0.5 percent of NIH spending on research in 1993, 0.9 percent in 1999. The trend was similar for engineering. NIH increased its funding substantially in percentage terms (69.9 percent) but not as a share of its portfolio (from 1.1 to 1.4 percent).

Overall, NIH continued to focus on the life sciences, accounting for most of the 28 percent increase in total

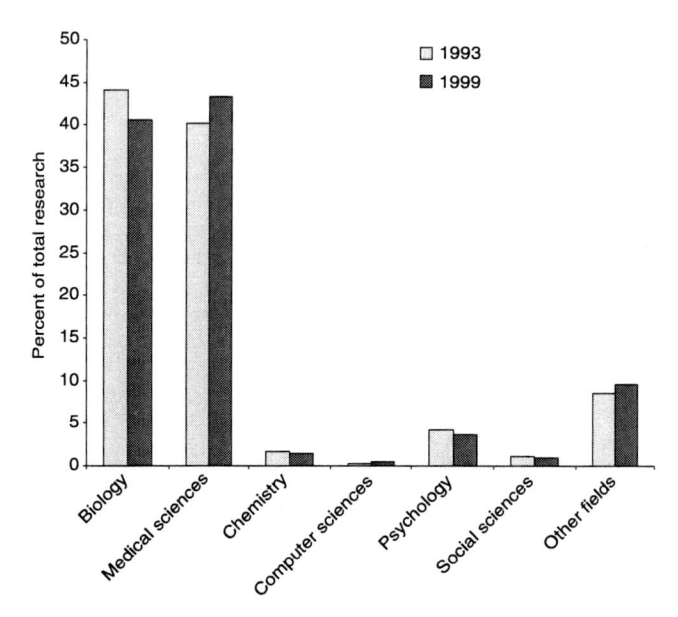

FIGURE 4-3 Research funding by field, National Institutes of Health, FY 1993 vs. FY 1999.

federal funding, and especially the medical sciences. There has been little diversification, at least with respect to the physical sciences and engineering. Mathematics and computer science support has increased substantially but still constitutes less than 1 percent of NIH's research budget.

A similar pattern holds for NIH graduate student support. The number of full-time graduate students in science, engineering, and health fields whose primary source of support was NIH increased 4.8 percent from 1993 to 1999 (Annex Table 4-5). The greater part of the increase in NIH support for graduate students went to those in health fields and the biological sciences. NIH-supported graduate students in health fields increased by 746, or 32.9 percent, and those in biological sciences increased by 4.1 percent. While their numerical increases are not as great, NIH-supported psychology graduate students increased 9.6 percent and NIH-supported engineering students increased 6.3 percent. An increase of 12.2 percent in biomedical engineering students supported by NIH accounts for much of the engineering increase. The rising tide at NIH, however, did not lift all boats. NIH-supported graduate students in the physical sciences declined by 19.2 percent and in computer science by 35 percent.

National Science Foundation

Among federal research agencies, NSF has the broadest portfolio and the most discipline-based organization and funding procedure. How the agency has distributed its budget increases is therefore of particular interest.

In the 1993 to 1999 period, NSF gave larger than average (19.3 percent) increases to the life sciences, computer science, several fields of engineering, and the social sciences, and this pattern is expected to continue in 2000 (Figure 4-4, Annex Table 4-6). Life sciences research went from 15.9 percent of the NSF research budget to 16.4 percent. Computer science funding increased from 6.7 percent to 11.9 percent of the NSF research budget. Civil engineering and metallurgy/materials engineering went from 1.5 percent to 1.6 percent and 1.1 percent to 4.5 percent, respectively. Social sciences went from 3.0 percent to 4.4 percent.

During the same period NSF gave less than average increases to mathematics research and most fields in the physical sciences, environmental sciences, engineering, and psychology. In some fields, NSF funding increased (astronomy, chemistry, atmospheric sciences, oceanography) and in some fields it declined (physics, geology, math, chemical engineering, electrical engineering, and mechanical engineering), but all of these fields consumed a smaller share of the NSF research budget in 1999 than in 1993. Nevertheless, although research funding for the physical sciences did not do as well at NSF as some other fields, astronomy and chemistry had a level of funding that was slightly larger in 1999 than 1993 and physics was not cut nearly as much as elsewhere, which moderated the government-wide reductions for these fields.

In dollar terms, there were substantial shifts away from the physical sciences and geology and toward computer science and metallurgy/materials engineering. Shifts in other fields were smaller in terms of changes in the NSF portfolio, although perhaps quite large for a particular field.[2] If the physical sciences had still accounted for 24.9 percent of the NSF research budget in 1999 as they did in 1993, those fields would have received $96 million more than the $528 million NSF actually spent in 1999. Geology would have received $183 million rather than the $110 million NSF spent in 1999. The life sciences would have had a little less ($12 million) if the allocation had not shifted from 1993 to 1999. Computer science research received about $9 million more in 1999 than it would have using the 1993 percentage. The big dollar shifts were toward oceanography and some subfields of engineering. Funding for oceanography was $111 million more than it would have been if NSF had not doubled its share of the research budget since 1993. Similarly, funding for metallurgy/materials engineering research was $84 million more than if NSF had not quadrupled its share. There was also a large increase in other engineering, which received $128 million more than it would have.

The physical sciences, environmental sciences (except

---

[2] Psychology, for example, accounted for a shift of $16 million dollars in the NSF portfolio from 1993 to 1999, but this would have nearly quadrupled its actual funding in 1999.

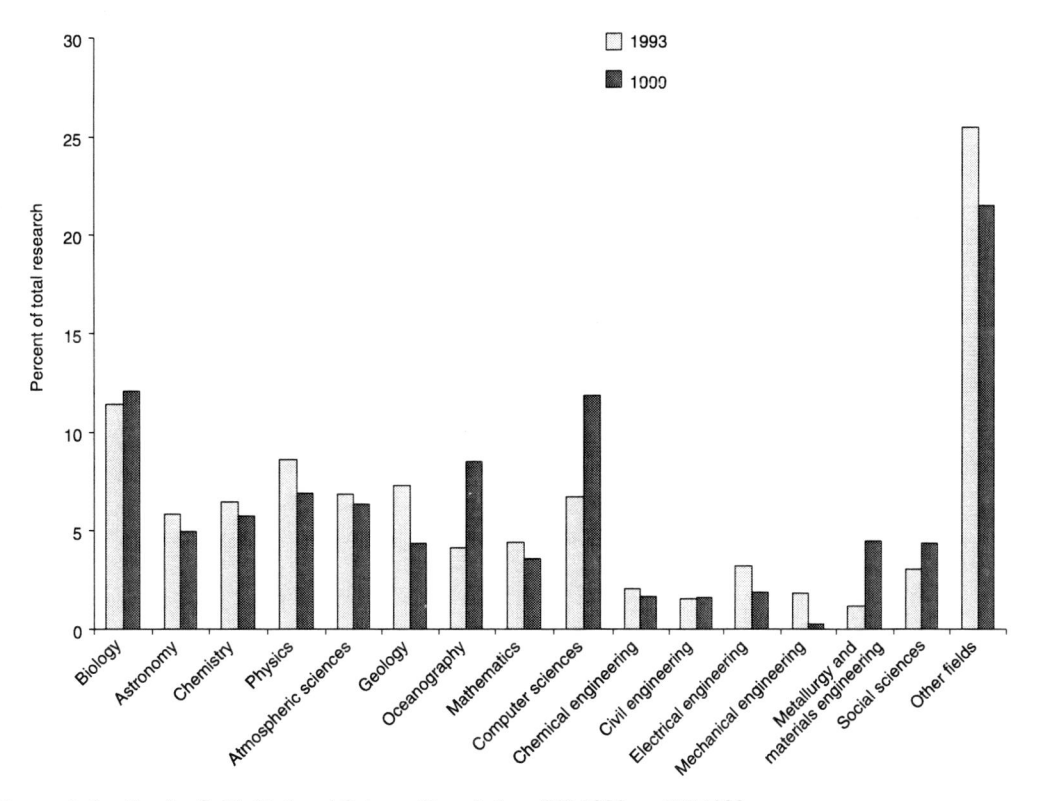

FIGURE 4-4 Research funding by field, National Science Foundation, FY 1993 vs. FY 1999.

for oceanography), math, and psychology were a smaller part of NSF funding in 1999 than in 1993. But the same fields also received smaller shares of DOD research funding. The percentage of NSF spending on life sciences research increased, but it also did so at DOD. When added to the large increase at NIH, the increases by NSF and DOD helped push the percentage of federal research funding spent on life sciences from 40.1 percent in 1993 to 46.0 percent in 1999.

Oceanography was another field that increased at both NSF and DOD, giving that field a large boost despite decreases at Commerce and Interior. A greater percentage of NSF research funding went to engineering research, compared with a smaller percentage of DOD's. Most of the increase in engineering research at NSF was for metallurgy/materials engineering. That increase of $88.1 million did, however, partially offset DOD's reduction of $283.0 million. The NSF increase together with DOE's increase of $256.4 million more than offset the DOD reduction. The increase in the NSF budget for social sciences research of $45.9 million also helped offset decreases at DOD, DOE, and USDA of $22.3 million, $23.0 million, and $20.7 million, respectively.

In short, with some exceptions—psychology, mathematics, chemistry, and astronomy—NSF increased funding of fields with increased funding overall and reduced funding of fields whose combined federal support was stable or declining in the 1990s, thus reinforcing rather than offsetting the changes occurring elsewhere. Of course, given the relatively modest size of the NSF budget, increases in NSF funding would not be sufficient to compensate for the substantial cutbacks in some fields at DOD and DOE. In chemistry research, for example, which was down by $126.2 million overall in 1999 compared with 1993, NSF's increase of $7.9 million in 1999 over 1993 did little to offset decreases totaling $181.3 million at DOD, DOE, and other agencies.[3] NSF had more effect in astronomy, where its increase ($1.9 million) was larger relative to cuts at DOE and NASA ($15.7 million).

The pattern of NSF graduate support is more mixed. There were increases in some fields whose research support was growing but also in some fields whose research funding was declining. Overall, the number of full-time graduate students in science, engineering, and health fields whose primary source of support was NSF increased 2.4 percent from 1993 to 1999 (Annex Table 4-7). The largest numerical increases in NSF-supported graduate students were in computer science, which increased by 30.1 percent, electrical engineering, which increased by 15.1 percent, and the biological sciences, which increased by 8.8 percent. There were substantial increases in several

---

[3]There were also small offsetting increases by NASA, NIH, and EPA totaling another $47.2 million.

additional fields. NSF-supported graduate students in mechanical engineering increased by 9.1 percent, in metallurgy and materials engineering by 13.3 percent, other engineering by 16 percent, and the social sciences by 7.3 percent. There were also large reductions in several fields. NSF-supported graduate students in aerospace engineering declined by 38.0 percent, in physical sciences by 9.5 percent, and earth, atmospheric, and ocean sciences by 17.4 percent.

ANNEX

TABLE 4-1 Trends in DOD Support of Research by Field, 1993 to 1997, 1999 (constant dollars)

	Percent change		Share of total		
	1993–1997	1993–1999	1993	1997	1999
Total, all fields	−26.6%	−22.4%	100.0%	100.0%	100.0%
Life sciences, total	−28.2%	13.6%	7.8%	7.6%	11.4%
Biol (excl. environmental)	−29.8%	67.7%	1.8%	1.7%	3.9%
Environmental biology	−52.3%	−56.9%	1.1%	0.7%	0.6%
Agricultural sciences	653.4%	−100.0%	*	0.0%	0.0%
Medical sciences	−29.0%	−9.7%	4.7%	4.5%	5.4%
Psychology, total	−28.6%	−58.8%	2.1%	2.0%	1.1%
Physical sciences, total	−48.2%	−46.1%	14.1%	10.0%	9.8%
Astronomy	−88.4%	1.7%	0.3%	*	0.4%
Chemistry	−25.7%	−32.3%	2.9%	3.0%	2.6%
Physics	−62.8%	−57.8%	10.0%	5.1%	5.4%
Environmental sciences, total	30.9%	11.2%	5.5%	9.8%	7.9%
Atmospheric sciences	−1.7%	−22.7%	1.2%	1.7%	1.2%
Geological sciences	−86.8%	−92.7%	1.8%	0.3%	0.2%
Oceanography	25.3%	88.9%	1.8%	3.1%	4.4%
Math and computer science, total	−3.1%	0.2%	12.0%	15.9%	15.5%
Mathematics	−48.4%	−34.7%	1.7%	1.2%	1.4%
Computer science	2.0%	1.9%	9.9%	13.7%	13.0%
Engineering, total	−27.3%	−28.7%	51.2%	50.7%	47.1%
Aeronautical	−6.8%	44.2%	4.6%	5.8%	8.5%
Astronautical	23.6%	−64.4%	2.2%	3.7%	1.0%
Chemical	−60.0%	−55.4%	1.5%	0.8%	0.8%
Civil	−43.5%	−57.7%	2.1%	1.6%	1.1%
Electrical	−39.6%	−31.2%	15.1%	12.4%	13.4%
Mechanical	−51.9%	−57.2%	7.4%	4.8%	4.1%
Metallurgy and materials	−27.2%	−49.7%	10.7%	10.6%	6.9%
Engineering, other	3.4%	11.6%	7.8%	11.0%	11.2%
Social sciences, total	−95.9%	−100.0%	0.4%	*	*

* Less than 0.05 percent.

TABLE 4-2 Full-time Graduate Students Whose Primary Source of Support is the Department of Defense by Field, 1993–1999

	1993	1994	1995	1996	1997	1998	1999	Change 1993–1999 Number	Change 1993–1999 Percent
Engineering, total	5,139	4,717	4,810	4,538	4,773	4,316	4,352	−787	−15.3%
Aerospace	749	605	535	492	501	459	438	−311	−41.5%
Chemical	139	128	164	169	169	160	163	24	17.3%
Civil	328	321	290	215	232	192	157	−171	−52.1%
Electrical	1,764	1,664	1,706	1,651	1,938	1,803	1,842	78	4.4%
Mechanical	797	782	823	739	766	728	713	−84	−10.5%
Metallurgy/Materials	518	426	468	468	441	342	320	−198	−38.2%
Engineering, other	844	791	824	804	726	632	719	−125	−14.8%
Sciences, total	4,176	4,351	4,196	3,933	3,928	3,643	3,322	−854	−20.5%
Physical sciences	1,187	1,316	1,198	1,073	1,037	994	883	−304	−25.6%
Earth, Atmos., Ocean. Sci.	517	494	410	393	366	336	339	−178	−34.4%
Mathematics	399	372	322	351	363	283	227	−172	−43.1%
Computer science	1,327	1,345	1,419	1,349	1,434	1,307	1,213	−114	−8.6%
Agricultural sciences	37	35	32	38	39	47	28	−9	−24.3%
Biological sciences	273	347	359	365	373	356	337	64	23.4%
Psychology	163	175	175	139	113	128	124	−39	−23.9%
Social sciences	273	267	281	225	203	192	171	−102	−37.4%
Health Fields, total	435	381	333	331	320	300	363	−72	−16.6%
Total	9,750	9,449	9,339	8,802	9,021	8,259	8,037	−1,713	−17.6%

SOURCE: NSF/SRS Survey of Graduate Students and Postdoctorates in Science and Engineering, Fall 1999.

TABLE 4-3 Trends in DOE Support of Research by Field, 1993 to 1997, 1999 (constant dollars)

	Percent change		Share of total		
	1993–1997	1993–1999	1993	1997	1999
Total, all fields	−4.4%	2.1%	100.0%	100.0%	100.0%
Life sciences, total	−17.4%	−7.2%	7.2%	6.2%	6.5%
Biol (excl. environmental)	−17.0%	−6.4%	5.3%	4.6%	4.8%
Environmental biology	−54.0%	280.2%	0.1%	0.0%	0.2%
Agricultural sciences	−100.0%	−100.0%	0.0%	0.0%	0.0%
Medical sciences	−1.5%	−2.9%	1.4%	1.5%	1.4%
Psychology, total	0.0%	0.0%	0.0%	0.0%	0.0%
Physical sciences, total	−19.0%	−26.8%	58.1%	49.2%	41.6%
Astronomy	−100.0%	−100.0%	0.4%	0.0%	0.0%
Chemistry	−11.4%	−31.0%	7.2%	6.6%	4.8%
Physics	−27.7%	−25.3%	47.5%	35.9%	34.8%
Environmental sciences, total	6.1%	−8.3%	8.9%	9.8%	8.0%
Atmospheric sciences	−11.5%	−8.3%	2.7%	2.5%	2.4%
Geological sciences	−54.7%	−33.1%	3.4%	1.6%	2.2%
Oceanography	−10.7%	−36.3%	0.2%	0.2%	0.1%
Math and computer science, total	84.2%	167.1%	6.0%	11.5%	15.7%
Mathematics	15.9%	32.9%	2.0%	2.4%	2.6%
Computer science	183.9%	338.7%	3.0%	8.9%	12.9%
Engineering, total	10.6%	45.7%	19.4%	22.5%	27.7%
Aeronautical	0.0%	0.0%	0.0%	0.0%	0.0%
Astronautical	0.0%	0.0%	0.0%	0.0%	0.0%
Chemical	6.1%	−18.5%	3.0%	3.3%	2.4%
Civil	6.1%	26.8%	0.9%	1.0%	1.2%
Electrical	−48.1%	−35.9%	1.3%	0.7%	0.8%
Mechanical	−61.6%	−60.9%	1.2%	0.5%	0.4%
Metallurgy and materials	279.6%	343.1%	1.9%	7.7%	8.4%
Engineering, other	−21.1%	33.0%	11.1%	9.2%	14.5%
Social sciences, total	−100.0%	−100.0%	0.0%	0.0%	0.0%

TABLE 4-4 Trends in NIH Support of Research by Field, 1993 to 1997, 1999 (constant dollars)

	Percent change		Share of total		
	1993–1997	1993–1999	1993	1997	1999
Total, all fields	12.2%	33.5%	100.0%	100.0%	100.0%
Life sciences, total	13.6%	35.2%	85.8%	86.8%	86.8%
Biol (excl. environmental)	3.3%	22.9%	44.1%	40.6%	40.6%
Environmental biology	–99.2%	–99.1%	0.1%	*	0.0%
Agricultural sciences	0.0%	0.0%	0.0%	0.0%	0.0%
Medical sciences	20.9%	43.8%	40.2%	43.3%	43.3%
Psychology, total	–0.3%	18.6%	4.2%	3.7%	3.7%
Physical sciences, total	–5.9%	11.9%	1.9%	1.6%	1.6%
Astronomy	0.0%	0.0%	0.0%	0.0%	0.0%
Chemistry	–4.6%	13.6%	1.7%	1.4%	1.4%
Physics	–15.5%	0.5%	0.2%	0.2%	0.2%
Environmental sciences, total	**	**	0.0%	0.3%	0.3%
Atmospheric sciences	0.0%	0.0%	0.0%	0.0%	0.0%
Geological sciences	0.0%	0.0%	0.0%	0.0%	0.0%
Oceanography	0.0%	0.0%	0.0%	0.0%	0.0%
Math and computer science, total	118.6%	160.2%	0.5%	0.9%	0.9%
Mathematics	85.4%	120.6%	0.3%	0.4%	0.4%
Computer science	159.2%	208.5%	0.2%	0.5%	0.5%
Engineering, total	42.8%	69.9%	1.1%	1.4%	1.4%
Aeronautical	0.0%	0.0%	0.0%	0.0%	0.0%
Astronautical	0.0%	0.0%	0.0%	0.0%	0.0%
Chemical	0.0%	0.0%	0.0%	0.0%	0.0%
Civil	0.0%	0.0%	0.0%	0.0%	0.0%
Electrical	0.0%	0.0%	0.0%	0.0%	0.0%
Mechanical	0.0%	0.0%	0.0%	0.0%	0.0%
Metallurgy and materials	0.0%	0.0%	0.0%	0.0%	0.0%
Engineering, other	42.8%	69.9%	1.1%	1.4%	1.4%
Social sciences, total	–6.0%	11.9%	1.1%	0.9%	0.9%

*Less than 0.05 percent.
**NIH funding of environmental research was zero in 1993; it was $35.0 million in 1998 in 1997, and $39.4 million in 1999. FY 2000 funding was estimated to be $31.4 million.

TABLE 4-5 Full-time Graduate Students Whose Primary Source of Support is the National Institutes of Health by Field, 1993–1999

	1993	1994	1995	1996	1997	1998	1999	Change 1993–1999 Number	Percent
Engineering, total	794	782	768	731	766	754	844	50	6.3%
Aerospace	5	5	1	0	3	3	3	–2	–40.0%
Chemical	119	143	136	148	121	111	127	8	6.7%
Civil	30	37	31	33	41	35	39	9	30.0%
Electrical	86	83	84	71	70	79	85	–1	–1.2%
Mechanical	70	71	82	63	70	71	87	17	24.3%
Metallurgy/Materials	10	13	11	7	9	5	6	–4	–40.0%
Engineering, other*	474	430	423	409	452	450	497	23	4.9%
Sciences, total	15,077	15,168	14,906	14,757	14,590	14,556	15,154	77	0.5%
Physical sciences	2,051	2,074	1,886	1,783	1,639	1,631	1,657	–394	–19.2%
Earth, Atmos., Ocean. Sci.	41	36	30	30	27	21	22	–19	–46.3%
Mathematics	74	68	63	61	66	68	78	4	5.4%
Computer science	99	95	93	80	78	75	64	–35	–35.4%
Agricultural sciences	32	47	19	17	21	15	17	–15	–46.9%
Biological sciences	11,314	11,464	11,400	11,302	11,299	11,304	11,774	460	4.1%
Psychology	1,163	1,098	1,094	1,218	1,198	1,226	1,275	112	9.6%
Social sciences	303	286	321	266	262	216	267	–36	–11.9%
Health Fields, total	2,266	2,345	2,437	2,444	2,731	2,828	3,012	746	32.9%
Total	18,137	18,295	18,111	17,932	18,087	18,138	19,010	873	4.8%

*In 1999, there were 452 students in biomedical engineering whose primary source of support was NIH. They comprise 90 percent of the 497 "engineering, other" students in this table and 53 percent of all engineering graduate students whose primary source of support was NIH.
SOURCE: NSF/SRS Survey of Graduate Students and Postdoctorates in Science and Engineering, Fall 1999.

TABLE 4-6 Trends in NSF Support of Research by Field, 1993 to 1997, 1999 (constant dollars)

	Percent change		Share of total		
	1993–1997	1993–1999	1993	1997	1999
Total, all fields	10.1%	19.3%	100.0%	100.0%	100.0%
Life sciences, total	1.6%	22.7%	15.9%	14.7%	16.4%
Biol (excl. environmental)	3.3%	26.3%	11.4%	10.7%	12.1%
Environmental biology	8.1%	26.6%	4.1%	4.0%	4.3%
Agricultural sciences	0.0%	0.0%	0.0%	0.0%	0.0%
Medical sciences	0.0%	0.0%	0.0%	0.0%	0.0%
Psychology, total	−66.2%	−73.3%	0.8%	0.2%	0.2%
Physical sciences, total	−6.1%	0.7%	24.9%	21.3%	21.0%
Astronomy	−3.2%	1.6%	5.8%	5.1%	5.0%
Chemistry	−2.3%	5.8%	6.5%	5.7%	5.7%
Physics	−27.1%	−4.7%	8.6%	5.7%	6.9%
Environmental sciences, total	1.8%	9.8%	21.4%	19.8%	19.7%
Atmospheric sciences	−6.8%	10.2%	6.8%	5.8%	6.3%
Geological sciences	−32.8%	−28.4%	7.3%	4.4%	4.4%
Oceanography	136.2%	145.3%	4.1%	8.9%	8.5%
Math and computer science, total	42.4%	60.8%	11.5%	14.8%	15.5%
Mathematics	2.0%	−2.6%	4.4%	4.1%	3.6%
Computer science	75.2%	109.5%	6.7%	10.7%	11.9%
Engineering, total	67.9%	66.2%	12.9%	19.7%	18.0%
Aeronautical	−100.0%	−100.0%	0.2%	0.0%	0.0%
Astronautical	0.0%	0.0%	0.0%	0.0%	0.0%
Chemical	−7.6%	−4.1%	2.1%	1.7%	1.7%
Civil	20.9%	22.9%	1.5%	1.7%	1.6%
Electrical	−35.1%	−30.0%	3.2%	1.9%	1.9%
Mechanical	−80.5%	−81.7%	1.8%	0.3%	0.3%
Metallurgy and materials	361.3%	369.7%	1.1%	4.8%	4.5%
Engineering, other	245.1%	226.0%	3.0%	9.3%	8.1%
Social sciences, total	42.8%	72.5%	3.0%	3.9%	4.4%

TABLE 4-7 Full-time Graduate Students Whose Primary Source of Support is the National Science Foundation by Field, 1993–1999

	1993	1994	1995	1996	1997	1998	1999	Change 1993–1999 Number	Change 1993–1999 Percent
Engineering, total	4,559	4,763	4,579	4,591	4,611	4,719	4,959	400	8.8%
Aerospace	158	139	121	101	109	112	98	−60	−38.0%
Chemical	730	749	759	777	708	756	744	14	1.9%
Civil	522	587	530	534	529	544	544	22	4.2%
Electrical	1,283	1,342	1,324	1,317	1,344	1,304	1,477	194	15.1%
Mechanical	812	800	743	770	841	908	886	74	9.1%
Metallurgy/Materials	459	505	495	504	514	501	520	61	13.3%
Engineering, other	595	641	607	588	566	594	690	95	16.0%
Sciences, Total	8,882	9,110	8,982	8,739	8,653	8,622	8,769	−113	−1.3%
Physical sciences	3,623	3,703	3,601	3,385	3,372	3,318	3,278	−345	−9.5%
Earth, Atmos., Ocean Sci.	1,366	1,409	1,387	1,242	1,201	1,122	1,128	−238	−17.4%
Mathematics	470	518	474	435	386	384	441	−29	−6.2%
Computer science	1,006	1,047	1,054	1,051	1,087	1,171	1,309	303	30.1%
Agricultural sciences	76	87	92	97	102	91	107	31	40.8%
Biological sciences	1,382	1,382	1,411	1,494	1,541	1,544	1,504	122	8.8%
Psychology	314	289	288	289	277	283	310	−4	−1.3%
Social sciences	645	675	675	746	687	709	692	47	7.3%
Health Fields, total	89	117	100	82	98	118	121	32	36.0%
Total	13,530	13,990	13,661	13,412	13,362	13,459	13,849	319	2.4%

SOURCE: NSF/SRS Survey of Graduate Students and Postdoctorates in Science and Engineering, Fall 1999.

5

Trends in Nonfederal Support of Research

In addition to the federal government, research is also supported by states, philanthropic foundations and individuals, nonprofit institutions including universities themselves, private investors, and, of course, public and privately held corporations. Together these sources account for about 63 percent of the nation's basic and applied research spending.

The most dramatic change in the late 1980s and 1990s was the growth in corporate and other private investment relative to federal government expenditures. Industry support of basic and applied research (excluding development) increased 80 percent in real terms between 1990 and 2000 to a level exceeding 50 percent of all research spending in the United States, up from slightly more than 40 percent in 1990. Because of its very small real growth, the federal share dropped from 48 to 37 percent in the same period. Research expenditures by the states, universities, and other nonprofit institutions increased 55 percent in the robust economy of the 1990s, but because of the higher growth rate in corporate R&D, their share of the nation's total research spending remained steady at about 11 percent. Venture capital and so-called angel investing in technology-based start-up firms increased nearly 25 times from 1990 to 2000 to more than $100 billion; but because it primarily supported corporate infrastructure, product development, production and marketing rather than basic and applied research in these new firms, we do not consider it here.[1]

Our purpose in this section is not to describe exhaustively trends in nonfederal support—a very tall order—but to review what national data series can tell us about the changing composition of the nonfederal research portfolio in relationship to the federal portfolio. These data series include NSF surveys of research-performing universities and research-sponsoring state governments and industry. Data on philanthropic organizations' contributions to research are collected by the private nonprofit Foundation Center.[2]

The principal question we pose is whether spending by the nonfederal sector has amplified or offset changes in the research field allocation of national government expenditures. In particular, did trends in nonfederal support favor the life and especially biomedical sciences or did the physical sciences and engineering fields that lost ground in the federal portfolio changes benefit from nonfederal sources of support in this period? Answering even that general question is enormously diifficult because of the lack of adequate data and lack of comparability among data sets. For example, in some data sets research cannot be distinguished from development, so we address each source separately and, of necessity, in a very preliminary way.

NONFEDERAL SUPPORT OF UNIVERSITY RESEARCH AND DEVELOPMENT

According to reports from research-performing universities and colleges, nonfederal support of research and development in the mid-1990s grew at a slightly faster rate than federal support—28.2 percent in constant dollars between 1993 and 1999—to reach approximately 8 percent of total expenditures by these institutions. This includes

---

[1] Lawrence M. Rausch. 1998. *Issue Brief: Venture Capital Investment. Trends in the United States and Europe.*, p. 1. Arlington, VA: National Science Foundation. The magnitude of these investments is highly dependent on market conditions and is declining steeply in early 2001. Moreover the technological focus of venture capital investments can change dramatically and rapidly.

[2] See the Appendix for details. A second source of data on corporate expenditures on research and development (undifferentiated) by a slightly different universe of businesses differently classified, is Compustat's compilation of information filed with the U.S. Securities and Exchange Commission.

institutional support and external support from industry, foundations, and other nonprofit institutions.

The distribution of nonfederal support is reported in the same field categories used in the Federal Funds Survey, but basic and applied research are not reported separately and development expenditures are included in the data. The 1993-1999 results are shown in Annex Table 5-1. The portfolio differs significantly from that of federally funded university research—with an even greater emphasis on the biological and medical sciences—but the directions and magnitude of changes in the mid-1990s closely parallel federal spending trends in all but one outstanding case. R&D in the medical sciences exhibited even faster growth in nonfederal than in federal support (44.1 percent vs. 28.9 percent) and consumed the largest share—27.5 percent of all nonfederal support—by the end of that period. The biological and agricultural sciences also experienced relatively rapid growth—32.2 percent and 20.1 percent respectively—and constituted 15.8 and 13.0 percent of the total portfolio, respectively. Together, the life sciences represented 58 percent of R&D funding from sources other than the federal government in 1999. On the other hand, nonfederal support of chemistry R&D increased only 14.2 percent and represented a small share (2.6 percent) of nonfederal funding. Support of physics increased by 8.0 percent in real terms but represented only 2.4 percent of nonfederal funding. Support of computer science, in concert with federal spending trends, and electrical engineering, in contrast to federal trends, grew substantially—by 35.0 and 37.5 percent, respectively—but to levels representing small shares of nonfederal funding (2.4 and 3.2 percent, respectively).

STATES' SUPPORT OF RESEARCH

The states' role in research and development expanded in the 1980s and 1990s beyond their traditional role in agriculture and agricultural extension and support of higher education to include technology-based economic development. Most states established science and technology offices, many produced strategic plans, and a number launched new spending programs. State expenditures increased at a slightly faster rate than federal spending throughout the period 1965 to 1995.

The most recent, and in important respects unique, comprehensive survey of this activity is a one-time snap shot taken in 1995 when NSF/SRS commissioned a survey by the State Science and Technology Institute (SSTI) of the Battelle Memorial Institute in Ohio.[3] SSTI found that states were spending approximately $2.46 billion of state revenues each year on research and development (compared with the federal government's $70 billion). Not included in the survey were state higher education funds used at institutions' discretion to support R&D activity or overhead on R&D. Nevertheless, over 80 percent of state funds earmarked for R&D went to universities. State agencies and their laboratories accounted for only 11 percent of expenditures, with the remaining 8 percent distributed to companies and nonprofit institutions.

As with nonfederal research activity in universities, the largest recipients of state support were the biological and medical sciences (nearly 40 percent of the total), followed by engineering and environmental science, with the remaining funds distributed among physical sciences, computer science and math, and social sciences as shown in Table 5-2.

Is there any reason to believe this allocation has changed in the past several years? One significant new element of the states' fiscal posture is the substantial windfall that states will receive over several years as a result of the master agreement settling their liability litigation against the tobacco manufacturers. The disposition of these funds is entirely up to the affected state legislatures. In FY 2000 and 2001, 44 legislatures have appropriated $8.2 billion, with the bulk of this money in the form of general funds, endowments and trust funds being devoted to tobacco prevention, health care services, education, tobacco farmer support, and various other purposes. In just two years, however, 12 states have dedicated $207 million (8.5 percent of state research and development spending in 1995) to research, all in the biomedical sciences. A $1 billion Florida endowment will generate an estimated $35 million per year for peer-reviewed biomedical research. Michigan has created a $50 million biomedical research trust fund administered by the state's public universities, and Colorado, Maryland, Illinois, and Kansas are planning other health research ventures.[4]

More diversified are a handful of recent state initiatives to establish centers of research excellence in particular fields. Although based at universities, the centers are required to establish industry alliances and raise matching funds. California has established three such centers in nanotechnology; information technology and telecommunications, and biotechnology/bioengineering/bioinformatics-funded by the state at $100 million each for four years. Georgia's Research Alliance program will match private contributions with nearly $250 million in grants over 10 years for biotechnology, environmental, and telecommunciations research. Alabama, Illinois, and

---

[3]State Science and Technology Institute, 1999. *The Survey of State Research and Development Expenditures: FY 1995*, Columbus, OH: Battelle. The results are summarized in John Jankowski. 1999. *What Is the State Government Role in the R&D Enterprise?* Arlington, VA: National Science Foundation.

[4]National Conference of State Legislatures. August 1, 2000. *State Allocation of Tobacco Settlement Funds, FY 2000 and FY 2001*, Washington, D.C.

Wisconsin each have plans for $100 million initiatives in biotechnology and biomedical research.

PHILANTHROPY

Philanthropic giving also accelerated with the economy and rise in the value of investment portfolios in the 1990s. The American Association of Fundraising Council Trust for Philanthropy estimates that charitable giving to all causes increased 10 percent or more per year in the latter half of the 1990s.[5] Individual donations and bequests represented nearly three-quarters of the more than $200 billion given in 2000, about 2 percent of gross domestic product. Although there is no single comprehensive source of public data, approximately 1,000 independent, corporate, and community foundations are surveyed annually by the nonprofit Foundation Center and asked to report the distribution of their contributions. Excluded from this survey are the Howard Hughes Medical Institute[6] public charities such as the American Cancer Society (with a research budget of $115 million in 2000) and other disease organizations. Education, health, arts and cultural, human services, and civil rights and social action purposes represent well over 80 percent of foundation grants, but increasingly scientific and engineering research is a significant beneficiary. In 1994, research grants constituted approximately 7.5 percent of the grants of foundations reporting; in 1999, the share had grown to 11.2 percent. Medical research accounts for the largest share of the total, and its share increased from 32 to 37 percent in that six-year period. By contrast, the share going to the physical sciences and "technology" declined from 18.3 to 12.5 percent. The distributions among several categories, unfortunately not well defined and perhaps overlapping, are shown in Annex Table 5-3.

INDUSTRY RESEARCH INVESTMENT

Between 1990 and 2000, internally funded corporate research and development spending significantly outpaced other indicators of corporate activity such as sales, capital investment, and employment growth, let alone publicly funded R&D. The expenditures were highly concentrated in a few industrial sectors—primarily pharmaceuticals, other chemicals, electronic components and equipment, transportation equipment, scientific instruments and, increasingly nonmanufacturing industries such as computer and data processing services and research, development and testing services. By 1999 the largest R&D spenders in manufacturing were electronics and pharmaceuticals.

A closer examination of internally financed basic and applied research in these and other sectors reveals two characteristics that distinguish public and private spending patterns. See Annex Table 5-4. First, industrial research spending is volatile. Despite the overall growth in industrial R&D, research spending fluctuated sharply in nearly every R&D-intensive sector and without apparent conformity to the business cycle. For some industries the low point occurred early in the decade, for others at the midpoint, and for still others late in the decade. Moreover, year-to-year changes were in many cases quite sharp, as high as 30 percent and frequently in the range of 10 to 20 percent, both up and down. The exceptions to this cyclicality were the service industries as a group and electronic components, which exhibited fairly continuous growth at least from the middle of the decade.

Electronic components, particularly in contrast to pharmaceuticals, illustrate a second characteristic of industrial research. Its character varies greatly across sectors and even over time. In drugs and medicines, for example, basic research represented an average of about 14 percent of all private sector pharmaceutical R&D in the 1990s, while in computers and electronic components basic research never exceeded about 4 percent of R&D and in most years ranged from less than 1 percent to about 3 percent.[7]

While the corporate sector also favored biomedical research in the 1990s as well as some other areas of growth in the federal portfolio (e.g., computer science/software), there was significant investment growth in some areas where federal support was falling—e.g., electronic components/electrical engineering—but this was highly skewed toward product and process development and away from fundamental research. Moreover, research spending in the semiconductor/electronic components sector is by no means certain to continue to increase in a far more uncertain economic environment than that of the latter part of the 1990s.

---

[5]Growth slowed to a little more than 6 percent in 2000. American Association of Fundraising Counsel Trust for Philanthropy, *Giving USA*, at www.aafrc.org.

[6]A nonprofit medical research organization under the U.S. tax code not subject to the same regulations as private foundations.

[7]Although the level of basic research support is low in a number of industries there is little evidence in the NSF data that it is declining as frequently asserted. In fact, in none of 10 industries in Table 1.1 has the basic research share of R&D declined over the decade. For a more thorough examination of research funding trends and needs in information technology see National Research Council. 2000. *Making IT Better: Expanding Information Technology Research to Meet Society's Needs*. Washington, D.C.: National Academy Press.

ANNEX

TABLE 5-1 Non-Federally-Funded Academic R&D in 1999 dollars

Field	1993	1999	Change in Number 1993–1999	Percentage Change 1993–1999
Total	8,923,176	11,442,264	2,519,088	28.2%
Engineering	1,448,558	1,818,848	370,290	25.6%
Aeronautical/Astronautical	58,893	77,417	18,524	31.5%
Chemical	146,017	170,248	24,231	16.6%
Civil	242,317	312,623	70,306	29.0%
Electrical	267,564	368,054	100,490	37.6%
Mechanical	192,953	237,660	44,707	23.2%
Metallurgy/materials	165,738	166,846	1,108	0.7%
Engineering, other*	375,074	486,000	110,926	29.6%
All sciences	7,474,618	9,623,416	2,148,798	28.7%
Physical sciences	689,454	740,169	50,715	7.4%
Astronomy	104,352	112,084	7,732	7.4%
Chemistry	262,373	299,610	37,237	14.2%
Physics	259,324	280,225	20,901	8.1%
Environmental sciences	500,736	588,913	88,177	17.6%
Atmospheric	55,553	65,513	9,960	17.9%
Earth sciences	193,171	223,695	30,524	15.8%
Oceanography	143,402	198,165	54,763	38.2%
Mathematical sciences	77,158	103,580	26,422	34.2%
Computer science	205,782	277,735	71,953	35.0%
Life sciences	4,983,013	6,671,036	1,688,023	33.9%
Agricultural sciences	1,236,836	1,485,804	248,968	20.1%
Biological sciences	1,368,009	1,809,185	441,176	32.2%
Medical sciences	2,181,345	3,142,768	961,423	44.1%
Psychology	128,720	154,739	26,019	20.2%
Social sciences	622,799	789,682	166,883	26.8%
Other sciences	266,956	297,562	30,606	11.5%

NOTE: Because of rounding, detail may not add to totals.

*Engineering, other includes bioengineering/biomedical engineering in 1999.

SOURCE: National Science Foundation/Division of Science Resources Studies, Survey of Research and Development Expenditures at Universities and Colleges, Fiscal Year 1999.

TABLE 5-2 1995 Recipients of State Research (Basic and Applied) Support by Field (Percent)

Biological sciences	27.2
Engineering	12.7
Medical sciences	12.2
Physical sciences	7.6
Environmental sciences	7.5
Social sciences	6.5
Math and computer science	3.9
Psychology	1.8
n.e.c.	20.6

TABLE 5-3 Foundation Grants for Research in Millions of Current Dollars

Field	1994	1999
Medical	$189.9	$381.4
General	$105.9	$184.6
Physical Science	$71.4	$73.2
Life Science	$33.3	$91.8
Technology	$36.8	$50.4

SOURCE: Foundation Center, Foundation Giving Trends, Washington, DC, 1999.

TABLE 5-4 Corporate Funded Industrial Research (Basic and Applied) in Millions of Current Dollars

Industry	1990	1991	1992	1993	1994	1995	1996	1997	1998	*1999
Drugs and Medicines	—	4064	4992	—	—	4832	4204	5003	4987	4756
Other Chemicals	—	3327	3008	—	—	2946	3430	3026	3797	3724
Petroleum Refining and Extraction	—	1378	—	—	—	891	—	761	846	—
Office Computing and Accounting Machinery	—	1850	—	1161	846	1439	1775	4081	8493	2575
Other Machinery (except Electrical)	—	1065	—	955	991	1405	1165	1291	1160	—
Communications Equipment	—	1132	—	—	—	769	806	1290	—	1590
Electronic Components	—	1025	1053	—	1627	2235	—	4732	—	4617
Other Electrical Equipment	—	1147	—	—	—	754	—	1383	—	—
Transportation Equipment	2467	2334	1542	1380	1522	2332	2764	2505	—	4026
Professional and Scientific Instruments	2102	2907	2802	2449	2460	2685	2069	2290	2479	—
Non-manufacturing	7395	8774	7771	6215	5980	7796	8021	9897	10422	13956
Computer/data processing services	—	—	—	—	—	2099	1793	1929	—	1047
Research, Development, Testing	—	—	—	—	—	—	1923	2362	2508	3990

— Not reported to avoid disclosing proprietary information.
*North American Industry Classification System employed in 1999. All other years, Standard Industry Classification System. Figures may not be comparable.

6

Findings, Conclusions, and Recommendations

This report updates and extends the previous analysis of trends in federal research funding to FY 1999, the latest year for which there are data on actual obligations for research by field. It has looked more closely than the 1999 study at trends in basic and applied research, research performed by universities and colleges, and graduate education. In addition, we have examined changes in the structure of agency support of some fields and changes in the research portfolios of some of the agencies with the largest research budgets. The key findings, conclusions, and recommendations resulting from this study are presented below.

FINDINGS

Agency Research Budgets Are Up

What has changed and not changed since the previous STEP Board analysis? First, federal research funding in the aggregate turned a corner in FY 1998. After 5 years of stagnation, total expenditures were up 4.5 percent in FY 1998 over their level in 1993. A year later, in FY 1999, they were up 11.7 percent. By 1999 the research budget of every major R&D funding federal agency was increasing again and, with the exceptions of the Departments of Defense and Interior, was larger than in 1993. FY 2000 and FY 2001 saw continued growth in budget authority for research.

Second, increases in appropriations to the National Institutes of Health kept federal research funding from falling lower in the mid-1990s and accounted for 61.8 percent of the net growth in research spending from FY 1997 to FY 1999. Indeed, the rate of NIH budget growth doubled in 1999, the first year of the 5-year campaign to double NIH's budget. The annual increase in NIH spending on research, which was between 4 and 6 percent in the 1996-1998 fiscal years, jumped to 12.5 percent in FY 1999 and was projected to be 11.9 percent in 2000. NIH's share of federal research expenditures increased from 32.1 percent in 1993 to 38.4 percent in 1999 and an estimated 40.4 percent in 2000. Substantial increases in NIH budget authority appropriated in FY 2001 and proposed by the current administration for 2002 and 2003 promise to sustain this pace of growth.

Research Fields Continue to Diverge

The sharp divergence in support of different fields of research that developed after 1993, although moderated, has continued. The life sciences received 46 percent of federal funding for research in 1999, compared with 40 percent in 1993. During the same period, the share of the federal portfolio represented by the physical sciences and engineering went from 37 to 31 percent. More recent actions on federal budgets for research, including doubling of the NIH budget over the 5 years ending in FY 2003, will increase the current divergence between the life sciences and other fields unless other fields receive substantially larger increases than proposed.

More specifically, whereas 12 of the 22 fields examined had suffered real loss of support in the mid-1990s (four by 20 percent or more), by FY 1999 the number of fields with reduced support was seven, but of these five were down 20 percent or more—physics, geological sciences, and chemical, electrical, and mechanical engineering. The fields of chemical and mechanical engineering and geological sciences had less funding in 1999 than in 1997. Other fields that failed to increase or had less funding after 1997 included astronomy, chemistry, and atmospheric sciences. One field that had increased funding in the mid-1990s, materials engineering, experienced declining support at the end of the decade. Its funding was 14.0 percent larger in 1997 than in 1993, but that margin fell to 3.0 percent in 1998 and 1.5 percent in 1999.

The fields whose support was up in 1997 and has continued to increase include aeronautical, astronautical,

85

civil engineering, and other engineering, biological and medical sciences, computer science, and oceanography. Of these, the number of fields whose support was up 20 percent or more from 1993 levels increased from one in 1997 to six in 1999. Funding of some fields increased somewhat from 1997 to 1999 but not enough to raise them back up to their 1993 levels. Those include electrical engineering and physics. Fields that, like overall research expenditures, turned a corner were environmental biology, agricultural sciences, mathematics, social sciences, and psychology. Their funding, which was less in 1997 than in 1993, exceeded the 1993 level by 1999.

NIH growth accounts for a large part but not all of the increased support of the biological and medical sciences. DOD and VA also increased their funding of those fields. The decline in the support of many of the physical science and engineering fields is partly attributable to the fact that the budgets of their principal sponsoring agencies (e.g., DOD, DOE, and NASA) did not fare as well as the NIH budget and partly to the fact that the agencies with growing budgets, especially NIH and NSF, did not increase their support of those fields and in some cases reduced it. At the same time, some fields—e.g., computer science, oceanography, and aeronautical engineering—experienced substantial growth, even though their largest 1993 funders were agencies with shrinking budgets—e.g., DOD and NASA. They did so by maintaining their level of funding of agencies with declining budgets and by picking up additional support from other agencies.

The patterns in federal funding of basic research and research performed at universities are somewhat more favorable than the trend in total research support, suggesting that by the late 1990s agencies were tending to protect basic and university research relative to applied research and other performers. At the aggregate level, funding of basic research was 16.6 percent larger in 1999 than in 1993, compared with 6.8 percent for applied research. University research was 19.9 percent more in 1999 than in 1993, compared with 7.2 percent for all other performers (e.g., industry, federal laboratories, other nonprofit research institutions).

Basic and university-performed research are also characterized by sharp divergence among fields, however. In basic research, 14 of the 22 fields had more funding in 1999 than in 1993, compared with 11 in 1997, and the number with 20 percent or more funding increased from five in 1997 to 8 in 1999. But basic research funding was less in eight fields, three by 20 percent or more (chemical and mechanical engineering and geological sciences). In university research, 15 of 22 fields had more funding in 1999 than in 1993, nine by 20 percent or more, compared with 10 and 4 fields, respectively, in 1997. The amount of university funding remained less in seven fields, two of them by 20 percent or more (mechanical engineering and geological sciences).

In most fields, trends in basic research funding were similar to those for total research. Where total funding was up, basic research funding was also up, and vice versa. There were some interesting discrepancies between overall and university research trends, however. For example, although total funding of chemical engineering research was down substantially in 1999 compared with 1993 (by 25.9 percent), chemical engineering research at universities was up slightly (by 2.2 percent). And while mathematics research was up by 6.4 percent overall, mathematics research at universities was down by 13.5 percent.

Production of Doctoral Scientists and Engineers Is Down

The number of Ph.D.'s awarded in science and engineering by U.S. colleges and universities declined 5 percent from 1998 to 1999. The number of Ph.D.'s awarded in the sciences peaked in 1998 at 21,379 and declined 3.6 percent to 20,616 in 1999. The number of Ph.D.'s in engineering peaked earlier in 1996 at 6,305 and has since declined by 15.4 percent to 5,337 in 1999. Because in most fields it takes 7 or more years to complete Ph.D. requirements, these declines must be attributable largely to factors other than changes in federal research support. Nevertheless, in the years ahead the ongoing decline in enrollment in most fields will reinforce the drop in graduate school output of Ph.D.'s.

Sharp Differences in Graduate Enrollment Trends Among Fields

From 1993 to 1999, trends in federal funding for university research, full-time graduate enrollment, and numbers of doctorate recipients reveal two divergent patterns among science and engineering fields. Fields in which federal funding for university research was down from 1993 to 1997 have nearly all had declines in both graduate enrollments and doctorate recipients from 1993 to 1999. Fields with increasing federal funding for university research, however, exhibit a range of divergent trends in graduate enrollment and doctorate production. These trends depend on a variety of factors, including the state of both the industrial and academic research labor markets and the supply of undergraduates.

As funding for most of the physical, environmental, mathematical, and social sciences declined in the 1990s, so did the number of graduate students in these fields, the number of students federally supported, and the number of federally funded research assistants (RAs). In physics, geology, atmospheric sciences, and mathematics, the decline in the number of federally funded RAs was approximately 20 percent between 1993 and 1999. Nevertheless, two fields with increasing research support—astronomy and ocean sciences—also experienced reductions in federally funded graduate students, although less drastic.

In engineering the pattern was similar with the exception of electrical engineering, where the number of federally funded RAs (especially through NSF) increased as research support declined. Federally supported graduate students in computer science increased along with research funding, as expected.

In the life sciences, biology and the medical sciences exhibit different trends in graduate enrollment although both fields are benefiting from increasing federal research support. The number of graduate students in the biological sciences grew only marginally in the 1990s and the number of federally supported RAs actually declined. On the other hand, the number of postdoctoral fellows in the biological sciences has increased. In the medical sciences overall graduate enrollment and the number of RAs in particular grew nearly 40 percent.

Trends in Nonfederal Research Support

Together, states, philanthropies, foundations, other nonprofit institutions, and industry are sources of 63 percent of the nation's basic and applied research spending, and their share increased in the 1990s as federal expenditures reached a plateau.

Although the data are much more limited, it appears that states and philanthropies have shared the research priorities of the federal government in the last decade. For both states and foundations, biomedical research consumes a majority of research funding and has grown at a faster rate than support of other scientific and engineering fields. If anything, this orientation is reinforced by patterns in the growing number and size of individual donations to research and research facilities and in the disposition of funds received by the states in settling their suits against the tobacco manufacturers.

Data on the composition of industry-funded research are not comparable to the data on federal expenditures because they are classified by the industry sector of the reporting parent firms, not by product line or constituent business, let alone by research discipline. Nevertheless some observations on the 1990s are appropriate and relevant. First, only a few industrial sectors are research intensive. Pharmaceutical industry research spending was the highest as a percent of sales of any industrial sector and has been growing rapidly. On the other hand, the information technology sector is spending more on research absolutely and has had a higher rate of growth. For example, real spending on R&D by the electronic components industry increased 17 percent from 1996 to 1998, in contrast to the sharp drop in federal support of electrical engineering research. Nevertheless, except for a few industries such as pharmaceuticals, only a small fraction (less than 5 percent in computers and semiconductors, for example) of all corporate research and development is basic research. Moreover, private research investment is quite volatile, sometimes subject to wide fluctuation from year to year with or independent of the business cycle.

CONCLUSIONS

The recent shift in composition of the federal research portfolio is significant. Although nonfederal entities increased their share of national funding for R&D from 60 to 74 percent between 1990 and 2000, the government still provides almost one-half of all basic research support and nearly one-third of total research support. Reductions in federal funding of fields of the magnitude that occurred in several fields in the 1990s have national impact, unless there are corresponding increases in funding from nonfederal sources. There is little evidence of compensating actions by states, foundations, or the private sector. Industry has been investing more in R&D but little of it supports long-term research except in a few cases such as pharmaceuticals.

The funding trends leading to shifts in the federal research portfolio will continue under the administration's budget plan, especially the build up in funding of the biomedical sciences relative to other most other fields. They will continue for several more years, at least until the fulfillment of the campaign to double the NIH budget from 1998 to 2003. The administration's request for NIH for FY 2002 would increase its budget authority for research by 12.9 percent over the FY 2001 level in constant dollars, and reduce all other non-defense research by 1.5 percent. As a result of the strategic policy review, DOD's research budget is likely to increase again; but based on trends in the department's portfolio from 1993 to 1999 there is little indication that funding for fields previously cut would be rebuilt.

There are compelling reasons for the federal government to invest across the range of scientific and engineering disciplines.[1] The most important problems in science are increasingly interdisciplinary. Examples include genomics and bioinformatics, which rely on mathematics and computer science as much as biology for progress; nanotechnology, which depends on chemistry and chemical engineering, physics, materials science and technology, and electrical engineering; and understanding of climate change, which relies on collaboration among oceanographers, atmospheric chemists, geologists and geophysicists, paleontologists, and computer scientists.[2] Historically, of course, progress in physics and chemistry

---

[1] The rationale for a diverse portfolio is articulated in NAS, NAE, IOM. 1993. *Science, Technology, and the Federal Government: National Goals for a New Era.* Washington, D.C.: National Academy Press; and National Research Council. *Allocating Federal Funds for Science and Technology,* 1995. Washington, D.C.: National Academy Press.

[2] Donald Kennedy, "A Budget Out of Balance," *Science,* 291 (23 March 2001):2337.

made critical contributions to the development and biotechnology and genetic engineering. The development of magnetic resonance imaging (MRI) used extensively in medical diagnoses was based on developments in physics, mathematics, and computer science.

Another reason for investing across a wide range of science and engineering disciplines derives from the high level of uncertainty associated with science. It is not possible to know where breakthroughs will occur or what practical applications they may have when they do occur. Important advances in one field sometimes come from apparently unrelated work in another field. For example, who knew in 1945 that the discovery of nuclear magnetic resonance in condensed matter by basic research physicists would lead to the development of MRI technology 30 years later?[3] Because of increasing interdisciplinarity and uncertainty about when and where advances will take place or pay off it is prudent to invest in a broad portfolio of research activities. Successive reports by committees of the National Research Council/National Academy of Sciences have recommended as an explicit goal of research policy maintaining U.S. parity with or superiority over other countries' capabilities in all major fields of science and engineering.[4] Private sector groups such as the Committee for Economic Development and the Council on Competitiveness have also called for sustaining federal support of the full range of research fields.[5]

There is cause for concern about the current and prospective allocation of funding among fields in the federal research portfolio, in particular, with respect to most of the physical sciences and engineering, whose funding, in contrast with the biomedical sciences, has with few exceptions stagnated or declined. We are not suggesting that every field of research merits constantly increasing or even stable support. Portfolio management should not be viewed in static terms, i.e., a single year's budget, nor in isolation from all other sources of research support—states, institutions, philanthropies, and industry. Nevertheless, it is not clear that the current allocation is optimal from a national viewpoint. It is also not necessarily optimal from the standpoint of advances in biomedical research or of computer science research, another field in which federal funding has increased substantially relative to other fields. Improved health and a strong information technology industry will rely on progress in a range of fields of fundamental research, including physics, chemistry, electrical engineering, and chemical engineering, all fields with less funding at the end of the 1990s.[6] Similarly, it may not make sense to cut geology research at a time of renewed concern about how to increase production of fossil fuels while minimizing environmental damage.

Although it may be wise policy to reduce the linkage between research funding and training support,[7] research allocation decisions should take into account the need for trained people in a field. Although federal funding is one factor among many in determining graduate enrollments and production of Ph.D.'s in a field, enrollments and the number of Ph.D.'s awarded were generally down in fields that had less federal funding in 1999 than in 1993, reducing the supply of new talent for positions in industry, academia, and other employment sectors. Curtailing research in a field may constrict the supply of trained people who are capable of exploiting emerging research opportunities. This effect is both direct, in that federal funding of university research supports the education of a significant number of graduate students in most fields, and indirect, in signaling to prospective graduate students that some fields offer poor career opportunities. Many graduates with master's or doctoral degrees in science or engineering work in industry, including the majority with doctorates in engineering, chemistry, and computer science and 40 percent of those with doctorates in physics and astronomy. Most of the rest work in universities, where they conduct research and train the next generation of scientists and engineers.[8]

The current system for allocating research funding does not necessarily ensure that national priorities are taken into account. In the highly decentralized U.S. system of support for science and engineering, most research funding is tied to the missions of federal agencies rather than national needs more broadly conceived, such as technological innovation and economic growth. If a mission changes—for example, defense strategy in the post-

---

[3]National Academy of Sciences. March 2001. *A Life-Saving Window on the Mind and Body: The Development of Magnetic Resonance Imaging.* Washington, D.C.: National Academy of Sciences. At: www/beyonddiscovery.org/beyond/BeyondDiscovery.nsf/files/PDF MRI.pdf/$file/MRI PDF.pdf.

[4]National Academy of Sciences, National Academy of Engineering, and Institute of Medicine. 1993. *Science, Technology, and the Federal Government: National Goals for a New Era.* Washington, D.C.: National Academy Press; and National Research Council. 1995. *Allocating Federal Funds.* Washington, D.C.: National Academy Press.

[5]Committee for Economic Development. 1998. *America's Basic Research: Prosperity Through Discovery*, pp. 34–35. New York: Committee for Economic Development; Council on Competitiveness. 2001. *U.S. Competitiveness 2001: Strengths, Vulnerabilities and Long-Term Priorities*, pp. 38–41. Washington, D.C.: Council on Competitiveness.

[6]Harold Varmus. March 22, 1999. "The Impact of Physics on Biology and Medicine." Plenary Talk, Centennial Meeting of the American Physical Society, Atlanta, At: www.mskcc.org/medical_professionals/president_s_pages/speeches/the_impact_of_physics_on_biology_and_medicine.html.

[7]A position taken by the Committee on Science, Engineering, and Public Policy in its report, *Reshaping the Graduate Education of Scientists and Engineers*, Washington, D.C.: National Academy Press, 1995.

[8]National Science Foundation. 2001. *Characteristics of Doctoral Scientists and Engineers: 1999 (Early Release Tables)*, Table 7. At: www.nsf.gov/sbe/srs/srs01406/tables/tab7.xls.

Cold War world—the mix of sponsored research may change and the support of certain fields of research may decline for reasons that are entirely defensible in terms of the affected agency's priorities but not in terms of the research opportunities in and productivity of those fields and their potential contributions to other national goals.[9]

In the mid-1990s, when research budgets were flat or shrinking, agency leaders and congressional overseers had to make choices about which research to fund and which to sacrifice. The evidence of priority setting within agencies is encouraging. As the shift in the Defense Department's focus illustrates, agencies did not simply spread their research budget losses or gains evenly across research fields. But it appears that the decline in support of certain fields was unplanned and unevaluated from the perspective of their research productivity, production of knowledge and scientific and engineering talent relevant to progress in other fields, and contributions to other national needs. Some fields, such as computer science, that might have been more adversely affected by dependence on agencies with declining research budgets or changing priorities were able to increase funding by shifting or diversifying their sources of support among federal agencies. Others, such as electrical engineering, were not able to find other support.

Improvements in data and analysis would support a better informed process of allocating federal funding for research. Current surveys are valuable and underutilized tools for assessing the nation's allocation of resources to the conduct of science and development of technology, but their utility could be improved by modest changes in the surveys and in the presentation of their results. Moreover, there are significant gaps in information, especially on non-university performers of federal research and on non-federal research sponsors — states, philanthropic institutions, and businesses at a fine level of detail. There needs to be a good deal more qualitative evaluation of the output of research fields and the effects on outputs of changes in funding levels as well as more rigorous analysis of the influences on the supply of and demand for scientists and engineers with advanced training.

RECOMMENDATIONS

Evaluations and Adjustment of the Research Portfolio

This report documents large shifts in federal research funding that occurred in the mid-1990s, when federal funding was flat for several years and that for the most part have persisted, although federal funding began to increase again after 1997. The decade ended with the support of five fields in the physical sciences and engineering below their funding levels in 1993 and several other fields at about the same levels of funding, whereas support of a few fields increased substantially.

The evidence suggests that the increases for a few fields were the product of deliberately chosen priorities of Congress and the administration, but the decline in support of other fields was more the product of isolated decisions of agency officials and congressional committees focused primarily, albeit appropriately, on particular agencies' missions rather than on the productivity or quality of work being done in those disciplines or their potential contributions to broader national goals.

More work needs to be done to determine how the fields with declining support were affected and what budget adjustments need to be made. This requires some sort of centralized review. Given the imperfect correspondence between how agency research budgets have fared and how research fields' support and graduate training have fared, simply increasing the research funding of certain agencies (e.g., DOD, DOE, or NSF), irrespective of how they have been allocating research funds, may not by itself shift funding to fields with declining support.

There is, however, an accepted mechanism for establishing research priorities across agencies. It involves the President's selection of an area of research emphasis—for example, high performance computing or global climate change—and mobilization of the resources of the Executive Office of the President, especially the Office of Science and Technology Policy and the Office of Management and Budget, to evaluate needs and opportunities, determine current spending patterns, and assign new resources.

For the FY 2001 budget the directors of OSTP and OMB included balance in the government-wide research portfolio as a criterion for making R&D budget decisions. As a result, the President's budget proposal that year did provide increased funding for some agencies, in part to bolster support of certain fields.[10] In the early 1970s, in circumstances similar to current ones, when funding for physical sciences and engineering research was reduced by cuts in the DOD, NASA, and Atomic Energy Commission budgets, OMB and Congress encouraged NSF to seek additional funding equal to about 10 percent of its budget to support scientifically valuable programs that were being dropped by other agencies. The appropriators obliged.[11]

Other reports have urged OSTP or its director, the President's Science and Technology Adviser, and OMB to

---

[9]National Science Board. March 28, 2001. "The Scientific Allocation of Scientific Resources" [Discussion Draft for Comment], pp. 3.

[10]Neal Lane and Jacob J. Lew. June 3, 1999. "FY 2001 Interagency Research and Development Priorities" [Memorandum for the Heads of Executive Departments and Agencies].

[11]Milton Lomask. 1976. *A Minor Miracle: An Informal History of the National Science Foundation.* NSF 76-18. Washington, D.C.: U.S. Government Printing Office.

take the lead in reviewing the federal research portfolio with respect to national goals rather than departmental or agency priorities alone. The NRC committee chaired by Frank Press called on OMB and OSTP to determine if the aggregate budget for science and technology would provide the resources to enable the United States to perform at a world class level in all major research fields and to be preeminent in selected fields. It urged Congress to examine the total resources budgeted for science and technology before parcelling out the budget to the appropriations subcommittees for consideration.[12] Most recently, the United States Commission for National Security/21st Century, chaired by former Senators Gary Hart and Warren Rudman, called for better coordination of R&D efforts within the executive branch and Congress.[13]

Recommendation 1. The White House Office of Science and Technology Policy (OSTP) and the Office of Management and Budget (OMB), with assistance from federal agencies and appropriate advisory bodies, should evaluate the federal research portfolio, with an initial focus on fields related to industrial performance and other national priorities and a recent history of declining funding. Examples are physics, electrical engineering, chemistry, chemical engineering, mechanical engineering, and geological sciences. Fields with flat funding or only small real increases through the 1990s also merit attention. These include materials engineering, atmospheric sciences, mathematics, psychology, and astronomy. The conclusions of the evaluation should be reflected in budget allocations.

Recommendation 2. Congress should conduct its own evaluation of the federal research portfolio through the budget, appropriations, or authorization committees.

Recommendation 3. For the longer term, the executive branch and Congress should sponsor the following types of studies: (1) in-depth qualitative case studies of selected fields, taking into account not only funding trends across federal agencies and nonfederal supporters and international comparisons but also subtler differences in the foci, time horizons, and other research characteristics that are obscured by quantitative data; (2) studies of agency research portfolios and decision making to understand the reasons for shifts in funding by field and the extent to which the health of individual fields and interrelationships among fields are taken into account; and (3) studies of methodologies for allocating federal research funding according to national rather than merely departmental criteria and priorities.

Recommendation 4. The executive branch and Congress should institutionalize processes for conducting and, if necessary, acting on an integrated analysis of the federal budget for research, by field as well as by agency, national purpose, and other perspectives.

Data Improvements

This report uses a valuable federal research funding data set initiated by NSF in 1970 and annually updated through a survey of agencies that support R&D. Data on support by broad and detailed fields of research at both the basic and applied levels are available by department and agency, including major subunits. For the six largest R&D agencies, these data are available for one category of performer—universities and colleges. A number of other NSF surveys on research and development spending and on the training and employment of scientists and engineers are also valuable tools for assessing the nation's allocation of resources to the science and technology enterprise.

In addition to the perennial issue of how rapidly data can be collected, verified, and published,[14] several factors stand in the way of these data being readily accessible by and highly useful to policy makers. The following observations for the most part have been made by other reports and the committee's recommendations anticipated by other groups, including the Academies' Science, Technology and Economic Policy Board.[15]

• Data need to be presented in a manageable and meaningful form. Among other steps, expenditure data should be reported in constant dollars to show real trends unaffected by inflation.
• More information should be available on performers of federally funded research and development other than universities and colleges. In particular it would be useful to

---

[12]National Research Council. 1995. *Allocating Federal Funds for Science and Technology*, pp. 8–14. Washington, D.C.: National Academy Press.

[13]The Hart-Rudman Commission calls for doubling the U.S. R&D budget and strengthening the capacity of OSTP to coordinate agency R&D activities, but notes that currently the Science and Technology's Adviser's Office is inadequately funded, staffed, and used to fulfill its functions.

[14]At the time of completion of the review of this report (June 2001), the most recent data on actual federal R&D obligations are for FY 1999, ending September 30 of that year.

[15]For example, National Research Council. 2000. *Measuring the Science and Engineering Enterprise*. Washington, D.C.: National Academy Press; and National Research Council. 1997. *Industrial Research and Innovation Indicators*. Washington, D.C.: National Academy Press.

know the field allocation of funds spent by government laboratories, in industry, and by nonprofit institutions.

- More information should be available on nonfederal sponsors of research and development. State governments have been surveyed only once in recent years. Philanthropic contributions are reported only for major foundations and not in a form consistent with federal statistics on research funding. Although it may not be possible to ascertain the field allocation of industrial research funding, it should be possible to derive a more accurate picture of the composition of industrial R&D than classification of corporate-level reporting by major industrial sector permits.

- It should be easier to link related data sets—for example, research funding and graduate student enrollment by field. This requires use of the same classification of research fields and definitions of research activity across surveys.

- While continuity of data series is important for evaluating long-term trends, data also need to reflect contemporary reality including the emergence of new fields of research and the reorientation of others.

As our understanding has grown of the contribution of science and engineering to economic performance and other national goals, so has the importance of good data. Our national data sources need to be expanded and improved to support better policy making.

Recommendation 5. NSF should annually report and interpret data from its survey of federal R&D obligations in a form (e.g., adjusted for inflation) and on a schedule useful to policy makers. Improvements in the data that should be given careful consideration include reporting of data on university research support by all agencies that support a major share of research in certain fields (e.g., Department of Interior in geological science and DOC in oceanography), obtaining data by field on performers other than universities (e.g., in industry and government laboratories), evaluating and revising the field classification, and making the field classification and research typology uniform across surveys (e.g., the surveys of academic R&D expenditures and earned doctorates as well as the survey of federal R&D obligations). Agencies should make sure that the data they provide NSF are accurate and timely.

Recommendation 6. Although it may be impractical to obtain data on industrial R&D spending by research field, NSF should administer the Industrial R&D survey at the business unit level to make data on the composition of private R&D more meaningful.

Recommendation 7. NSF should consider ways of obtaining data on the allocation of state expenditures on a regular basis.

Recommendation 8. The philanthropic community should cooperate in collecting and publishing data on a basis comparable to federal research statistics.

Analytical Improvements

The analysis reported here is simply a more thorough collection and integration of existing data. It raises as many questions as it answers.

One direction for improved analysis helpful to policy makers is to focus on innovation results and to develop better measures of effort than funding inputs and formal patent outputs. The funding trends observed in this report are only one aspect of innovation. They have important implications, but determining what difference the funding trends are making is a much more ambitious but important task. This is true even if the objective is to understand the impact of funding trends on research performance. Recent Academy experiments in international benchmarking of scientific performance in diverse disciplines has nevertheless shown that this can be done relatively quickly at modest expense.[16]

It is also important to explore more carefully the interrelationships between federal research funding and the development and use of human resources. The correlations between trends in funding and trends in graduate education documented in this report are intriguing, but many more factors are involved. Those factors include population flows (supply of baccalaureates in science and engineering), employment demands for trained personnel by field, and nonfederal sources of graduate support. One important question to address is the extent to which federal research funding determines the number of advanced science and engineering degrees produced, compared with the need for such personnel in the workforce.

Recommendation 9. NSF and other federal agencies funding research should support benchmarking studies that compare inputs and outputs across countries and sponsor other efforts to develop techniques for assessing the productivity of various fields of research.

Recommendation 10. NSF should continue and expand its efforts to develop innovation indicators other than

---

[16]National Academy of Sciences, National Academy of Engineering, and Institute of Medicine. 2000. *Experiments in International Benchmarking of U.S. Research Fields*, Washington, D.C.: National Academy Press.

R&D expenditure inputs, collect data on them, and fund researchers to analyze them. Other agencies (e.g., NASA, DOD, DOE, and the National Institute of Standards and Technology) interested in the role of federal research in technological innovation, could fund or jointly fund such analyses.

Recommendation 11. Researchers, professional societies, industry associations, and federal research agencies should explore the relationships between federal research funding and other factors (e.g., population flows through the educational system, domestic and foreign student demand, labor market conditions, etc.) in the development and use of scientific and engineering talent. Only then can we evaluate the trends in student enrollment and in graduate study programs' output and determine how to influence those trends if that is the conclusion of the analysis.

Appendix

Note on Sources of Data

This report relies primarily on a series of annual surveys conducted by the National Science Foundation's Division of Science Resources Studies (NSF/SRS). The following descriptions of these surveys emphasize the information collected that is relevant to the subject of this report. Privately collected data on charitable foundation giving supplement these surveys.

SURVEY OF FEDERAL FUNDS FOR RESEARCH AND DEVELOPMENT

(http://www.nsf.gov/sbe/srs/sffrd/start.htm)

The Federal Funds Survey is conducted annually and includes retrospective reports of 32 federal agencies and their major subdivisions on obligations actually incurred during the past fiscal year and those expected to be incurred during the current and following fiscal years. The information is collected in a number of categories (i.e., research field, character of research, and performer) that can be cross-tabulated in useful ways for an analysis of trends in federal research spending. Obligations are commitments to spend money, regardless of when the funds were appropriated and of whether actual payment may be made later, for example, under multiyear contracts. In most cases respondents are agency budget analysts who consult with R&D program managers in their agencies.

Character and field of research. Obligations for research are classified as basic research or applied research in seven broad research fields and in 26 narrower natural and social science and engineering fields, called subfields in this report. Although the nomenclature corresponds to academic disciplines and departments, in the Federal Funds Survey it also is applied to research performed in industry and government laboratories and by other nonprofit institutions. The field categorization used by the Federal Funds Survey is further discussed in Chapter II. NSF/SRS does not try to collect information on obligations for "development" by research field because of the difficulty of categorizing highly applied work that may draw on many disciplines (for example, in the development of a military aircraft).

Uncharacterized research. The agencies also report funding of research "not elsewhere classified" or "n.e.c." for each broad field (i.e., life sciences, n.e.c.; engineering, n.e.c.) and for research that cannot be attributed to any broad field (i.e., other sciences, n.e.c.). These may be multidisciplinary or interdisciplinary projects that do not fall within any of the broad fields or subfields. The n.e.c. categories represent the majority of research in the social sciences and psychology (60.4 percent and 86.6 percent, respectively) and are quite large in engineering (28.3 percent) and environmental sciences (19.4 percent), but they are much smaller in other major fields. They have been growing in most major fields but not very rapidly. All n.e.c. research combined was 15.5 percent in 1993 and 16.8 percent in 1999.

Two-year projections. The survey asks agencies to estimate future research allocations for the current and next fiscal years for the seven broad fields but not for the 26 subfields. For the fiscal year in which the survey is administered agencies' estimates reflect enacted appropriations levels and are presumably fairly realistic. For example, the latest survey was conducted between February and September 2000, when agencies were in the middle or late stages of obligating the FY 2000 budget and had a good idea of what the final amounts would be. For the subsequent fiscal year (FY 2001 in the case of the latest survey reported), the estimates reflect probable administration budget request levels, which frequently differ from actual appropriations. In the case of the National Institutes of Health, for example, congressional appropriations have consistently exceeded executive branch requests.

Performers. Agencies report how much they obligate for basic and applied research by performer (i.e., industry, universities, nonprofit institutions, and in-house and contract laboratories) but with one exception do not separately report these figures by field of science and engineering. The six largest R&D supporting agencies report research performed by universities and colleges by field and also by whether it is basic or applied research. However, research performed in industry or government laboratories is not reported by field.

Anomalies. Unexplained discontinuities in the data usually prompt NSF/SRS or its contractor to inquire about the source of anomaly, which may be a genuine change in priorities or a reclassification. Beginning with FY 1996, the reporting unit for NSF, for example, changed its procedures for classifying research obligations by field. The change most affected engineering, where the amount classified as "n.e.c." by NSF jumped from 20 percent to 40 percent of engineering research, while mechanical engineering dropped from 13 percent to 2 percent of NSF engineering research funding. Because NSF is the second largest funder of mechanical engineering (after the Department of Defense), the total amount of funds for mechanical engineering appeared to drop by 30.1 percent from FY 1995 to FY 1996, although almost certainly any shift in NSF's portfolio was not as significant. A similar shift into the n.e.c. category occurred in the classification of physical science research, which especially affected physics. The NSF-reported increase in oceanography research and drop in geology research from 1995 to 1996 may also have involved reclassification of some activities from one category to another rather than a real change.

Features of our analysis. In this report, the current dollar expenditure data from the Federal Funds Survey are converted to constant 1999 dollars, using the official deflators issued by the Office of Management and Budget (OMB) in February 2001.[1] Subfields of the social sciences and psychology are not considered in this report because of the high proportion of research in both major fields reported as "n.e.c." "Engineering, n.e.c.," called other engineering in this report is included in the analysis because it encompasses a series of discrete fields (e.g. biomedical, nuclear, etc.) constituting a significant part of the discipline rather than a residual category for unclassifiable or multidisciplinary research. Accordingly, our analysis is based on trends in 22 subfields, counting social sciences and psychology as subfields. Most of the analysis is based on actual obligations through FY 1999, the last year for which subfield data are available. In some instances, trends in broad fields are reported through FY 2000, because of the reliability of the estimations for that year in contrast to the estimations for FY 2001. In describing trends in the affected fields the report tries to take into account the affects of the 1996 changes in NSF classification criteria affecting reported obligations in certain fields.

SURVEY OF RESEARCH AND DEVELOPMENT EXPENDITURES AT UNIVERSITIES AND COLLEGES

(http://www.nsf.gov/sbe/srs/sseeuc/start.htm)

The university R&D expenditures survey has collected data annually from a sample of education institutions that grant science and engineering degrees and perform a minimum level of separately budgeted R&D. Three years ago the survey was expanded to a census of all research universities. Respondents are usually central administrative staff who consult with their academic departments that are receiving support.

Character and field of research. The major fields and subfield classifications used in this survey are virtually the same as those used in the Federal Funds Survey, but institutions are not asked to disaggregate R&D into basic, applied, and development categories. Thus, funds for research and funds for development cannot be distinguished as they are in the Federal Funds Survey.

Unclassified research. Academic respondents may avail themselves of the same "not elsewhere classified" categories in each major field and overall. "N.e.c" research is highest in engineering (22 percent in a recent survey), lowest in the life sciences (4 percent), and about 10 percent overall, or lower than reported in the Federal Funds Survey.

Sources of support. NSF asks for total expenditures by field and federal expenditures by field. This enables one to derive data on nonfederal sources of support but *not* to disaggregate these data further, for example, to determine how state government or industry or philanthropic support varies by field and over time.

Discrepancies between the surveys. The university survey results show higher levels of support for academic research overall and in most fields than do the Federal Funds Survey results. For example, federal obligations for academic electrical engineering research declined in constant dollars by more than 30 percent between 1993 and 1997. But according to the academic R&D survey, federally funded R&D expenditures in that field increased

---

[1]Office of Management and Budget. 2001. *Historical Tables, Budget of the United States Government: Fiscal Year 2002*, Table 10.1. Washington, D.C.: U.S. Government Printing Office.

[2]National Research Council. 2000. *Measuring the Science and Engineering Enterprise: Priorities for the Division of Science Resources Studies*, pp. 94-95. Washington, D.C.: National Academy Press. The National Academies' report observes that the gap between federal obligations to universities and the level of federally funded R&D expenditures by universities opened in 1992 and has been growing, to about $1.9 billion in 1997. A much larger discrepancy exists between the results of the Federal Funds Survey and NSF's Survey of Industrial R&D with respect to the size of federally funded R&D expenditures in industry (p. 47).

by 27.2 percent.[2] The omission of development funds from the Federal Funds data on university research and the inclusion of development funds in the data reported by academic institutions account for some of the difference between the results of the two surveys, especially in fields such as engineering where development comprises about 60 percent of academic R&D compared with 13 percent of academic R&D in science. A second and possibly larger contributor to the difference is that the academic R&D survey counts twice some funds that derive from the federal government but are transferred from one institution to another.[3] Third, obligations (reported in the Federal Funds Survey) differ from actual expenditures (reported in the academic R&D survey) from year to year. Fourth, Federal Funds Survey respondents tend to assign more research to n.e.c. categories than do academic respondents, perhaps in part because it is easier for institutions to identify departments receiving the funds than for federal officials to assign a field of research.

Features of our analysis. Because of double counting of federal dollars, we rely on the Federal Funds Survey data to analyze the field distribution of government support. Nevertheless, the Academic R&D Expenditures Survey provides the only data on university funds by research field from other sources (e.g., state government and industry), and the latter are cited in Chapter 5.

SURVEY OF GRADUATE STUDENTS AND POSTDOCTORATES IN SCIENCE AND ENGINEERING (GSPSE)

(http://www.nsf.gov/sbe/srs/sgss/start.htm)

The graduate student survey collects data on the number and characteristics of graduate science and engineering students and postdoctorates enrolled in U.S. institutions offering postbaccalaureate programs in science and engineering. The final 1998 survey universe consisted of 722 responding units at 601 master's- and doctorate-granting institutions in the United States. Survey questionnaires are completed for each department in each responding unit at an institution either centrally or by departmental staff.

Variables. Data variables drawn on for our analysis include enrollment status, postdoctorate status, primary source of support, mechanism of support, and field of study.

Field of study. The major fields and subfield classifications are in some respects more detailed than those in the Federal Funds and Academic R&D Expenditures Surveys. For example, there are 14 instead of 7 engineering fields, 17 biological sciences fields, and 23 "health" fields. In two cases, subfields in the Federal Funds Survey are combined in the GSPSE data. "Aerospace engineering" indicates both aeronautical and astronautical engineering. "Biological sciences" incorporates environmental biology.

Unclassified students. In GSPSE there are departments that are classifiable by broad, but not fine, field. Thus there are residual categories such as "physical sciences (and biosciences, psychology, engineering, etc.), other." These residual categories comprise from less than 1 percent to more than 25 percent of their broad field category.

Primary source and mechanism of support. Respondents are asked to identify the primary source of support for each graduate student and postdoctorate. For graduate students, sources of support include federal agencies (e.g., Department of Defense, National Institutes of Health, other HHS, National Science Foundation, Department of Agriculture, NASA, etc.) and nonfederal sources (institutional support, self support, other U.S. and other foreign). GSPSE also asks respondents to cross-tabulate source of support against the following mechanisms of support: graduate fellowships, graduate traineeships, graduate research assistantships, graduate teaching assistantships, and other types of support.

Features of our analysis. In this report we have aggregated subfields in the GSPSE to arrive at a classification closely corresponding to that of the R&D data. We use the GSPSE category of "Health Fields" as most comparable to the Federal Funds category of "Medical Sciences."

SURVEY OF EARNED DOCTORATES (SED)

(http://www.nsf.gov/sbe/srs/ssed/start.htm)

The doctoral survey is a census of individuals receiving research doctorate degrees from U.S. institutions since 1958. Graduate schools are responsible for collecting questionnaires from doctoral recipients and submitting them to be compiled in the Doctorate Records File (DRF), which maintains data on the number and characteristics of all recipients since 1958. The population for the 1999 survey consisted of all individuals receiving a first research doctorate from a U.S. academic institution in the 12-month period ending on June 30, 1999. The total

---

[3]Reporting on a workshop requested by the Senate Commerce, Science, and Transportation Committee, the Congressional Research Service of the Library of Congress concluded:

There is general agreement among the workshop participants that the source of the discrepancy is a result of a changing research environment—such as more cooperative research ventures under which a significant fraction of the funds received by universities can be counted twice. As funds get transferred between different academic institutions involved in joint research efforts or between different parts of the same institution, tracking the funds becomes more difficult and can lead to double counting....The (federal) agencies believe that they can accurately account for R&D funds obligated to universities.

Michael E. Davey and Richard E. Rowberg. January 31, 2000. *Challenges in Collecting and Reporting Federal Research and Development Data*, p. 17. Washington, D.C.: Congressional Research Service.

universe consisted of 41,140 persons in approximately 392 institutions.

Variables. The DRF contains a wide range of data on the demographic characteristics, citizenship status, educational history, field of study, financial support, and planned employment of doctorate recipients.

Field of study. Major fields and subfields in the SED are roughly comparable to those of the Federal Funds Survey with one exception. The SED collects data on fine fields within the major field of earth, atmospheric, and ocean sciences. However, published tables on citizenship status do not disaggregate this major field.

Citizenship status. The DRF provides five citizenship categories: native-born U.S. citizen, naturalized U.S. citizen, permanent resident, temporary visa holder, and unknown citizenship. Trends in permanent and temporary visa holders can be divergent, as they were in the 1990s, for idiosyncratic political reasons. The Chinese Student Protection Act of 1992, which allowed Chinese students in the U.S. at the time of the Tianamen Massacre to become permanent residents, generated a dramatic shift in Chinese Ph.D.'s away from temporary to permanent visa status. The overall trend in foreign students' enrollment in doctorate programs is best observed by looking at the larger category of non-U.S. citizens. The citizenship variable has also been clouded in recent years by a significant increase in the "citizenship unknown" category.[4]

Features of our analysis. For cross-survey comparison, the component fields of geology, atmospheric sciences, and oceanography in data from the Federal Funds Survey and the Survey of Graduate Students and Postdoctorates have been aggregated to match the DRF data. We also aggregate the native born and naturalized citizens into one U.S. citizen category and temporary visa holders and permanent residents into one non-U.S. citizen category.

SURVEY OF STATE RESEARCH AND DEVELOPMENT EXPENDITURES: FY 1995

The state R&D survey was a one-time NSF/SRS-sponsored survey conducted and published by the State Science and Technology Institute of the Battelle Memorial Institute in Columbus, Ohio (STTI/BMI). The survey identified only directly targeted R&D funds, not general education purpose funds used by universities for research expenses or to cover the indirect costs of research. Previous intermittent NSF surveys of state agency R&D excluded funds directly appropriated to academic institutions, making comparisons over time difficult if not impossible.

Character and field of research. The SSTI/BMI survey asked respondents to categorize research into major fields but not subfields, to characterize research as basic, applied, or development, and to further distinguish research by budget function such as health, agriculture, economic development, and support of the science and technology infrastructure. Thus, respondents reported the share of engineering research directed at economic development (20 percent) and the share of biological research directed at agricultural production (35 percent).

Uncharacterized research. State respondents were able to employ a "not elsewhere classified" category, overall representing about 21.1 percent of research reported in the 1995 survey.

FOUNDATION GIVING TRENDS

The private nonprofit Foundation Center compiles reports from a sample of approximately 1,000 large independent, corporate, and community foundations, most recently in 2000. The sample was expanded in 1991 to include more smaller and corporate foundations, introducing a discontinuity in the data series. Excluded from the sample are grants by wealthy individuals and expenditures of private research institutes (e.g., Howard Hughes Medical Institute) whether or not established by philanthropic bequests.

Classification of grants. Expenditures are classified by function such as art and culture, education, and health. "Science and technology" is further distinguished as general science, physical science, technology, life science, and "other;" but general science includes grants to improve science education below the college level. "Medical research" is a subcategory of health rather than science and technology. In general, interpretation of the data is complicated by the fact the same expenditures may be reported under two or several categories. In the case of the physical sciences, year to year fluctuations are common and attributable to the fact a number of large foundation donors (e.g., Keck, Kellogg) primarily fund large capital projects.

SURVEY OF INDUSTRIAL RESEARCH AND DEVELOPMENT

(http://www.nsf.gov/sbe/srs/srs01410/start.htm)

NSF/SRS has sponsored and the Bureau of the Census has conducted an annual industry survey since 1953. The survey is directed to the central corporate headquarters of U.S.-based public and privately held, U.S.- and foreign-owned corporations and asks them to report separately annual corporate domestic spending on R&D regardless of business unit or product or service lines, together with sales, employment, numbers of employed scientists and engineers, and cost of R&D per scientist/engineer. Respondents are asked to identify funds from the federal government, the principal source of non-self-financed R&D. But

---

[4] A. Sanderson and B. Dugoni. *Summary Report 1997: Doctorate Recipients from United States Universities*, p. 18. Chicago: National Opinion Research Center.

R&D performed in-house is not distinguished from contract R&D or grants to non-profit institutions. As a Census Bureau survey the identity of respondents is strictly confidential. Data are not reported where their publication might reveal the identity of the single or a small number of respondents.

Character of research. Activity is classified as basic research, applied research, or development according to standard definitions that are uniform across NSF/SRS R&D surveys.

Classification. Respondents and responses are classified according to the U.S. Standard Industry Classification (SIC) code at the three- and four-digit levels. From one survey to another, a firm may shift from one classification to another either because of acquisition or because of a shift in business emphasis (e.g., computer manufacturing to computer services), but all of its R&D falls in a single classification regardless of how diversified its business operations. Because of the confidentiality requirement, reclassifications of firms are not made public. In 1999 firms were classified under a new scheme, the North American Industry Classification System (NICS). To avoid a sharp discontinuity in the data series, NSF/SRS reclassified the data from the previous two calendar years, 1997 and 1998, but cannot assure users that the adjusted data are strictly comparable to the 1999 results.

COMPUSTAT R&D DATABASE

An alternative source of industrial spending data is the the Standard and Poor's Compustat database, which contains information required to be reported annually to the U.S. Securities and Exchange Commission (SEC) on so-called l0K forms by publicly held firms headquartered in the United States. Banks, utilities, and insurance companies are not required to report R&D expenditures. In addition to domestic and foreign R&D spending, the information includes other characteristics such as corporate sales, employment, exports, foreign sales, profits, and capital investment. Because the data are mandatory and public, they are available more quickly than NSF survey results and the respondents can be identified. On the other hand, basic and applied research and development are not distinguished and therefore the data are not used in this analysis.[5]

---

[5] For a Compustat-based analysis of the distribution of R&D by field see Carl Shepherd and Steven Payson. 1999. *U.S. Corporate R&D Vol. I: Top 500 Firms in R&D by Industry Category.* Washington, D.C.: U.S. Department of Commerce and National Science Foundation. This analysis is being updated.